UNDERDOG

UNDERDOG

Confessions of a Right-Wing Gay Jewish Muckraker

SUE-ANN LEVY

SIGNAL
McCLELLAND
& STEWART

Signal is an imprint of McClelland & Stewart, a division of Penguin
Random House Canada Limited, a Penguin Random House Company

Signal and colophon are registered trademarks of McClelland & Stewart,
a division of Penguin Random House Canada Limited,
a Penguin Random House Company

Library and Archives Canada Cataloguing in Publication
is available upon request

ISBN 978-0-7710-4800-5
eISBN 978-0-7710-4802-9

Typeset in Frutiger Serif Pro by M&S, Toronto
Printed and bound in USA

McClelland & Stewart,
a division of Penguin Random House Canada Limited,
a Penguin Random House Company
www.penguinrandomhouse.ca

1   2   3   4   5   20   19   18   17   16

This book is dedicated to the memory of my adopted
aunt Lena Alexander and my beloved uncle Jeffrey Lyons
(Brother Jeff), both of whom were larger than life,
who called it the way they saw it and who both
passed away suddenly in the summer of 2015
before Underdog *went to print.*

It is also dedicated to the love of my life,
Denise Alexander, the woman who helped make
my life whole again at the age of fifty, who encouraged me
to write this book and who never got tired of
helping with the drafts and rewrites.

CONTENTS

BEGINNINGS

Although I've completed ten half marathons and too many ten-kilometre events to count in my ten years as a runner, I'm probably the least competitive runner there is. This is in stark contrast to how focused I can be in my efforts to scoop the competition with a story. When I run, I rarely pay attention to how fast I'm going or to the obstacles in front of me. I just run around them. I usually sport one of the latest Garmin watches and a Fitbit, but I do that more to clock how far I've gone and how many calories I've burned, being ever mindful of the cardio burn of running and that endorphin rush that tends to come about twenty minutes into my route. My three- to four-times-weekly jog has become not just a workout but my special escape from all the stresses of life, a time to deal with personal issues and come up with a list of column ideas. I first took up running at the age of forty-eight, the same week I decided to seek therapy so I wouldn't turn fifty still being angry about my past. And I am not even referring to living in a closeted relationship for twenty years, but rather to having been brutally assaulted not once but twice in my life, the first time left for dead by my assailant.

I am not a runner who finishes a route quickly. More often than not I have the distinction of being the slowest in my running group. I like to take notice of my surroundings, people watch, and observe the goings on of my adopted city of Toronto. I pass my long runs of two to three hours by challenging myself to find at least one story about the city along the way. I often say I've gotten to know Toronto's neighbourhoods far better when I've trained for the half marathons than as a journalist for twenty-six years running.

Taking in the world around me is so important to me that I get annoyed if I have to run alongside someone. While training in the winter of 2014–15 with my running group for my first half marathon in three years, I invariably found myself either at the back of the pack or content to do the runs at my own pace. My running coaches have a hard time believing I can run for up to three hours by myself, but I have no problem doing so. It isn't just the rather late age I took up the sport, or that I have the furthest thing from an optimal runner's body, carrying far too much weight above the waist. Rather, it's just that after years of running away from obstacles in my life, I was content to deal with them at my own pace. I enjoy the freedom to cherish the peacefulness of the world around me, at all times of the year, cold weather or warm, snowstorms or searing heat. What I lack in speed, I make up for in endurance. As in other areas of my life, I am an underdog when it comes to running. But I always reach the finish line.

I have approached my calling – investigative journalism – with the same endurance I put into my running. My readers know this, and I choose to believe that the politicians, bureaucrats, advocates, and activists I write about know that I am not one to back down or run away from controversy or intimidation. I am most satisfied when I'm chasing or breaking exclusive stories rather than allowing myself to be spoon-fed the party line, as far too many of my journalistic colleagues tend to be happy to do these days. No doubt that's the easier route to take, and the most popular, but it's not what the public deserves.

Like my columns in the *Toronto Sun*, this book pulls no punches. I say it the way I see it, in a cheeky and certainly tell-all manner. I hoped, by writing it, I might motivate others to pursue what makes them happy and to be honest about themselves. I hope I can also inspire and give others the courage to deal with their traumas, to come out, and to say what is on their minds. After pretending I was someone I wasn't for so many years, I have no regrets about speaking out now.

The theme of the book is its title: *Underdog* – whether I'm talking about my own personal struggles or the causes I've championed. I write about political underdogs like the late Rob Ford and my own uphill (and losing) battle to try to win the hearts and mind of voters as the first openly gay and married Progressive Conservative candidate in the Toronto provincial riding of St. Paul's. I challenge the myths perpetuated by the Liberals and those who align with the left about each other and the ways they indoctrinate voters into believing they truly are compassionate, tolerant, and open-minded. I question what truly motivates politicians like Barack Obama, Kathleen Wynne, and former mayor David Miller, suggesting they are more enchanted with the image they see in the mirror than truly driven by a need to change the agenda and help those who elected them. I suggest that most politicians are really in it because they're narcissistic, that they're far too concerned with getting re-elected, and that they're essentially too cowardly to do what's right. I respect very few of them. I also tackle the rise in anti-Semitism dressed in the guise of criticism of Israel. If ever an entire people could be called underdogs, Jews are it. I advocate for the poor and homeless, who have far too often been used as props for photo ops by poverty pimps more concerned with keeping themselves employed than with truly helping the vulnerable. I take on waste, mismanagement, and the abuse of tax dollars by politicians, few of whom seem to care about the endless burden they pass on to the people who pay the bills. I am not afraid to tell Ontario's empowered unions that they are bankrupting the province with their ridiculous 1950s-style demands, or to advise Muslim cabbies – who are licensed to serve the public – that if they don't want to take my dog in their car (for religious reasons), perhaps they should find another line of work.

In my Twitter handle, I state – with a certain amount of pride – that I'm a shit disturber. My friends and my readers often tell me, accompanied by a laugh, that I really like to stir it up, both in my columns and in my radio spots. There's no doubt that I get under the skin of many of those I write about. But it's anything but a "shtick." I often feel I'm merely saying what is on the minds of many – those who don't have a soapbox or are too afraid for whatever reason to speak up. As I do in my columns, I hope that in this book – with its many behind-the-scenes anecdotes and my cheeky observations of all things political – I will help inspire people to pay more attention to what politicians of all stripes are doing or not doing for them; will give readers the other side of the story from the endless, mind-numbing political spin often repeated (without question) by all too many of my media colleagues; and will provoke discussion, whether you love me or you love to hate me.

CHAPTER ONE

Underdog

I t was like a flip of a switch. His arrogance and dismissive-ness made me so angry I walked up to Joe Pantalone in Toronto city council during a break in 2008, looked him in the eye, and told him off. Deputy mayor at the time and a long-serving politician, Mr. Pantalone – who had taken on the job of council's first Tree Advocate – had just stood up and delivered a blistering attack on a poor, innocent semi-retired couple for allegedly allowing their tiny home to "deteriorate." Mr. Pantalone, clearly suffering from short man's syndrome, blamed their home's lousy foundation for the problems they were experiencing with an out-of-control Norway Maple tree. The weed tree's aggressive roots had infiltrated the home's foundation, their pipes, and basement. When I happened on the scene, Perry Thompson and his wife had already spent $17,500 on repairs to rectify the damage. They were beside themselves because their insurance company had warned them their policy might be cancelled if the tree

1

didn't come down. The couple felt they were being "held ransom" by this crazy out-of-control tree. And they were.

Toronto's tree police – drunk with their own power to decide what stays and what goes in the city's urban forest – had flatly denied the couple's request to take down the tree, dismissing the clearest evidence of the damage it had done. For heaven's sake, it was a weed tree known to be invasive, to have a highly aggressive root system that smothers other plants and wildflowers, and to even have the power to raise sidewalk pavement. Yet the city's tree police and Mr. Pantalone had passed judgment without once visiting the couple's small house, as I had. Shaking with anger at his arrogance and the way he'd abused his power, I approached Mr. Pantalone and told him he had no right to judge the couple that way and that he owed them an apology. Taken aback at the reprimand, he tried to defend himself and then beat a retreat as hastily as he could. That wasn't the only time I'd reacted like this; the misuse and abuse of power, not to mention the city's often bordering on irrational intransigence, had and has a way of setting me off.

Whether it was this couple with a weed tree, or the Ontario seniors who'd been mistreated, students who'd been bullied while the school principal and teachers stood by and did nothing, or what I clearly came to recognize as a homelessness industry happy with keeping its pawns (street people) living out on the sidewalk or in the city's parks to guilt the politicians into spending more money on shelters, drop-in centres, and social workers, with no desire to reverse the cycle of dependency – all of this made me (and continues to make me) crazy mad.

Helping the underdog became a crusade because I could relate to each and every one of the people I've featured in a column or story. That's not to say I've ever been homeless, but I've known, from a very young age, what it's like to feel intimidated, bullied, mocked, helpless, powerless, and betrayed by those in positions of trust. Once I found my courage and the voice to go with it, I was determined to speak for others, remembering what it was like to be that little girl from Hamilton, the one who for many years felt she was on the outside looking in at others who seemed to have it all.

That feeling of being powerless became evident to me at the young age of twelve, when I was outed by a religious school teacher. Yes, a Sunday school teacher. I'm not referring to the fact that he revealed I was gay. He could have hardly known that. My coming-out story would unfold many, many years later. I'm talking about being labelled an outsider. One Sunday morning, when he was supposed to be teaching us lessons from the Bible, this teacher decided, instead, to sit us in a circle and analyze us. When he got to me, he announced to my fellow twelve-year-olds that I was an "outsider." I'm really not sure to this day what caused him to come to that conclusion. Did I appear vulnerable or lacking in self-esteem? Or was it already clear that I didn't fit in? It doesn't really matter. For an awkward, chubby twelve-year-old desperately trying to be accepted by her peers, that day became forever burned in my memory because of the collateral damage it caused.

I came home in tears, absolutely devastated by what had been said. My father Lou, livid at the idea that a Sunday school teacher would overstep his authority in this way, angrily complained to the principal of religious studies at our synagogue. I'd been labelled very publicly. The kids who heard the word "outsider" felt empowered, or at the very least enabled, by what that teacher had said. As kids will do, my circle of religious school peers carried on their bullying unchecked. Those years in junior high school are a blur to me now except for my attempts to run away from the constant insults my tormenters hurled at me. They called me fat, they called me "four eyes" for wearing thick glasses to correct my extreme nearsightedness and even for being an A student.

Because I developed physically earlier than some, the rabbi's daughter was fond of telling everyone who would listen that I stuffed popcorn in my bra, joking that she could hear it crackling as she chased after me. I can laugh about it now, but at age twelve I was mortified whenever she said it. (Ironically, popcorn has turned out to be one of my favourite treats.) That marked the beginning of my attempts to prove my peer group wrong, to be the best I could be at whatever I did – and to stand up for what's right. The shift certainly didn't happen overnight. It took me years to recover from the verbal abuse and the many, many other obstacles that life threw my way, but in the process I developed both a strong work ethic and an unshakeable self-esteem. I was no longer the underdog. The Sunday school teacher ended up teaching me something other than religion, but a lesson just as important: That those in positions of authority cannot always be trusted to do what's right; that respect for one's elders should be earned and not simply given. I'm convinced that my irreverence with politicians and others in power and my constant need to question authority grew from being let down by those in positions of trust, starting with that teacher.

I did have strong, loving influences in my life that showed what it was to be compassionate under the most difficult of circumstances. Whenever I could, I sought comfort and unconditional love at the home of my father's mother – my Bubby

Becky. Every Thursday I'd walk the twenty minutes from my junior high school to her house, eager to be embraced by her warm hug and to hear the same words week after week, said in her thick Eastern European accent: "You vant chips?" What she meant were french fries, lovingly made from scratch – as was every dish served in her home. We both looked forward to those weekly lunches. She didn't care that Thursdays were her busiest day – the day she prepared gefilte fish and her sweet, chewy bagels for her weekly Shabbat dinners using the techniques she'd brought from her native Poland. Most often when I'd turn up I'd find her kneading the bagel dough or pounding the whitefish into gefilte fish. Her home was a safe harbour for me. She was in her late sixties and I was not yet thirteen. But we had an undeniable kinship. She was not just loving but incredibly sharp. I admired her for her strength, her forthrightness, and her kind heart. One afternoon, because she wanted to buy me a Hanukkah gift, we took the bus together down to the old Eaton's in downtown Hamilton to purchase the latest rage at the time – white go-go boots à la Nancy Sinatra. I'm sure they looked ridiculous on me, but my Bubby Becky knew my heart was set on those boots. I can't remember if I ever ended up wearing them that much.

She had a hard life but did what she felt was right. There was no casting her husband aside when my Zayda suffered a serious stroke. She was in her late seventies when that happened, and she cared for him at home until she could no longer continue to do so physically. Her strength, compassion, and loyalty to her loved ones have undeniably rubbed off on me, and I'm a better person for it.

When I got to high school, barely thirteen after accelerating a grade in elementary school, I found comfort with a rather eccentric group of "browners." What we lacked in athleticism and grooviness, we made up for in smarts. One old friend with whom I've renewed acquaintance in recent years I fondly named Frigga Factfinder the First. I probably did it back then because I was envious of her brilliance and ability to retain facts. I can't for the life of me say why I came up with Frigga, other than to speculate that even then I was fond of alliteration. Gwen Rousseau (Gwen Roper in those days) was serious about her studies. But she was always a good sport with a genuine twinkle in her eye and a zest for life, which she has to this day. And she was brilliant – destined to spend most of her career as a nuclear engineer. Another close friend, Rosemary Euringer (née Reid), and I shared a passion for languages as well as many, many laughs about our similar family situations. Both of us had outspoken and at times demanding mothers, both of them married to men who were nurturing fathers.

I served on student council and on house council as social and publicity coordinator. I even fulfilled a term as senior representative on Hamilton junior city council, unwittingly setting in motion a lifetime of political involvement. Quickly bored with the less than creative and often tedious instructional methods of many of my high school teachers, I said what was on my mind and challenged them continually, probably to the point of rubbing every last one of them the wrong way. Many years later, in the mid-nineties, when I covered the education beat for the *Toronto Sun* and started writing about teachers who went the extra mile, I had trouble remembering any in my own high school who had inspired me. I sought my challenges outside school, filling up my spare time by playing roles in amateur theatre productions, taking voice and piano lessons, and competing in the voice category in the yearly Kiwanis Festival.

My favourite sub-category was Broadway show tunes. As I stood up there competing – usually I won silver because there was another young lady who always captured the golds – I imagined myself on the Broadway stage performing in some musical, preferably from the fifties or sixties. What I lacked in talent, I made up for in bravado, although I joke that I'd never have made it on the Broadway stage because I lack rhythm. But I didn't feel the slightest bit shy performing a role on stage.

Nevertheless, my maternal grandmother, Frances, who was amazingly well plugged in to the world long before the Internet, found out about a music camp in northern Michigan called Interlochen. With her urging, I spent three summers there as a camper. It was pure heaven for me. I not only studied drama and voice but spent the summer immersed in classical music, developing an appreciation for it that I maintain to this day. For someone used to being bullied and mocked by my peer group in Hamilton, the summers offered a sense of freedom. It was refreshing to be the underachiever in a sea of highly talented overachievers. It was hard to single out anyone for their appearance when we all looked less than stylish dressed in the Interlochen uniform of blue corduroy knickers, red knee socks, and a bland blue blouse. The knickers certainly weren't kind to those with an extra twenty pounds either, and they could be impossibly hot in the summer. But I didn't care. My three summers there expanded my horizons and helped me develop a sense of independence. I found myself bunking with fellow campers from all over the United States and from as far away as Japan. I still have the Japanese prints my friend Natsuko Oshima, a talented violinist, sent to me after we spent a summer together as cabin-mates.

At camp and at school – wherever I went and whatever I did – I hid my inner frailties with an outer toughness, a constant habit of questioning authority, a sarcastic wit, and a need to say exactly what was on my mind. My use of sarcasm and my unfiltered tongue were even noted in reviews from camp counsellors and particularly by high school teachers, and would get me in trouble many times over the years. When I was off for two months in grade twelve because of a serious illness and missed my initial set of exams, my teachers were forced to estimate my first-term marks. Most treated my extended absence as if I'd cut school, giving me barely passing grades – even though I'd been an A student for the first three years of high school and had been in an enrichment program for four years. I still can't help but think those estimated grades – some of them barely passing ones – constituted payback from some of those teachers who'd been subjected to my sarcasm. Perhaps they felt it just deserts. Nevertheless, knowing what I know now (after years of covering the education beat) about how some teachers bring their personal and political agendas into the classroom and try to poison impressionable students, I would bet that I was caught on the wrong end of that same vindictiveness. Still, recognizing that those first-term estimated marks would preclude me from graduating with an 80 per cent average or higher and from having my name permanently inscribed on the school's walls as an honours student, I marched into the vice-principal's office and pleaded with him not to take them into consideration. I pointed out that I had raised my marks to well over 80 per cent in the second term. Alas, I did not manage to move him.

To satisfy my thespian aspirations, I adopted the habit from the age of eleven or twelve of rewriting my favourite Broadway musicals and performing them – with my brother in a supporting role – to honour family members at special occasions. At my Bubby and Zayda's fiftieth anniversary party, my brother and I performed many of the songs from *Fiddler on the Roof*, rewritten in their honour. The title song, "Fiddler on the Roof," became "A Bubby at the Stove" and "Matchmaker" was rewritten as "Clothesmaker, Clothesmaker," a tribute to my Zayda, who eked out a living as a tailor in a dusty shop in the north end of Hamilton. When I couldn't think of a suitable musical to adapt, I'd write poetry for my family members and recite it to them on their special occasions. It may sound rather hokey now, but it was all done with love and creativity. My maternal grandmother, the same one who encouraged me to go to Interlochen, noticed how much I loved writing – and that I seemed to be talented at it. Not wanting me to "end up waiting tables as a would-be actress" she encouraged me to redirect my desire to attend drama school into a career in journalism. Sadly, Frances lived long enough to see me finish journalism school but not to see me become a successful journalist. She died of advanced breast cancer at the young age of sixty-six.

I flourished in the journalism program at Ottawa's Carleton University. It was the perfect place to explore my newfound interest in politics. I threw myself into the federal political scene – both writing about ground-breaking female politicians like Flora MacDonald and Barbara McDougall and working behind the scenes on Progressive Conservative Joe Clark's leadership campaign. My uncle, Jeff Lyons, a long-time member of the Conservative backroom, had encouraged me to get involved in his friend's campaign, believing it would be good experience for a journalism student. Jeff had known Joe Clark from his student days when they were both part of the federal Progressive Conservative Student Federation. They remained close friends all their lives until, sadly, my dear uncle died of a massive heart attack while jogging on a hot July day in the summer of 2015. But back in my student days, my uncle unwittingly, or perhaps knowingly, set in motion my passion for politics, which I would indulge both as a journalist covering the municipal, provincial, and federal scene, and as a one-time provincial candidate.

To the envy of my classmates, I was able to experience the thrill of a leadership convention right on the floor with the Joe Clark delegates. The position also led to an opportunity I never anticipated while a journalism student. Exactly one year after I'd finished my journalism degree at Carleton and was already living and working in Toronto – when Mr. Clark defeated Pierre Trudeau to become prime minister of a minority government – I was invited back to Ottawa by Allan Lawrence to serve as his press secretary. Mr. Lawrence, ever the gentleman with his staff, had dual responsibilities as solicitor general and minister of consumer and corporate affairs. I was hired to assist him with the latter portfolio. It was a dream job and truly a heady experience for a twenty-two-year-old budding journalist. During my nine months on the job – before the government fell on a non-confidence vote – I spoke to media across Canada on the issue of exploding 1.5-litre glass pop bottles (which were banned) and on a variety of highly technical corporate issues involving the banks and oil companies. I had only been out of journalism school for a year, but I learned phenomenally fast. I had to since Mr. Lawrence, often busy with his other demanding portfolio, let his staff take care of many issues on his behalf. I learned very quickly, when the government fell – and the moving van took my worldly possessions back to Toronto once again – that politics is indeed a fickle game: that you can be on top of the world one day and out of a job the next. I would have never traded those nine months for anything, however, and think it was during this time that I started to trust my political instincts, as young as I was.

After returning to Toronto from that brief sojourn in federal politics in Ottawa, I spent the next five years immersed in the rigours of part-time MBA studies while working full-time in a communications job at Queen's Park. Between toiling at my day job, studying at night, and trying to have a romantic life, I had a good excuse not to tackle my worsening psychological problems.

Acquiring an MBA at night, especially when one's undergraduate is in the arts, is arduous and certainly not for the faint of heart. But it was a perfect way of keeping myself busily distracted. Although I dated a series of very decent young men during my university days and throughout my twenties, my attraction to women forever haunted me, as much as I tried to suppress it. I believe it may have started as early as the age of thirteen, when I found myself having crushes on my female teachers and on some classmates. I wasn't to act on it for years – in fact I was afraid to do so – but I found myself forever confused throughout my university years, thinking at the very least I was bisexual. I simply pushed those feelings away, resolving to be the best I could on the heterosexual dating scene as in all other areas of my life.

My confusion was no doubt exacerbated by my unwillingness to deal with the torment of a vicious assault at the hands of a stranger during my final three months at Carleton University. The stranger – who came to my apartment on the pretext of subletting it once I finished my university year – beat me over the head several times with a lead pipe and tried to strangle me. He came within inches of murdering me. After that traumatic assault, my life went into auto-pilot. I was not encouraged to seek counselling. The message I got from my family was to put it all behind me. In fairness, it was a different era back then, and it was the norm to sweep many psychological and emotional issues under the carpet. My only choice was to keep moving and try to forget, or at least deny, the trauma. I felt that if the figurative treadmill onto which I'd forced myself ever stopped, I'd fall off and shatter into a million pieces. But the ordeal haunted me, no matter how much I tried to forget it.

I made sure I filled every waking hour to avoid dealing head-on with the trauma of the assault, together with the pain of living in the closet. I had a hard time being alone with myself. No matter how hard I tried, I had trouble sleeping through the night, often being startled awake at 4 a.m. by a full-blown anxiety attack. To get a proper night's rest, I took sedatives. Although I was careful never to get addicted to the drugs, for years I'd start my day in a groggy, hungover state. I always said I was not a morning person. But most often it was because I had such trouble getting a decent night's sleep or was battling the after-effects of the drugs. To the world, I presented a brave front, always in control, always highly driven. Privately, if I'd stopped to think about it, I'd have realized I was both a mess and a mass of contradictions. It was a very long twenty-five years before I recognized that I needed help and sought counselling.

At each family gathering, as I watched distant family members making a big deal of getting married and having children, I forever felt the outsider, which was nothing new for me. Jews have a long and complicated relationship with guilt, and I take some pride in the fact that I was able to put a special twist of my own on it. Ironically, my overachieving side made me feel guilty that I was letting my family down. Unlike many closeted lesbians, I did not end up marrying the men I dated throughout my twenties, thirties, and even forties – despite the ever increasing pressure from my family to do so. But my maternal grandfather, Irwin's, third wife – with whom I had a very close relationship – didn't stop trying to fix me up well into my forties. I loved her dearly for her efforts.

I had a special intellectual connection with my grandfather Irwin, a self-made man who created and operated the first chain of grocery stores in Hamilton. We enjoyed long discussions about politics, government waste, our Jewish heritage, and many other issues. I respected his wisdom, his work ethic, his refusal to succumb to the ravages of old age, his mastery of the game of golf, and his entrepreneurial spirit, especially considering he was forced to survive and raise a family during the Depression. He, in turn, respected me as a journalist. But being from a different, far more chauvinistic era, he couldn't understand why I had not followed the traditional route of marriage and children. I never really felt I lived up to his expectations, a point always left unstated until about a year before he passed away. While at my parents' home for dinner and well into his nineties, he let the martinis do the talking. Made even more unedited than normal due to the early stages of dementia, he told me he thought I was a good journalist but that he plainly didn't agree with my "lifestyle." It was amazing to me that he even knew the word *lifestyle* or that he even had some inkling that I was gay. I was upset for days by what he had said, although it didn't surprise me. But in hindsight, it was likely his disapproval that kept my family from speaking about the subject and that contributed to keeping me in the closet for so many years.

While I clearly had a tendency to say what was on my mind, I didn't find a platform or the confidence to champion others like me until I made my mind up to ditch a twelve-year well-paying career in public and government relations and pursue my real calling in journalism. To the shock of my friends, family, and work colleagues, I decided to start my career all over again at the age of thirty-two. It was a calculated risk. I figured I had more to gain than lose and that I had to do it before I became far too comfortable with the much higher salaries in what we journalists quasi-affectionately call "the dark side." I ended up at the *Bracebridge Examiner*, a weekly in Muskoka, where my ex had a summer home. The public relations agency I left, probably not quite believing or trusting my decision to join a small-town newspaper, told me they'd keep the door open for three months, in case I discovered the error of my ways. I never looked back. Within a month, I knew I was right. Although I had taken a circuitous route, at long last I was fulfilling my late grandmother's prophecy.

I did everything but deliver the paper. I asked to help lay out each weekly edition and to learn to write headlines on production day, on top of my writing and reporting duties. Within three months I was working for the *Gravenhurst Banner*, covering town council and trying to effect change with critical editorials. Again, I figured I had nothing to lose, considering I was only getting my journalistic feet wet. Boy, was I naive. The town councillors, not used to having the spotlight shone on them, didn't much appreciate an outsider, particularly one who knew a number of cottagers from Toronto, writing editorials about what I believed to be their poorly thought out and wasteful decisions. One councillor, who later became Gravenhurst's mayor (after I left town), called me one day crying after I criticized him in an editorial. He informed me he'd never been treated that way. (That was in 1989. He should ask politicians in Toronto what they think of me now.) My cottager friends from Toronto loved what I wrote. The town councillors obviously felt differently. They were so upset, I joked that I'd better find a job in Toronto before I was run out of town. Lucky for me, the owner and publisher of the papers, Ted Britton, supported my efforts 100 per cent. He was as irreverent as me. I would often hear him telling off some local politician or another on the phone. He did not seem to care if the powers that be threatened to withdraw their advertising dollars, and he owned enough papers in Muskoka to have a powerful presence. He, too, felt it important that the truth get out, and had the integrity not to be bullied into backing down from his convictions. Sadly for the citizens of Gravenhurst and Bracebridge, and for freedom of the press, he sold the papers to Metroland, a subsidiary of the Toronto Star conglomerate, in 2005.

After seven months in Muskoka, I was eager to get back to Toronto. I put out feelers and was offered a job at the *Canadian Jewish News*. That would get me back to the city, but my real ambition was to work at a daily newspaper. I called my old friend from journalism school, Peter Howell, for advice. He had been at the *Toronto Sun* for years and had just moved to the *Toronto Star* when I contacted him. He told me to use my connections – namely then publisher Paul Godfrey, a close friend of my uncle. As much as I abhorred the thought, having prided myself on doing it on my own, I wasn't too proud to realize that the connection would get me a foot in the door. I soon realized the rest was up to me. Les Pyette, the *Toronto Sun*'s colourful editor-in-chief at the time, agreed to meet with me, but he wasn't going to make it easy. I marched into the interview with Mr. Pyette full of bravado, claiming that despite my lack of journalism experience, I was not afraid to tell it like it is. I waved my editorials from Gravenhurst in Mr. Pyette's face as what I hoped would be proof of my irreverence. He agreed to give me a tryout in the business section, but with no guarantees I'd get hired. I grabbed the opportunity, thanking the *Canadian Jewish News* for their kind offer but telling them I couldn't take their job. A month later, I was moved over to news as a general assignment reporter, and I never looked back. My ballsy efforts earned me the nickname "The Feisty Girl from Gravenhurst" – a name that has stuck to this day, at least for Les, and despite the fact I'm not from Gravenhurst.

By then, I was several years into what was to be a twenty-year relationship with my ex, and I remained deeply closeted for the first sixteen years of my career at the *Toronto Sun*. I was as much, if not more, married to my job at the newspaper. I threw my energy and passion into it with abandon, which helped me cope with my deteriorating personal life. The years flew by, all becoming a blur of shift work, fascinating assignments, and a willingness to work overtime. Early in my career at the *Sun*, in 1991, I was assigned to cover the funeral of Dr. Carolyn Warrick, who was viciously stomped to death in the underground parking lot of her downtown condo by two druggies looking for cocaine money. The story struck too close to home. I hadn't told anyone about my 1978 near-death experience because I had convinced myself that it was far behind me and that I was better off than most victims of such heinous crimes for having been able to get on with my life. But Dr. Warrick's vicious killing haunted and nagged at me for days after. I'm not sure I even understood or cared to examine why at the time because I had buried the trauma so deeply. A consummate perfectionist and highly driven, I was determined to be the best at keeping up a tough facade. While I clearly chose to remain in the dark and ignore my own personal hell, something inside me motivated me to start my journey to expose the truth and advocate for others who didn't have a voice. The more I worked those brutally long hours, the less time and energy I had to think about, or rather acknowledge, my personal issues – until 4 a.m., when the anxiety attacks would hit. But even those were attributed to relatively minor worries at the time.

MY PERFECTIONISM LIKELY GOT NOTICED at the paper. But it was only a few years later that I realized the way it was recognized was perhaps not the way I would have preferred. After eighteen months as a general assignment reporter, I was put on the city desk as assistant city editor, which meant that, depending on the shift, I'd either be assigning stories to reporters or batting cleanup – that is, helping to put the paper to bed. For the three years I was on the "desk" – as we called it – I worked with a terrific team (we actually had a team of editors and reporters in those days). Assigning stories helped me develop a sound sense of news judgment, and I did enjoy working with our team of reporters, even the prima donnas. But it took me away from what I had grown to love so much: writing and digging for stories. I wanted very badly to show my stuff by developing a "beat." For months, I pleaded with my bosses to let me leave the city desk to develop contacts and hopefully get breaking stories as the new education beat reporter. It took some convincing, but they finally agreed. Even though I had no kids of my own in the school system, I sensed from the few stories we'd been covering that the system badly needed a wake-up call, and no one at our paper was calling them on it. It was in this same system that Ontario Premier Kathleen Wynne got her political feet wet, first as an activist for an organization called the Toronto Parent Network and subsequently as a trustee with the Toronto District School Board.

What bothered me, virtually from the outset, was the tremendous lack of transparency in the school system and the coziness between the very entitled trustees and the bureaucrats they were charged with overseeing. Within weeks of being on the beat, I journeyed up to York Region to cover a protest by parents over a plan by the region's Catholic school board to lay off two thousand teachers in order to balance their budget. The protest took place in front of their brand new and scandalously expensive headquarters – shockingly bad optics that seemed to go right over the heads of the bureaucrats who ran the board and the trustees who rubber-stamped their decisions. It was a mild April evening, and when I pulled up, hundreds and hundreds of parents and teachers were marching in protest. The group subsequently marched inside the Catholic board's new twenty-two-million-dollar monument to itself to attend that evening's public board meeting, only to find the meeting room doors locked and a phalanx of security guards barring entry to all. I was appalled that the trustees didn't have the guts to face their teachers and the taxpaying public head on. It was arrogant and undemocratic, and it suggested they had much to hide.

From that day forward, I promised myself that I'd force school trustees and those I started calling the "educrats" to come clean to the public who elected them. In mid-1994, I set about exposing the bloated salaries and the expensive meals at fancy restaurants and lavish junkets taken by the top brass at all Metro-area school boards – the same top officials who were crying that they had no cash for school programs and new textbooks or money to fix their facilities. As I hoped, it created such consternation and bad will among parents it forced the education brass into full damage control.

As is the case in the news business, one revelation led to another. When a group of "reform-minded trustees" decided to try to shake up the highly secretive Toronto Catholic board and shine a light on the overspending of its leaders, I was the "go-to" journalist. The group, which called itself the Sunshine Trustees, met in secret one weekend at trustee Mike Del Grande's home to discuss their concerns with their school board colleagues. Mr. Del Grande became a trusted and respected source both while at the school board and subsequently at City Hall. Whenever he called or e-mailed me with the words "I've got juicy juicies," I knew he had something interesting to share. Mike and his fellow Sunshine Trustees were a ballsy bunch. They had their hearts in the right place and helped transform a secretive organization overseen by a not-so-benevolent dictator (education director Tony Barone).

For wanting what was best for the kids in the classroom, the Sunshine Trustees were intimidated, threatened, and even accused of not being Christian.

But it was always the same story with the entrenched school board bureaucrats and trustees. The kids were forever their lowest priority. Perquisites and power came first, and appeasing the teachers' unions and other special interests second. Little wonder there was limited money left to buy new textbooks and other resources for the classroom. Sadly, now, having recently delved back into affairs at the highly dysfunctional Toronto District School Board (TDSB) as an investigative journalist, I can vouch that not much has changed in the past twenty years. If anything, it has probably gotten worse. A shocking two thirds of the current TDSB is comprised of left-leaning trustees, many of whom could not have won their wards without heavy financial and campaign support from a variety of teacher and staff unions or the very public backing of an NDP city councillor. Take downtown trustee Ausma Malik, who captured her ward despite a checkered past that included being a keynote speaker at a pro-Hezbollah, anti-Israel "peace" rally in front of the U.S. consulate in July 2006. She had NDP councillors Mike Layton and Joe Cressy shilling for her when her questionable past came out, accusing those who dared criticize her – including me – of being Islamophobic. The unions are no better. They are well known to target certain wards where they'd want to take out a fiscally conservative trustee. Just ask former trustees Elizabeth Moyer or Mari Rutka, both of whom were bullied by the administration and then toppled in the October 2014 school board elections by heavily union-backed and NDP-leaning trustees. To try to silence Ms. Moyer before she lost her seat, several members of the TDSB administration, I believe, cooked up an accusation that she'd sexually harassed two (male) bureaucrats. And what did Ms. Moyer and Ms. Rutka do to deserve this scandalous treatment? They both dared to bring to light the board's many fiscal issues and stood up to the former board's education director, Donna Quan, now shuffled off with a $600,000 package, by the Liberal government to a cozy gig within the education ministry. Naturally the unions, who expect their quid pro quo, are now calling the shots. The TDSB's collective inability to close underused and costly schools (a decision that could cost a few teachers their jobs) is proof of how beholden the trustees are to the unions.

The bullying and intimidation filters down from the top. For all their talk and the money school board bureaucrats and trustees have spent on anti-bullying campaigns, I am forever amazed at how many school principals and superintendents – right up to the top of the org chart – have tried to bully into submission or ignore parents who dare speak up, hoping they'll give up and go away. That continues to this day. I realized this when I wrote in March 2014 about the case of fourteen-year-old Mylissa Black, who'd been bullied for four years at her Scarborough public school – despite repeated efforts by her parents to get some resolution to the problem. The school board brass ignored their repeated calls, the principal did very little, the trustee was MIA, and the bullying continued until I did a story about it. And then there were the lousy teachers. Even with a College of Teachers and a formal complaints process in place, it is almost impossible to get rid of a bad teacher unless sexual assault, violence, or criminal acts are involved. It is well known in the system that the incompetent, the verbally abusive, and even the physically abusive ones are just quietly shuffled from school to school.

During my time as the *Sun*'s education beat reporter, I met many devoted teachers who just wanted to be left alone to teach and wanted nothing to do with the politics and the activism of their unions. But I also saw the deadwood – those who continued to teach almost by rote and felt no shame bringing their political views into the classroom, rather than retiring and freeing up a spot for someone with fresh ideas and a passion for the profession. I saw the deadwood at Queen's Park during the province-wide teaching strike (against then premier Mike Harris in 1997) and sadly, I still see the same kind of whiners protesting today against the possibility of not getting a raise, or being required to account for their sick days, or having their preparation time better controlled. I was shocked to see the uber-militancy among the teachers in the crowd at an Elementary Teachers Federation of Ontario (ETFO) conference in August 2015. There was much talk from the entitled ones about "solidarity," as they protested for their rights and for fairness, but almost no talk about the kids, whom they hold ransom whenever the provincial government doesn't give them what they think they are due. It doesn't matter which government is in power: the teachers' unions love to play one against the other to see who gives them the most.

THE TRUSTEES – PARTICULARLY THOSE IN TORONTO – often use the school board as a stepping stone to enter municipal politics, and whenever they succeed they repeat the same patterns of mismanagement and overspending. It was a natural move for me to go from reporting on the school boards to covering Toronto

City Hall. But when I was asked if I would go to City Hall in 1998, I didn't see the link and wasn't particularly thrilled with the idea. I thought I'd be bored covering stories on garbage collection, water rates, road construction, and city planning. Because of my political background and my experience working for the province in the 1980s, I thought the Queen's Park beat would be more interesting. But my time at City Hall turned out to be fifteen years of incredible career and personal growth. I never forgot the advice of one of my mentors and a *Toronto Sun* founder, the late and perennially politically incorrect Bob MacDonald, who told me to get to know the real people who made City Hall tick, and not to run with the pack. From very nearly the day I began there, I was determined not to rely on the "party line" from the mayor's office or from the city's top bureaucrats, who knew that if they played the game well and waited it out, they could outlast any change in political leadership.

I took Mr. MacDonald's advice and got to know the people on the frontlines, and very well. I was interested not only in understanding how they did their jobs but in hearing directly from them what it was like to work in what I considered a top-heavy, bloated bureaucracy. The fact is, I like getting my hands dirty and hanging out with those who do, not with the rather drab bureaucrats who fill the offices of City Halls everywhere. I did a ride-along in the back of an ambulance, a stinky shift on a hot August day on a garbage truck, and another with a fire crew in heavy gear on a sweltering night in August. I rode with the bike cops down dark alleys off Toronto's Yonge Street, looking for drug dealers. The clerks in charge of the various City Hall committees became my friends and confidants. We met for coffee and shared the latest gossip and personal milestones. When dear senior clerk Patsy Morris died of cancer at fifty-nine in the fall of 2011, we stood together at her grave mourning the loss of a trusted friend. The security guards were also my friends, ordinary people doing their jobs who knew everything that was going on.

I felt like I had nothing to lose, and hence it came naturally for me to ask unpopular questions, and to be willing to investigate a politician and then confront that politician the very same day my story appeared. It was as if I was making up for lost time. I loved – not too strong a word – taking on councillors and highly placed bureaucrats; the CUPE unions; the firefighters; the thin blue line and their thin-skinned chief, now-retired and Liberal MP Bill Blair; socialist mayor David Miller; the hateful Queers Against Israeli Apartheid (QuAIA) element that invaded the Pride Parade; the intolerant left; and any element of government waste that dearly cost taxpayers.

My job allowed me to become the voice for residents who'd been intimidated by the city and by politicians who'd abused their power. I championed openness and transparency in budgeting and fought against wasteful spending on everything from councillor office budgets to pet projects like the late Jack Layton's plan to build pre-fab housing costing fifty thousand dollars per unit for the 110 squatters living illegally on contaminated lands bordering Lake Ontario. Mr. Layton's and council's lack of political will to deal with Tent City squatters for years – until the encampment grew virtually out of control – earned Toronto an unflattering article in the *New York Times* in June 2002. Even with this wake-up call, it took the politicians three months to get up the nerve to turf the squatters from their campsite.

I tackled sacred cows like the billion-dollar revitalization of Canada's largest social housing project – Regent Park. My three-month investigation revealing that the poor had largely been kicked out of the community to make way for rich speculators and friends of the developer earned me a Sun Media investigative reporting award – and the wrath of left-of-centre media colleagues, who after my stories appeared took turns attempting to discredit my research and prop up the developer, Mitch Cohen of Daniels Corp. Like the poverty pimps who preyed on the poor and homeless, developers were largely considered off-limits for the media at City Hall.

My attempts to hold politicians' feet to the fire earned me a long list of left-of-centre councillors who refused to take my calls and openly bragged about it – Kyle Rae, Paula Fletcher, Janet Davis, Adam Vaughan, Joe Mihevc, Maria Augimeri, Sandra Bussin, and Howard Moscoe to name just a few. But this didn't stop me from pursuing them every time I had a story on them. I often joked that it was a good thing I took up running since I could often be seen chasing more than one politician and six-figure bureaucrat across the council floor or out of a committee room for a comment.

Mr. Rae was perhaps one of the best examples of a councillor notorious for trying to intimidate me into silence. Aside from the fact that by the time I got to City Hall, bullying attempts just made me more intent on pursuing a story or stories, for much of the time I was on the municipal beat, I was living in Yorkville. Mr. Rae was my councillor and I was very troubled by his attempts to put skyscrapers on every corner of what was once a charming neighbourhood of three-storey buildings and upscale shops. The residents' associations with which I was connected fought vociferously against his attempts to "Manhattanize" Yorkville. It was an uphill battle. Mr. Rae was well known to be beholden to the many developers who were building the condo projects. All they had to do was donate the maximum amount to his election campaigns and their approvals sailed through the City Hall approval process. One project that was particularly contentious was the Four Seasons Hotel Toronto – a Menkes project – which included two towers of forty-six and thirty storeys containing both hotel rooms and pricey condos. No one was against the revitalization of the top of Bay Street, and the project is impressive, but at ten times the density rules, it set a terrible precedent for Yorkville. When I approached Mr. Rae during the council debate on the project in 2006 to question him about why he was ramming it through despite very public neighbourhood opposition, he went ballistic. He took the floor and alleged to everyone at the meeting that I had accused him of taking bribes. I had done nothing of the sort, but I suppose by denouncing me publicly, he thought I'd be censured, or intimidated into silence. When that tactic didn't work, Mr. Rae seemed to set out from that day forward to try to make my life at City Hall as difficult as possible. He called my editor whenever I tried to do a story on him, refused to come out of his office each time I endeavoured to interview him for an issue, and was heard regularly to make snippy and bitchy remarks about my weight (considering he battled his own pudginess, that was particularly ironic) and my integrity, or lack thereof. When I finally came out publicly in 2007 and Councillor Doug Holyday asked him what he thought of my revelations, Rae snipped that I may be a lesbian, but I'm a "bad" lesbian.

No matter. I considered it all part of the fallout that came with being an outspoken columnist. I was and am an outsider. I wear it like a badge of honour now, and understand through much experience that journalists must be outsiders to tell the truth and represent their readers. Insiders can't or choose not to tell the truth or they wouldn't be insiders for long. There's a place for insiders, to be sure, but not as investigative journalists – as CBC's Evan Solomon knows well. I'm not putting myself on a pedestal, god knows, partly because I never had a choice in the matter: I was born an outsider.

CHAPTER TWO

Lightning Strikes Twice

On a Tuesday morning in September 2004, three days shy of my forty-eighth birthday, I walked into the office of psychiatrist Karen Abrams. I told Dr. Abrams, who specializes in women's mental health and violence against women issues at Toronto General Hospital, I didn't want to turn fifty still being angry at the world. Finally, after twenty-five years, I was determined to change my life, no matter how painful it would be to strip away the anger and denial.

By the time I got to Dr. Abrams, I was weary and desperately unhappy. I was so depressed that my family doctor put me on anti-depressants to help me cope at work – something I would have never considered in all the years I pretended to be someone I was not. I was tired of living a lie; of denying that the assault of twenty-six years earlier had not deeply affected and traumatized me; of pretending I was tough and on top of the world; of numbly letting my life fly by in a blur while I balanced precariously on a treadmill I couldn't stop.

If I'd ever toyed with the idea of seeking help before, I'd been so busy trying to keep all the pieces of my life together and doing everything I possibly could not to be "outed" as a gay woman, I suppose I didn't have time to look for help. There was always the question of finding the proper fit with a helping professional. In my line of work I'd heard horror stories about psychiatrists, psychologists, and even social workers. As fragile as I felt inside, I was astute enough to know that if I were to reveal my innermost secrets to someone, there had to be a professional bond, a real trust, and an understanding of and insights into my vulnerabilities.

Within a few sessions, I knew I'd found the right person. Karen was Jewish, she had a sense of humour and a tremendous empathy, and never once did she stand in judgment. I liken her work with me almost to that of an emotional tour guide. She let me talk and helped steer me in the right direction. I often describe my role as an investigative journalist, in getting to the bottom of mismanagement and corruption with any organization, as similar to peeling away the layers of an onion. That applied to me during my discussions with Karen. For the first year, I cried almost non-stop in every single forty-five-minute session with her as I revealed my deeply held secrets and anxieties. Slowly but surely – always with her guidance – I started to piece together the patterns of my life and the anger was replaced with an understanding of how I interacted with everyone, both friends and family. My emotional tour guide saw me through a sexual assault trial, my coming out, my breakup with my ex after twenty years of living in the closet, my wedding to Denise, and finally, but only in recent years, my acknowledgment of the deep denial I'd felt around my first assault. I know it was up to me to do the hard work, but I feel myself blessed to have had a therapeutic relationship with Karen.

The Sunday in August that led me to find Dr. Abrams began quite innocuously. Purchasing a storage bench from a store down the street from my condo, I offered the young salesman who served me an extra twenty-five dollars to assemble it after work. I thought nothing of inviting him into my condo because I lived only two doors down the hall from the lobby, which was manned with twenty-four-hour security. Besides, the store was a fixture in my Yorkville neighbourhood and I trusted the owners. I sensed something was wrong about twenty minutes into the young man's visit when he suggested he'd made a mistake putting the bench together. As I peered at what he indicated was the supposed problem, he grabbed me and began caressing my buttocks. I retreated, trembling and in silent horror, to my open-concept kitchen. When I next looked out at him, he had his penis out of his pants. Then, somewhat nervously, the words came tumbling out of him. He told me he'd felt a "vibe" from me and that he'd always had a fantasy about having sex with an older woman in a situation like the one in which he found himself. He asked if he could kiss me. When I told him absolutely not, he persisted. He was now standing in the middle of my living room with his penis fully erect. I would write in the victim impact statement I read in court nine months later that I felt this was not really happening to me. Numb, strangely calm, and fearing somewhere in the recesses of my mind that he would force himself on me, I tried to act as if nothing had happened. I eventually convinced him to zip up his pants and leave. I don't remember whether I paid him. I think I did. I do remember that a few minutes seemed like hours. Considering he could have raped me, I escaped relatively unscathed – physically at least.

Twenty-six years earlier, I had not been so lucky. The first time I was assaulted occurred on a raw and still bitterly cold St. Patrick's Day while I was in my final few months of journalism studies at Carleton University. With a job in Toronto awaiting me when I graduated that May, I decided to sublet my bachelor apartment, putting an ad in the local newspaper. After I'd arranged with the man who answered my ad a time on St. Patrick's morning for him to see my apartment, I asked the superintendent to be there with me. He refused, even chiding me for asking him. I was not a priority, he told me. Convincing myself that nothing could ever happen during the light of day and feeling foolish for asking the superintendent to be there, I didn't want to bother my boyfriend at the time either. As I later learned, it ended up being the perfect time for an assault. Most people were away at work, and the two neighbours who were there and heard my screams chose not to get involved. One later told the police that she thought it was a baby crying. The other believed my cries to be over a domestic issue and she didn't want to get involved.

Within a few minutes of his arrival, I made it pretty clear I was alone and that no one would be coming to keep me company during his tour of my tiny bachelor apartment. When I turned my back on him for just a moment, he struck, bludgeoning me several times on the back of the head with a lead pipe he had hidden in a pocket of his khaki-green duffle coat. With blood from my wounds streaming down my face and into my eyes, I could think of nothing but fighting back. As he continued to hit me, I turned around and tried to knee him in the balls while screaming at the top of my lungs for help. This only made him angrier and more desperate. To try to silence me, he pushed me to the ground, climbed on top of me, and squeezed his hands around my throat. At that point, all I could think of was how my family would take my death. With the blood roaring in my head and my own voice sounding like it was coming from within a deep tunnel, I finally and mercifully passed out. The Ottawa police later told me that was what saved me. Thinking he'd murdered me, my assailant fled. When I came to, I realized no one was coming to help. I don't know how I had the presence of mind, but I dragged myself to my front door and locked it.

Then I called my boyfriend, shrieking hysterically. His lovely grandmother kept me talking while my boyfriend hurried over to my apartment. When he saw me with blood pouring from my head, he panicked and called the fire department instead of the police and EMS.

Later, lying traumatized in the emergency ward of Ottawa General Hospital, I replayed the interchange with my assailant in my mind many times. He had given me clues, but I chose to ignore them. He kept one hand in his coat pocket as we spoke. He changed his story. At first he told me he was in a rush because he had to catch a bus to Arnprior, a forty-four-minute drive west of Ottawa. A few minutes later, just before he assaulted me, he said he was in a hurry to take a flight to Montreal. It took the doctors two dozen stitches to sew my head together. I was left with a dent at the top of my head and a scar above my eyebrow. I suffered a concussion, a blackened eye, and an inability to talk because of the abrasions to my neck and throat.

Upon my release from the hospital, far too traumatized to return to my apartment for fear he'd be back to finish me off, I spent the next few days at the home of my boyfriend's grandparents. The next morning, still reeling from the shock, I went to the police station, where I pored through books filled with various facial features to help the police artist compile a composite sketch. I wanted to ensure I did so before my memories began to fade. That composite would be distributed to every police vehicle and station in the city of Ottawa. The investigating officers told me that, from my description, my assailant easily had a hundred pounds on me. If caught, my attacker would be charged with attempted murder. But I was advised that a capture would most likely occur only if he attacked again. That wasn't what I wanted to hear.

I never returned to my apartment. After a few days back at home in Hamilton, where I recuperated from the beating, the emotional trauma hit me so hard I was afraid to return to Ottawa at all. I would only agree to go back to school and finish my degree if I could live somewhere where there was plenty of protection. My mother Judy flew up to Ottawa a week later, and with my boyfriend's help, I rented a room in the nurse's residence at another hospital. The residence had twenty-four-hour security, and that, at least, was a comfort. I finished my degree requirements, started my new job in Toronto a month later than originally planned, and graduated in November of that year. I suppose I also graduated from the school of hard knocks, so to speak.

When I returned to Ottawa to work in the job for newly elected Prime Minister Joe Clark's government a year later, I never followed up with the police to check on the status of the case. Eleven years later, when I started my journalism career at the *Toronto Sun*, I quickly came to realize that the Ottawa police, considered not the most efficient or effective at their crime-solving abilities, probably didn't go out of their way to solve the crime or even conduct a proper investigation. That said, I could hardly point fingers since I, too, had put the attack behind me.

That was my first mistake. I wish I could say the trauma dissipated, but when anyone is attacked so violently and left for dead, life can never be the same without counselling, or at the very least deep and long introspection. As a result, I spent the next two decades in denial, quick to erupt in anger when I felt overwhelmed, treated unfairly, or when even the smallest things didn't go my way.

As the *Sun*'s editor Lorrie Goldstein told me, the anger found its way into my writing. I'd never allowed myself the indulgence of looking within myself, preferring to engage in my drug of choice: workaholism. Already an obsessive-compulsive personality – meaning in my case that I needed to strive for perfection and fill every waking minute with activity – I was a perfect journalist, forever working long hours and going beyond the call of duty to get the story. The exclusive focus on work wreaked havoc on my personal life, keeping the spotlight off my closeted homosexuality.

In comparison to the first assault, the second attack was minor. But to my shock, it triggered memories of the first, resulting in a form of post-traumatic stress disorder. Within days of the second assault, I fell apart emotionally and sank into a deep depression. For weeks afterward, I would wake up in the middle of the night, panicking and in a sweat. I came to call my Fridays off "Black Fridays" because, with less to keep my mind preoccupied, I would spend much of the day crying. When I could see that, after the first week, the trauma wasn't subsiding, a kind counsellor at the Toronto Police Victim Services unit proposed I contact the Barbra Schlifer Commemorative Clinic – for women who have experienced violence – to make an appointment.

Unfortunately, I was told it would take at least a month for a spot to free up. I thought I could wait, but when my grandfather suddenly passed away, the combined stress and sadness proved insurmountable. A kind social worker friend of my ex, Ellie Levine, seeing that I was in chaos and knowing I didn't know where to turn, got me right in to see Dr. Abrams.

Over the weeks and months that followed, I was blessed to get support from the most unexpected places, in addition to that very generous social worker friend who hooked me up with Dr. Abrams. A few days after the second assault, and still in shock, I had coffee with the city's now retired auditor general, Jeff Griffiths. I tried to put on a brave face as I relayed to him what had happened. After all, my automatic go-to response – based on how I dealt with and was encouraged to deal with my first assault – was to try to make light of it and go on with my life. Mr. Griffiths was in the midst of a follow-up audit on the handling by Toronto police of sexual assault cases. His original review in 1999 had produced a scathing report with dozens of recommendations. After he heard what had transpired with the police response to my assault, he said it sounded to him like the cops had broken every rule of a protocol that had been put in place by then police chief Julian Fantino to ease reporting of such assaults and to ensure police investigators conducted regular and timely follow-up with victims. Mr. Griffiths would prove an invaluable friend and a sounding board, regularly reminding me of what the police were obligated to do. He was the kind of auditor general who was dogged about keeping up the pressure on those bureaucrats he audited. Five and ten years after his initial 1999 review, Mr. Griffiths did in-depth follow-ups to see how far the police had gone to implement his recommendations. His ground-breaking report has been reviewed and used by police forces across North America.

But it was not just the support from unexpected places that helped my healing. What kept me from succumbing to my crippling depression was a determination to get my day in court – the kind of closure I was denied twenty-six years before with my first assault. I soon realized that getting justice would prove to be as much of an uphill battle as facing my demons with Dr. Abrams. Like so many other victims of assault, sexual and otherwise, my ordeal had merely begun with the assault itself. Over the next nine months, I would feel repeatedly betrayed by a system that is supposed to help victims – by jaded cops untrained in sexual assault cases, by a women's support network that appeared to pick and choose who it helped, and by an overstretched legal system that tried to strong-arm victims into dropping their cases. I was careful throughout never to talk about my first assault, except to Dr. Abrams and a very few close friends as a way of explaining why I'd fallen so completely apart. Despite my profile as a journalist, I was forever afraid that if the cops or court officials found out what had happened to me twenty-six years earlier in Ottawa, they would take me even less seriously than they did at the time. (I quickly discovered why more than 80 per cent of Canadian women who suffer a sexual assault do not report it. Put simply, they are afraid of being victimized all over again by the police and the court system.)

Mine was a textbook case of incompetence and apathy by all parties involved. In the seventy-two hours following my assault, I found myself repeating my story eight times to the first responders and then to the investigating police officers located in the division representing my Toronto neighbourhood – as if I was being tested to see if my story would stand up under repeated scrutiny. In the first week after the assault, I came into the police station and recorded my statement, only to be told the camera hadn't worked, forcing me to repeat it a second time.

Although my assailant was arrested the day after the assault, right in the store employing him—Structube – his manager denied all culpability, claiming the incident had taken place outside the store and after working hours. She even refused to do the bare minimum and apologize for what had happened. To further rub my nose in it, my assailant retained his employment, and at that location instead of being transferred to another store or put on leave until the court case was settled.

The real culprit was the police. Given the circumstances – the store was right down the street from my condo – they could have made it a condition of my assailant's bail that he was not allowed within a safe distance of my residence. Instead, and without my knowledge until it was too late, he was merely ordered not to come within one hundred metres of my home, which is nothing – forcing me for the next nine months to live in fear that I'd run into him. And I did, three times.

When I told the investigating officer that it was difficult to walk by the store, he chided me, saying that if it were him and it bothered him as much as it bothered me, he would walk out of his way, even if it meant adding thirty extra minutes to his route to work, to avoid such an encounter. Disgusted with his lack of empathy, his victim-shaming and poor follow-up, I blew up at him, and he blew up at me. We eventually calmed down and reached a truce, and to his credit, from that day forward, he was much gentler and more helpful in his approach to my case. Just before Christmas (and nearly four months after the assault) he contacted me to say the Crown was considering dropping the charges but he'd be recommending against that. I made it clear I would not allow that to happen and thanked him for his vote of confidence.

The system set up to provide counselling support to victims in crisis wasn't much better. Aside from the Toronto Police Victim Services, which was only a stopgap measure, I found myself repeatedly pouring out my story to various counselling agencies, only to find out they either had a long waiting list or to not hear back from them again. I never once told any of them I was a journalist, although some probably recognized my name. Throughout, I wondered – if I'd presented as more vulnerable (and perhaps less affluent), would they have found me an opening much faster? I will never know.

The Barbra Schlifer Commemorative Clinic, about which I'd heard wonderful things, contacted me after three months – long after I started counselling with Dr. Abrams – to tell me a spot had opened up. That was not the only agency to leave me hanging. About two weeks after the assault, I met with the assistant coordinator with the provincial Victim/Witness Assistance Program who was charged with acting as an advocate as my case proceeded to a plea or to trial. I poured my heart out to her that day, never to hear from her again. It was only when I tried to reach her three months later that I found out she'd been assigned to a new job a few weeks after we met. No one new had been put on my case. I was left to fend for myself over the Christmas holidays, as I wrote my victim impact statement in preparation for a January pre-trial conference on the case.

The Victim/Witness Assistance Program reluctantly agreed to set up a meeting with the Crown attorney, Chris Punter, in early January after I insisted on it. And I did hear from a new case worker with the provincial courts in March, but it was long after I'd written my own victim impact statement, built up a wonderful support network, and taken significant steps on my journey of self-discovery with Dr. Abrams. By 2005, after seven years as a columnist at City Hall, I was well enough known to police and the courts for my scrappy approach to political reporting. Yet I never asked for, or expected, special treatment. I only wanted to be treated fairly and with respect. But when that didn't happen, I was more than dogged about getting my day in court. I wanted to be the voice for others in my predicament who did not have a voice, or who felt battered even more by the system. Still, it was only after I met with Mr. Punter and two officers from the Victim/Witness Assistance Program that I started to feel they were taking my case seriously. Although I never indicated who I was, Mr. Punter made reference to my column in the *Toronto Sun*, suggesting to me that it was partly my profile that had helped attach more of a seriousness to the case. I could only imagine how others without a column were treated. He told me my assailant wanted to plead guilty to common assault, but given the brazenness of the attack, the Crown would only accept a guilty plea to the original charge of sexual assault. That would get him listed on the national sex offender registry, but it was unlikely he'd get jail time because it was a first offence. Mr. Punter also offered little hope that any judge would include an order in the sentencing subsequently causing my assailant to lose his job. I insisted that I would deliver my victim impact statement in person to try to make whichever judge heard the case understand what it was like to walk regularly by Structube and see my assailant waiting on other women as if nothing had happened. The Crown agreed that would have far better impact, if I could handle doing it.

The court date to hear my assailant's guilty plea was originally set for March 9. I was still dreadfully ill from a version of Lyme disease I'd caught during a trek in South Africa the month before and from a severe allergic reaction to the drug given to me to treat it. But I dragged myself to court anyway with my uncle Jeff, only to be told the case was being put over because the judge scheduled to hear the plea was off sick.

Two months later, on May 3, I was back in court with my uncle. As I entered the appointed courtroom at 2 p.m., I was handed a typed apology from my assailant. Again the scheduled judge was not available to hear the guilty plea, but the Crown and the trial scheduling office refused to put the matter over as suggested by the defence attorney. Justice John Moore was found to be free and we were sent to another courtroom. Within minutes of hearing the guilty plea, he instructed me to come forward to give my victim impact statement. It was difficult not to break down as I provided an insight into the impact of the assault on my life and how it had felt to encounter my assailant more than once over the nine months I waited for my court date.

I pleaded with Justice Moore that any punishment meted out to my assailant should include forcing him to leave his job at Structube, especially since the store was not prepared to do the right thing. I told the court that day that I should not have to change my life for fear of running into him. "I should be able to go on feeling comfortable and at ease in my own neighbourhood," I told the judge. You could hear a pin drop in the courtroom when I finished my statement. I looked over and saw my uncle wiping tears from his eyes. Mr. Punter got up and argued vociferously for both the prohibition order and a suspended sentence, which would have left my assailant with a criminal record.

The defence attorney, who produced a psychiatric assessment that said my assailant would be unlikely to reoffend, informed the court, without a trace of irony in his voice given my just-delivered statement, that Structube would be happy to keep him on. To add insult to injury, unless the judge ruled otherwise, the store said it would resume sending him out on "house calls." Bear in mind this was the very store that had denied any and all responsibility for my assault even though it had been perpetrated by one of its employees, claiming my "house call" had happened after store hours.

Justice Moore reserved judgment, asking us to come back the next day at 2 p.m. for his decision. It was a difficult night for me, but I also took the delay as a sign he'd be giving my request serious consideration. Returning to court the next afternoon with my next-door neighbour – the very same one I first went to after the assault – my heart at first sank when the Justice ruled my assailant should get a conditional discharge, meaning no criminal record. I waited for the other shoe to drop. But it didn't. Justice Moore agreed with my sentiments, declaring that my attacker would be restricted from being within one kilometre of my home during an eighteen-month probation period.

He also went so far as to take direct aim at Structube for the way it had handled the matter. "Just as an aside, I really, really agree with Ms. Levy. I can't believe that he [the assailant] is still working there; that the store would keep him on," the judge said. "It is just incredible that they would want to keep him on, despite all the good qualities he might have."

It was a shock – although a welcome one – to all in the courtroom that day, including the investigating officer and the Crown attorney. I felt vindicated. Outside the courtroom – while her son was taken away to give a DNA sample for the Canadian sex-offender registry – the assailant's mother came up to me and apologized, through tears, for the trauma I'd been through. She suggested that she knew something was not right with her son. I thanked her for her graciousness.

My neighbour and I went home and cracked open a chilled bottle of wine to celebrate this small but important victory. The Crown attorney and investigating officer later suggested to me that it was a good thing I insisted on seeing the court case through. They felt this probably wasn't the first time my assailant had done what he had, and I'd probably stopped him from escalating behaviour that likely would have ended in rape.

A close friend was so incensed with the store's negligence, she urged me a few months later to use the judgment as a basis for pursuing legal action against Structube. I opted not to, for more than one reason. After twenty-seven long, painful years, I'd finally gotten my day in court. I did not want to relive the agony with a civil action. Discussing it with my editor-in-chief at the time, Lou Clancy, I decided I could do something far more positive by writing a two-part series for the *Toronto Sun* about how the judicial system had treated me. I felt strongly that if I could educate others while trying to effect changes, that would be more rewarding for me in the end. The series ran in July 2005. After it appeared, I was inundated with e-mails from readers who'd had their own experiences with the system. Half of the comments were from men who had known or were close to a sexual assault victim.

Although I feel like a ten-ton weight has been lifted from my shoulders, the trauma never ever goes completely away. How could it? While watching the stories unfold in the fall of 2015 of disgraced CBC radio host Jian Ghomeshi – who was awaiting trial on five counts of sexual assault and one of choking – and of the disturbing double life of entertainer Bill Cosby, my immediate reaction was to empathize with the victims of both men. I know from my own experience it takes strength and persistence to pursue a sexual assault charge and to deal with judicial systems that are still far too quick to either write off or blame the victim. In my mind, there is very little wiggle room for questioning the veracity of their claims. After all, how many women would want to put themselves through the ordeal of reliving an assault, over and over again, if it did not happen? Sadly, it became abundantly clear with both of these recent cases that the blame-the-victim culture is still very much alive and well. When Mr. Ghomeshi was acquitted of three charges of sexual assault and one of choking in late March 2016, I couldn't help but think the police and the Crown had failed in their job to build a respectable case and that not much had changed since 2005. I am not so naive as to fail to recognize that one's celebrity status – applicable of course to Ghomeshi and Cosby – is a powerful aphrodisiac and that made the women in both cases particularly vulnerable before and after the alleged assaults. What really incensed me, but what I certainly did not find surprising, was that officials with the CBC – the great bastion of political correctness, tolerance, empathy, yada, yada – sat on their hands and did nothing when the tales of how Mr. Ghomeshi abused his position with his female co-workers started to come to light.

I was delighted to see that their mishandling of this entire affair did indeed tarnish the CBC brand. The penalty was well deserved. I have no trouble saying that, after living my own nightmare and emerging, proudly, with nothing to hide. After many years of working through the pain and denial with Dr. Abrams, I am finally no longer ashamed to concede that lightning has indeed struck twice in my life. I am literal proof of that well-known adage that what doesn't kill you makes you stronger.

CHAPTER THREE

Secrets

For twenty years, I lived in a closeted relationship afraid to tell the truth about myself, convinced I would not be accepted by my family and that being out would severely limit my career ambitions. I lived that lie with one foot firmly planted in the heterosexual world and the other in the gay world, trying to make as "normal" a life as one could with a partner who was quite happy to keep our relationship secret, even long after I decided to come out. Heaven knows I am not the only gay person who lived a lie for a long time, but looking back now, I am amazed I did. Today, my past seems like a whole other life, lived by someone other than myself. Sometimes I wish I could get those years back, if only because living a lie as I did meant I gave up any and all chance of having children of my own.

My wife, Denise, is fond of teasing me that I have the memory of an elephant. I had to. I grew adept at talking about a straight life that didn't exist and remembering what I'd told to whom. Now I can't even fathom engaging in the kind of mental gymnastics or keeping all the stories straight that I was forced to then. Anybody who chooses to be closeted knows this routine. To the world beyond my front door, I was a single woman who happened to be very picky and was just waiting for the right man to come along. I survived in a kind of holding pattern, always deluding myself that one day down the road, this sexual diversion would end and I'd have a traditional marriage and children. Had I met Denise sooner, I suspect we would have had children of our own and been as regular a family as is possible as a same-sex Jewish couple. Regrettably, we met too late to consider having children; we do have a traditional Jewish home and are very tied to our faith and its traditions.

Whenever a family member or friend tried to fix me up, I'd reluctantly agree if only to throw them off the scent. It didn't hurt either that it provided me with enough stories I could tell to make them think I really was looking for a man to marry – and to divert attention away from my real life with my partner of twenty years. Still, I was able to live that lie for so long because I didn't present as a "typical lesbian." I'm what is referred to as a "lipstick lesbian," if only because I love to wear . . . lipstick – and designer clothes, jewellery, and other makeup. Still, back then I would always wince when I heard the word *lesbian*. It is only in the last decade that I've even been able to refer to myself as a lesbian. Fairly early into our relationship, my ex, a former journalist, decided to live outside Toronto in the summer to pursue a second career in real estate. For nearly eight months of the year, I saw her only on weekends, also making it easy to fool people into thinking I was really living alone.

Our dance of deceit started almost from the moment we met at a club playing tennis just as I was about to turn twenty-nine and she forty. There were three of us who became fast friends that summer, one very clearly heterosexual. But when my ex and I started spending as much time off the court sharing our innermost secrets, we discovered an emotional spark. We never really talked about who we were to each other or what our connection meant; we just kind of fell into it. With our significant age difference, I guess I also looked up to her as a mentor, both professionally and emotionally. After a few months together keeping separate apartments, we decided to rent a duplex apartment, but we agreed it had to have two bedrooms. The bed in the spare room would get a kind of fake roughing up before people came to visit. Before her parents grew too old to come to the family cottage, I'd sleep in a separate bedroom as if I was just a friend or roommate coming along for the weekend. We found out to our horror many years later that not even my ex's young niece and nephew were fooled by our fake bed or other living arrangements. To satisfy my nurturing instinct, my ex encouraged me to get my first long-haired dachshund, Shopsy. Although she wasn't really keen on dogs, she grew to love Shopsy and was heart-broken when we had to put her down. We travelled the world together extensively, but for years I even had a convenient excuse for that as well. My ex introduced me to the world of travel writing, and very soon after I joined the *Toronto Sun*, I found a niche writing ski stories for the paper on a freelance basis. We'd simply visit different resorts in western Canada and the U.S. as two friends and journalists on travel assignments. Later, when my travel writing portfolio expanded and I started to pursue assignments in southern destinations and exotic locales like Ecuador, South Africa, Australia, New Zealand, and Fiji – the latter three countries were visited during a fabulous six-week trip we took together for my first sabbatical from the *Toronto Sun* in 1999 – she became my photographer and travelling companion. While on assignment, no one questioned what we were to each other and we certainly didn't offer any explanation. Years later, when I confessed our couple status to skiing legend and Tory senator Nancy Greene – whom we dined and skied with during more than one visit to her resort at Sun Peaks, B.C. – she was not at all surprised. I still remember telling her about my long-held secret over drinks at Toronto's Canoe restaurant. We discussed how difficult the relationship could become with one partner refusing to come out of the closet. That conversation proved to be prophetic, even though it took me a year to realize that myself.

In 1989, at the age of thirty-two, after leaving twelve years in corporate and government public relations for a newspaper career and before I started working at the *Sun*, my ex encouraged me to seek the job in Muskoka so we could live together. We continued our little charade, telling everyone the arrangement was in the interest of saving money. When I started at the *Toronto Sun* seven months later, I didn't dare speak about my circumstances. As much as I'd found my home with a feisty paper, I suspected that a tabloid featuring Sunshine Girls wouldn't be too kindly disposed toward having a lesbian on staff. Sexism in the newspaper business was still prevalent in the early nineties. Anyone who denies it either doesn't know what they're talking about or is a liar. But editors who made chauvinistic comments to me on the city desk then wouldn't dream of acting that way now.

At thirty-six, having watched my younger brother get married, and afraid that I'd never be in the position to have children if I remained in a closeted relationship, I left my ex for several months. I purchased a condo with the idea of trying to date men and find a husband. But within months, we were back together. I plunged even deeper into the closet and threw myself into my journalism career, trying to convince everyone, particularly myself, that I was career-minded and not really meant to have children anyway. From that point onward, I was careful only to invite my family to my condo after my ex had left for Muskoka. Their trips to Florida in the winter months, when she lived with me, made it easy to continue living a lie. In many ways, I felt very ashamed that I'd let my family and myself down by not following the route of having a traditional Jewish home and marriage. It would take me a long, long time to realize that I had absolutely no reason to feel guilty. Now that I'm out, I am grateful that I did not end up marrying a man. But I did end up getting married to a kind and generous Jewish woman. I do not mean to insult the many gay women of my generation who did marry men, only to leave them and come out, perhaps because it became more acceptable in the eyes of family and society in general, or because they grew fed up with living a lie. But I'm glad I didn't put a husband and children through the emotional wringer as well. I have seen the toll it can take on those who had no option but to deal with the breakdown of their families.

The next thing I knew, I was forty-something and had found a strong voice at the *Toronto Sun*. Still afraid to come out, I nevertheless endeavoured to put my toe in the water by writing about LGBT issues. When I first got to City Hall, I covered Mayor Mel Lastman's decision to march in the Pride Parade as leader of the newly amalgamated city, despite his discomfort with the spectacle. I understand how he felt, considering my discomfort and absolute fear of admitting who I really was. To this day, my wife and I aren't comfortable with the public nudity at the parade, and believe it takes away from the true message of Pride Day. Each and every time I wrote about the Pride Parade or gay marriage – and I did so every year during my early days as the *Toronto Sun*'s City Hall columnist – I kept hoping I'd have the courage to come out myself. At least, I thought, in some small way I was serving as a voice for LGBT issues, even if I hadn't come to grips with my own sexuality at that point. Still, as the years went on, it became tremendously exhausting to live a double life. The more I carried on with the charade, the more I experienced extreme anxiety, insomnia, and depression.

It was New Year's Eve 2004 – and it happened quite innocuously. I was celebrating with my ex and some friends at her brother's cottage as we did every year. We'd have hors d'oeuvres and dinner, and then if it was cold enough, skate on a rink made by my ex's brother. Fuelled by a few glasses of wine, one friend, a woman older than me with grown children of her own, got into an intense conversation with me about my family. When I suggested that the relationship with my family had its share of troubled moments, she asked if that was because I was a lesbian. My heart started pounding at the idea that I'd been "busted," but that's where the conversation ended. A few days later, I thanked her for her forthrightness and for having the courage to say what I'd been so afraid to say for years. On New Year's Day, I woke up and told my ex, through tears and perhaps a tad dramatically (as I have a habit of doing), that I couldn't live in secret anymore and that if I did anything that year, I'd come out. I suspect at the time she was horrified but didn't think I would follow through on my vow to come out. She said repeatedly – both that day and in the months that followed – that she was quite content to remain closeted; that it had worked for nineteen years and things did not need to change. And for months I didn't follow through on my promise – until I was assaulted in the summer of that same year.

That assault, coupled with the loss of our beloved dachshund Shopsy quite suddenly from cancer two months before, proved to be the impetus I needed. I had made up my mind before I walked into Dr. Abrams's office that if we were to pursue a therapeutic relationship together, I'd come out, regardless of the consequences. I still remember the day I first came out to the doctor herself. I left a City Hall committee meeting for my forty-five-minute session – only my third meeting with her – more nervous at the thought of talking about my same-sex relationship than about my two assaults or my family dynamics. When she got to the point of asking me if I was in a relationship with a man, I shook my head and started to sob. I think I sputtered that I was with a woman and that no one knew, that she was the first. I was so beside myself I don't recall my exact words. It's kind of funny now. Dr. Abrams recently admitted to me that I even caught her by surprise seeing as I didn't present as a butch lesbian loaded with tattoos and body piercings. After crying my eyes out for most of those forty-five minutes, I had to return to City Hall that very same afternoon to write a column. That pattern would continue for at least a year – an emotional session followed by a day at City Hall feeling completely drained and looking a little worse for wear, but pushing myself to do my job and produce a column. I forever hoped no one would know what was tearing me up emotionally. But I know I had my days. A lovely woman who worked for the NDP caucus at Queen's Park confided in me years later that she called me during that year to ask if I wanted to speak to one of her caucus members on the City of Toronto Act. In a fit of pique, I told her I'd already had quite enough with all the damn socialists given my attempts to deal with the lunacy at City Hall under Mayor David Miller and that I was definitely not interested. Of course I can laugh about it now. But it was certainly an indication of how fragile I was as I worked to undo twenty years of closeted living.

With Dr. Abrams's support, I approached my coming out very strategically. I first told my closest friends, whom I could trust not to spill the beans to others, and then finally, after nearly a year, my family. Some knew long before my confession and were just waiting to hear it from me. My dear friend Rosemary Euringer, with whom I'd grown up in Hamilton, told me she'd wished I'd confided in her sooner – that she'd always suspected. I fooled former *Toronto Sun* reporter and another good friend, Moira MacDonald, so well that she surprised me with a male stripper for my fortieth birthday party. He came dressed as a police officer and handcuffed me for being mean to school trustees (I was on the education beat at the time). I enjoyed every minute of it and was touched that she and her dear late dad, Bob, went to such lengths for my birthday. When I did finally come out to her, it was over dinner in Toronto. She says she was not at all surprised that I struggled to get it out – except that throughout she was figuratively slapping herself upside the head with questions of how she missed it.

She recently told me she was sorry that I had to go through the "whole masquerade" of hiding my real life from friends.

I was the consummate actress. As the months went by and I began feeling more comfortable with my decision to come out, I reached out to some of my closer colleagues at the *Toronto Sun* and City Hall. The day I told my colleague and friend Zen Ruryk, alongside whom I worked for many years at City Hall, I closed the door and started crying with pent-up emotion because I'd lied to him so many times about my personal life. Zen, living up to his name, told me he'd always suspected something was up because I was too attractive not to be hooked up with a man if I'd wanted to. That's all he needed to say. We hugged and have been as close as brother and sister ever since. Support came from many places at the *Toronto Sun*. My Queen's Park colleague Chris Blizzard, upon hearing about my coming-out process, phoned me out of the blue one day to say she'd found a Jewish lesbian working in the Ontario government who'd be willing to talk to me and offer support. Chris did not need to do that but went out of her way to help. Nevertheless, it was still early in my journey and I never did call the woman for fear that my secret would get out in political circles. Now it seems silly to me, but I feared that I would not be able to cope with the potential fallout. At City Hall, I decided Conservative councillor Doug Holyday and his lovely assistants, Bev McVeigh and Judy Ambrose, would be the first to be told. I had built up such a relationship of trust with all three of them that I expected they would neither judge nor gossip. I was absolutely right. Four years later, when I married Denise, I insisted on inviting all of the members of the *Toronto Sun* and political families who had given me support and comfort during my year-long journey – including Chris; Zen and his wife, Jackie; auditor general Jeff Griffiths; and Doug, Bev, and Judy.

As time went on and I expanded my circle of those who knew, I felt like a huge weight was being lifted from my chest. I left my family to the end, first telling my brother after a 10K run we did together. When I said through tears that I was always afraid to come out for fear I'd be a bad example for my niece and two nephews, he told me not to think that for a minute. A few years later, my nephew Cooper, then ten, marched in my wedding, and to this day, all three of my brother's kids treat Denise and me like we're any other couple. Although I know young people still get bullied in school for being gay and I am not so naive as to think we as a couple don't have to be careful when we travel to certain countries and American states, it is thrilling to see how much more accepting kids of my niece and nephews' generation are. I often get asked now if I regret going through the pain and hardship I did, seeing as acceptance of gay marriage has changed so dramatically in the past five years – and especially south of the border within the last year. I try not to make a habit of dwelling on what could have been; nevertheless, I find myself trying to be as outspoken as possible about my marriage to Denise and about being gay, perhaps to make up for lost time.

I decided to tell my parents before the year was out and at a public restaurant, just in case things got out of hand (more on my part). It seems ages ago, but at the time I was a basket case. I don't remember how I managed to eat any of my dinner that night with all the tears. But I do remember telling them I'd always felt I let them down and my dad responding that my comment was nonsense, that he was proud of me and that I reminded him of Ellen DeGeneres. Okay, I thought, not so bad. My mother needed time to let it sink in, although she did admit she'd always suspected. The next week, when I told Dr. Abrams about what had happened, we both started to cry. I felt free at last, except for one very major issue. Sadly, throughout, my ex continued to vociferously resist my coming-out efforts – even though we had told her family that what they long suspected was true and they now embraced our relationship. She was extremely upset with me when I suggested to our Muskoka vet that we were a couple, although I would bet the vet knew all along, seeing as we made no secret that Shopsy had two mommies. I believe to this day that the combination of her having been married before, being eleven years older, and trying to practise real estate in a small town made her afraid to admit what we really had together. Whether the fear was realistic or not, it was real to her. The tension between one partner living in the closet and the other coming out to the world proved to be our undoing – although I wouldn't admit it at the time. In May 2005, when my assailant from Structube pleaded guilty in court to sexual assault, my ex was so fearful of being publicly exposed as my partner – even though at that point her family and my friends already knew we were a couple – that she opted not to come to court with me. After convincing me to pursue the case to the bitter end, she convinced herself that accompanying me would damage my case, though that made absolutely no sense. I suppose I had so much to deal with at the time, I pretended it didn't matter. But looking back, it hurt me terribly and was probably the beginning of the end for us.

In the spring of 2006, some six months before we split, I learned of a support group for lesbians endeavouring to come out, generously operated in their home by a lesbian couple, Carol Pasternak and Audrey Kouyoumdjian. The couple had both been married to men and had had children before meeting each other in 2002. I begged my ex to come with me to the group, but she adamantly refused. I will never forget Audrey's words when I first talked about how my ex and I had lived in the closet for so long, and raised the issue of her resistance to coming out. Audrey said, in her experience, such relationships usually don't last. In absolute denial, I responded adamantly that our relationship was different. But by that spring, we were fighting more than getting along and I started spending less and less time at my ex's cottage on weekends. When I ran my very first half marathon in Ottawa in May 2006 – after four long and arduous months of training – my ex didn't come to Ottawa to cheer me on. That same month, I went to visit my ex's mother in her assisted living apartment. Her mother was well into her nineties, gravely ill, and receiving twenty-four-hour care. She couldn't understand why her daughter and I were apart on a weekend when I was supposed to be at the cottage. She told me in her by then frail voice that she was so happy her daughter had someone with whom to spend her life. That was the funny thing. Even though she couldn't articulate the word *lesbian*, she accepted and was happy that we were a couple.

Nevertheless, Audrey's words were indeed prophetic. When my ex's mother passed away a little more than a month later, things really took a turn for the worse. By then I was out enough at the *Toronto Sun* to take three days of compassionate leave to be with my ex for the funeral and the shiva. But when I sat with her and the rest of the family at the funeral home to make the arrangements and to write the obituary, my partner of twenty years adamantly refused to have me listed with her as a couple in her mother's obituary. Her brother and sister-in-law tried to convince her otherwise, but, no doubt again out of fear of being "outed," she would not budge. To add insult to injury, she got very upset with her niece – who was delivering one of the final tributes at the funeral – for daring to suggest in it that we were a couple. Her niece was forced to mention me as a friend of the family. I was crushed beyond words, especially because I was by her side at the funeral and the shiva. I made it through another month of weekends at the cottage, but I knew I was just going through the motions. At that point, though, I didn't realize how quickly the relationship would come crashing to an end.

In the last week of July, I received a call from a lawyer telling me he had a great story for me – an issue symbolizing everything that was wrong with City Hall. He said his client, Denise Alexander, had just been to a meeting of the community council representing midtown Toronto, and her councillor, Michael Walker, was poised to pull a fast one by trying to yank her permit for a widened driveway. The city had approved the driveway three years earlier after she'd fulfilled thousands of dollars of landscaping requirements, and since then she'd been paying a permit fee to the city for the privilege of using it. As we later learned when I did a Freedom of Information search, the councillor had for almost a year been meeting behind the scenes with Denise's neighbours on either side.

Just a few months later, the neighbours sported Mr. Walker's campaign signs on their property and we learned after the election that they'd donated to his re-election campaign. That, sadly, is how easily most councillors are swayed to action, whether for the positive or the negative. Denise's lawyer was hoping a story could run before the vote on her driveway came to full council. I was reluctant to do it because my plate was full. But her lawyer persisted and without even knowing Denise, I found myself incensed at the idea of the system, yet again, abusing innocent taxpayers. So, on a Friday, as I was packing to go to my ex's cottage, I did a pre-interview with Denise by phone. It was just one question that forever changed both of our lives. I asked her why she thought her neighbours would engage in such harassment – meaning, what was in it for them? Denise told me it was "off the record" but she thought it was because she'd been living with a woman. I responded that if it made her feel better, I was gay too and I'd also had issues with my neighbours in the condo where I lived. I could never prove it, but I suspected some of them changed the way they interacted with me after I came out. If timing is everything, this was proof. One can only imagine what I might have said, or not said, had it been a year earlier and I was not yet out of the closet.

My conversation with Denise that Friday morning, while strictly professional, haunted me through my entire weekend in Muskoka, not because of the subject matter but because of her. She came across, even over the phone, as a highly intelligent woman with a fabulous sense of humour and a tremendous warmth. To add to my confusion, my ex decided not to show up to cheer me on as I participated in my first Try-a-Triathlon event that weekend. Upon my return home Sunday night, I phoned Denise to confirm my interview with her for the next morning. When she heard my dog, Kishka, barking in the background, she asked what kind of dog I had. I told her Kishka was a long-haired miniature dachshund, to which she responded that she had the same rare breed, four-teen-year-old Zigmund.

The next day, as I drove up to her house, I kept repeating the mantra "Oh please let her be fat and ugly." When I arrived and she opened the door, I knew it was game over. I was immediately taken by her twinkly turquoise blue eyes and her hot body. I was so discombobulated, I could barely concentrate on the interview, and for the first time in my nearly eighteen years at the *Toronto Sun*, I had to really force myself to keep focused on the story. The next day, when my story appeared and helped get Denise a deferral at council (a major feat considering how often community council issues were and still are usually rammed through without question at council), she called me at work to say thank you and to invite me for Friday night dinner, as "any good Jewish girl" would do. I don't know where I got the courage, but I told her I was in a relationship and that it would be very dangerous for me to come over for dinner, seeing as I felt a chemistry during the interview. But Denise wasn't taking no for an answer. She said it was just a thank-you dinner, and once she had placed the food on the table, if it would make me feel more comfortable, she would give me some duct tape to use in whatever way I needed to feel safe. (When I arrived that Friday night, she'd set the table using the duct tape as a napkin ring.) I was still unsure about going until I had dinner with a former *Toronto Sun* colleague, Trish Tervit, who'd also come out, but after she'd left the paper. When I asked her what she thought, she simply said, "Life is not a dress rehearsal."

Especially mine, I thought. Here I was at a point in my life where I'd overcome tremendous hurdles, including surviving two assaults and coming out. I wasn't going to stop here.

So a mere seven weeks before my fiftieth birthday, I went for that Shabbat dinner. It started at 7 p.m. and ended at 8 a.m. the next morning, when I went home. Nothing untoward happened. Denise and I just talked all night. From that point forward, it was only a matter of time before my relationship ended with my ex. She had planned to take me on a cruise of the Greek Islands, starting in Venice, for my fiftieth birthday. Through my travel-writing connections, I had gotten us one of the best rooms on the ship, but I decided that in all good conscience I could not go. By the time my birthday rolled around, we had split. She kind of faded out of my life, sadly, after twenty years together, along with many of her family members and friends with whom I'd spent so many hours and years. It was a divorce with no assets to divide because we'd lived such separate lives, financially and, as I realized later, emotionally.

To the surprise of the politicians, friends, and family members who attended the cocktail party thrown by my parents at Toronto's old Four Seasons hotel in honour of my birthday, Denise turned up as my date. She met everyone in my life for the first time that night, handling herself in her usual bubbly and infectious manner. She'd even taken the time to go to Holt Renfrew to pick out a little black dress for my then very trim size 8 figure to wear to the party. From that day forward, Denise, who has a talent for design and decorating and who had worked in fashion before meeting me, became my advisor and guru in these realms, although her equally wonderful talents in the kitchen have cost me that size 8 figure. Despite the reservations expressed by my friends and family about my jumping from one long-term relationship into another, I just knew that Denise was the woman I'd been waiting for all my life. I told everyone she was my fiftieth birthday present. I felt alive again. Two months after we met, Denise met me at the finish line with a bouquet of flowers following my second half marathon in Toronto, one that produced a time I will never be able to top, no doubt because of the adrenaline rush of showing off for a new love. Surprisingly, moving so quickly from one relationship to another wasn't as difficult as I thought it would be. I did have much to learn, however, about being open and out. Undoing twenty years of secrecy took time and patience. For the first few months, when Denise grabbed my hand as we walked along a Toronto street, I'd flinch and pull away, worried about what people would think.

The months went by and we settled into being a couple, travelling together first to Italy in March 2007 and to Israel in June. Both were reporting assignments, and Denise joined me on her own dime to visit two of her favourite destinations. We returned home from Israel just days before the 2007 Pride weekend, but at that point, the gay Pride festivities were merely something I could acknowledge more openly as someone who was finally out. We had no interest in being part of the parade. In fact, we'd been invited to two parties that day – one for Pride and another to celebrate Canada Day, which happened to fall that year on the same day. But when a column by freelancer Dave Menzies appeared in the *Sun* on the Friday before Pride Day, I decided that was a call for me to come out publicly. Mr. Menzies took offence with the gay agenda in general, and specifically with how mainstream the gay lifestyle had become. I was so upset reading it over breakfast, I started to weep. I decided that this wasn't so much about us going to a party and a parade. It was the point it made. Perhaps it says something that today Dave and I are good friends.

With Denise's and my editor's encouragement, I decided to write a column about my own twenty-year journey of living in and subsequently coming out of the closet. The column ran on Pride Day 2007. Denise, as bubbly and outgoing as she is, is at heart a private person. But she understood the need to make a strong statement about coming out after so many years of living a lie. And I had a "public voice" that perhaps could help others dealing with the same issues. The day before the column ran, I phoned my parents to warn them. I told my mother I felt I needed to do it for all kinds of reasons. My parents took the news well. In fact, on the Sunday morning when the column appeared (the *Sun* staff neglected to let me know that my picture and a headline would be on the paper's front page) my father called to say he hadn't choked on his English muffin seeing it in print. The response was overwhelmingly positive – I was inundated with e-mails, starting with a lovely one at 5 a.m. from John Tory. Buoyed by the outpouring of support, I decided unambiguously that I'd spent all too many years hiding who I was. I would not base my entire identity on being gay, but from that day forward, I resolved to write about my lifestyle and advocate for others still afraid to come out of the closet, if and when the opportunity presented itself. I certainly felt there weren't, and still aren't, enough journalists prepared to be public about it – even those embracing the left side of the political spectrum. I also felt, and continue to feel, it is important to show that the *Sun* – despite the bad rap it regularly gets from the left-wing media elitists – has no problem with me being out and open about my views.

A year later, having decided Denise was the woman with whom I wanted to spend the rest of my life, I concocted a plan to ask her to marry me while at a fancy dinner on her birthday. I booked a window-side table overlooking the Toronto skyline at the posh Canoe restaurant and arranged to have an engagement ring delivered in a dessert dome, along with a card expressing my love and passion for her. The evening went perfectly and she loved the ring. There was just one problem. It wasn't until the next day that Denise realized that I'd asked her to marry me. I hadn't actually used the word *marriage*, and Denise thought the ring was just a lovely birthday present. Being very close to the next table at the restaurant, I got a rare attack of shyness (I was still not used to being openly gay). I mistakenly thought the card spoke for itself.

When she realized my intentions and accepted, we were faced with the task of telling our families. My parents, realizing I was happy and settled at last, took it well. I suppose that once they accepted that I was gay and that I was deeply in love with another woman, marriage wasn't that big a leap for them. Unfortunately, the same couldn't be said for Denise's parents. Even though Denise's mother and father knew she'd dated women for many years, the reality of her marrying another woman in a traditional and very public ceremony was more than they could handle. For the longest time, her father steadfastly refused to attend our wedding and her mother would not agree to walk her down the aisle alone. Even though her very dear great-aunt, Lena Alexander (who passed away in June 2015), consented to be the stand-in for her parents, it tore me up inside watching Denise having to deal with the uncertainty and the hurtful possibility they would not attend. This was supposed to be a happy day, and for months it was overshadowed by her parents' refusal to attend. We spent many meetings with our rabbi, Debra Landsberg, discussing various options in case her father didn't come. We also had a number of backup plans in case, heaven forbid, it rained that June afternoon of our outdoor wedding. We had chosen Rabbi Landsberg because she was knowledgeable, warm, and compassionate, and because she understood that Denise came from a far more conservative Jewish background than I did and was having some trouble getting used to the Reform traditions. It didn't hurt, either, that she had been chair of a coalition of liberal rabbis in favour of same-sex marriage when the legislation first came before the federal Parliament. As far as Rabbi Landsberg was concerned, all that mattered was that Denise and I were both Jewish and intended to set up a traditional Jewish home. Still, at one point just before the invitations went out, we wondered whether, like some people, we should simply elope to some fabulous far-off location instead. But after debating this at length, we decided that we should do no less than get married in a traditional Jewish ceremony. We also felt that, out of respect for those who fought for the right for same-sex couples to get married, we should exercise that right. Besides, we loved each other, it had taken us a long time to find each other, and why should we not have the right to experience all the headaches of a heterosexual couple?

And that we did during the six months preparing for our wedding day, which auspiciously fell that year on Father's Day. The challenge wasn't just trying to pare down the invitation list to an affordable number (without slighting certain family members) or dealing with the fallout of certain very close members of Denise's family deciding not to come because of her father's decision not to attend. We wanted our outdoor, afternoon wedding to be elegant, meaningful, and full of charm, and that is where Denise came in. With her incredible sense of unconventional style and her tremendous creativity, my wife put together 101 details that gave our outdoor wedding (in the back garden of Sunnybrook Estates) charm, ambiance, and unequalled style. Somehow, her favourite travel destination, Venice, crept into the old-world music featured at and after the ceremony and into the decor. We even brought her Blackmoor sculptures and six-foot golden candelabras from our dining room to lend to the ambiance. But the pièce de résistance had to be our chuppah – which she also created herself and decorated with the seven fruits of Israel.

Three days before the wedding, Denise's father relented and decided to walk Denise down the aisle, with her mother on the other side. In the end, and very much to his credit, he admitted to us that it was a beautiful ceremony. Others, particularly Chris Blizzard, said that within minutes of the start of the ceremony they instantly forgot two women were marrying and thought of it as a traditionally Jewish ceremony presided over by a Reform rabbi and a cantor. We both wore custom-designed long white gowns. Instead of the bride circling the groom seven times, we circled each other three and a half times. Denise's cousin, Osnat, who came all the way from Israel, read our ketubah in Hebrew and I read the English words. At the end of the ceremony, before we were pronounced legally married, Denise and I broke the wine glass together (it was actually a light bulb wrapped in a napkin) – which symbolized that in times of happiness, we should never ever forget that life is fragile, something we have definitely experienced seven years into our marriage.

As if we didn't have enough on our plate, we spent the weeks leading up to our wedding in an adoption course with Jewish Family and Child Services and in a home study in preparation to possibly adopt a Muslim child from Israel. The fall before, just after I asked Denise to marry me, we travelled to Israel for a family bar mitzvah. During our visit, we drove up to Haifa to tour the Shabtai Levi Home – an orphanage serving Christian, Jewish, and Muslim children. Immediately after our return home, Denise's parents were to be honoured for their years of philanthropic efforts to sustain this home, and she wanted me to see what they did. While there, we met a sweet three-year-old Muslim boy who, as we were told then, would likely never find a permanent home because the Muslim community was not in the habit of adopting children. We also learned that while Israel would never allow Jewish children to leave the country for adoptive homes overseas, the same restrictions did not apply to Christian and Muslim children. We came home with a picture of this child, Rean, and set about trying to ensure that we were qualified to adopt him – a move that promised to be precedent-setting. As the months wore on and we learned that Rean's Arab social worker would not stand in the way of an adoption, we spent a good portion of our pre-wedding sessions with Rabbi Landsberg discussing how we would ease Rean's transition into life in Canada as well as how we should deal with his religious schooling. We completed the adoption course and were practically through our home study. But about a month before our wedding, we were suddenly informed by Shabtai Levi officials that Rean had been adopted out. To this day, we suspect he was not adopted but sent to a foster home – likely because the concept of a Canadian couple adopting him would have been far too controversial. We were not turned down for being gay but because of the potential political fallout of allowing an Arab child to leave Israel. Denise was absolutely heartbroken, and for the longest time afterward, kept his picture on the refrigerator. She still has his picture, even though he'd be ten years old by now. She was so heartbroken that when she was diagnosed a year after our wedding with a very painful chronic disorder called trigeminal neuralgia – one that is often exacerbated by stress, loud noise, and atmospheric changes – we decided, reluctantly, to abandon our idea of adopting a small child. Even though we'd both make good moms, we've had to content ourselves with devoting our love and attention to our three furkids.

We move as a married couple in circles of friends who are both gay and straight. I take Denise proudly to political events and introduce her as my wife. We rabble-rouse together as a couple about issues of concern to the both of us. I joke that I've made Denise even more political than I am, but that was hardly difficult. We are known as the go-to couple by the elderly residents of our gated Florida community, where we purchased a second home in 2010. In fact, a number of the elderly ladies there attended a sunset ceremony on the beach where we renewed our vows – a surprise I arranged for Denise for Valentine's Day in 2015. The idea was not just to celebrate our love for each other but to recognize the lifting of the ban on same-sex marriage in Florida at the start of 2015.

We've also had to adjust to all the issues that beset a typical straight married couple meeting later in life and having to combine two households. I can honestly say marriage between a same-sex couple is as challenging as one between a straight couple. We deal with the same family issues, the same concerns about money, and the same need to compromise between often dissimilar ways of doing things (even how we discipline our dachsies), of communicating, and of approaching everyday little things that can spark an argument. In our wedding speech, we summed up our union like this: we aren't opposites that attract, but rather, people with very different strengths that happen to complement each other. Denise jokes that I am her GPS and MBA – steering us in the right direction when it comes to both our finances and whenever we drive anywhere. I'm her office (also keeping our paperwork intact), and her memory. Denise has brought me an appreciation and understanding of beautiful things, a sense of humour and whimsy and learning how to slow down and make time for each other. Denise told the guests at our wedding that after we were married she'd make all the small decisions, but when a big decision came along, she'd let me make it. Oddly, in ten years together, there haven't been any BIG decisions. So far, I'm off the hook. After years of struggling to be true to who I am, I've learned to do what any good Jewish spouse should do: smile and say, "Yes, dear."

CHAPTER FOUR

The Good, the Bad, and the Beauty Impaired*

In case it isn't abundantly clear after three chapters, I like to stir up shit. Most of the time, I believe it's the right thing to do – to correct a wrong. Sometimes, it is possible to get carried away. Either way, it's done with the very best of intentions. Perhaps this explains why my equally outspoken wife and I share a love for and loyalty to long-haired dachshunds. We could have picked a perfectly well-behaved breed like a Labrador retriever, an obedient, highly trainable dog that would follow us anywhere wagging his or her tail at anything – in other words, a dog that would not give us the slightest bit of pushback. But no. We had to pick dachshunds – strong-willed, challenging, independent, deaf when it comes to the word no, and full of attitude. They're the dog version of political incorrectness. I've lost count of how many times Flora, our little female and the dominant one in our household, will look at us like we're out of our minds whenever we

* With thanks to Colin Mochrie for his description of political correctness.

try to reprimand her for misbehaviour like climbing on our kitchen table in search of extra dinner scraps. Kishka tells me off when I leave him alone for a couple of hours, barking at me to let me know he's displeased. But the fact is, we love them because they're feisty and comical characters who are never dull. They're also extremely loyal and loving. Sound familiar?

I would be lying if I said I didn't love attention. Most people in the media fall into the same category. My "shit disturbing" comes more than anything from a deep disdain for and despair over the kind of political correctness that leaves people walking on eggshells – censoring themselves from saying or doing what they truly feel is the right thing for fear of offending. I have grown so sick of watching powerful men and women, particularly those in public life, turn into complete wimps when asked for their opinion on any remotely controversial issue. We are so busy pandering to political correctness, we've lost sight of how much the special interests take advantage of our incredible fear of being politically incorrect. We throw money at politically correct causes – access, equity, and anti-racism grants for example – without asking for or expecting accountability. We are afraid to call our home-grown terrorists for what they are – bloodthirsty, mad, evil, murdering zealots – and we excuse their actions as those simply of the mentally imbalanced. We lose sight of the fact that these evil terrorist groups attract, even prey on, the mentally ill, and that invariably these kinds of disenfranchised people end up being radicalized. Who else would commit murder in cold blood and then allow themselves to be killed fighting for an extremist cause? Why must the politically correct have you believe it is all so complicated? 1 + 1 = 2, not 4. Caitlyn Jenner is a man. Rachel Dolezal is not trans-racial or black. She's white.

Cheating on your spouse is just plain wrong, despite what the online dating sites dedicated to just that will tell you.

Once in a while, I wish my fellow Canadians weren't so polite, at least when it comes to calling out political correctness. In my experience as a reporter and a columnist, I've witnessed few politicians with the guts to take on political correctness, knowing full well the special interests, the elitist left, and the chattering classes will attack them with a vengeance from the moral high ground where they have firmly planted their self-righteous selves. Whether you sided politically with Stephen Harper or not – and I happen to have supported him – he was absolutely right when he had the guts to call out Muslim women wearing the full niqab, insisting their faces should be shown during citizenship swearing-in ceremonies. Mr. Harper's comments came in early 2014 as he vowed to appeal a court ruling allowing women who typically dress in the full niqab to keep it intact while swearing in as new Canadians. Mr. Harper was mocked for saying the full veil – which allows Muslim women to show only their eyes, and which is dictated by a culture that is rigidly patriarchial – is rooted in beliefs that are anti-women. The opposition leaders, especially the vapid, immature, and narcissistic Liberal leader (now prime minister), Justin Trudeau, took turns insisting Mr. Harper was promoting Islamophobia. Ah yes, the federal Conservatives are Islamophobic. No, not pro-women; not pro-democracy; not pro-Canadian values. Islamophobic. Heaven forbid we should call a spade a spade. Accusations of hate, bitterness, some kind of phobia, and/or stupidity are always the go-to position for the self-righteous and politically correct. They've been levelled at me more than once.

What part of becoming a Canadian do these extremist Muslim women and their communities not understand? We are not in Abu Dhabi. We are in Canada, a country that not only respects all races and religions but respects freedoms and democracy. Being forced to cover oneself in a full tent, with hair, head, and face blacked out except for one's eyes, and walking several paces behind one's husband is not the least bit respectful of women's rights and freedoms. It is reminiscent of the Dark Ages. What part of that do the politically correct hysterics and assorted anti-Harper leftists not understand? It says these women are chattels and in need of being kept docile like the character of Kate in Shakespeare's *Taming of the Shrew* from 1592. Author and poet Margaret Atwood got right into the act in the middle of March 2015 with a series of bordering-on-childish tweets under the hashtag #dresscodePM. She tweeted such gems as "Is your face your 'identity?' Your signature, your fingerprints, your iris scan + your DNA might have something to do with it?" She also put up a picture on Twitter of Queen Victoria wearing her crown and veil (both of which did not cover her face), adding the tweet, "Not respectable." This is the same Ms. Atwood whose feminism comes out loud and clear in her poetry, who railed against misogyny in her 1985 novel *The Handmaid's Tale*, and whose 1969 novel *The Edible Woman* came about a decade into the second wave of feminism. Are we to take from her nonsensical Twitter comments that she is a feminist when it suits her? Or did Atwood and her fellow faux feminists hate Mr. Harper so much that in order to show him up, they took the ridiculous stance of defending women's right to wear this regressive veil? Or is their response simply political correctness in overdrive, a knee-jerk reaction against the right?

Still, I repeatedly shake my head wondering why they'd make absolute fools of themselves by condoning such a regressive, anti-feminist act.

I think I've made a decent career at the *Toronto Sun* by railing against examples of political correctness gone berserk, whether it be Muslim cabbies refusing to take me and my dog Kishka at the airport (because of religious beliefs that consider dogs unclean) or some heavily subsidized government program that made no sense to me. While on the education beat in the mid-1990s, and still deep in the closet myself, I had trouble understanding why the Toronto school board pushed for segregated classes for black and homosexual students. The special Triangle program, which operates to this day, is offered to students who are gay, lesbian, bisexual, and transgendered who can't operate in a mainstream program because they are experiencing homophobia or bullying. It seemed like a complete contradiction and pure hypocrisy to me that a board purporting to be politically correct and tolerant, that preaches inclusivity and offers anti-bullying programs up the proverbial yin-yang, would encourage such students to remove themselves from mainstream classrooms. How do they expect to educate straight students and demand acceptance of the LGBT lifestyle if gay and lesbian students are segregated in a special school? Besides, what kind of contradictory message does it send that while they allow LGBT students to pull out of mainstream classrooms, they are integrating students who suffer from autism or other learning disorders? Talk about a lack of consistency. Segregating gay and lesbian students always seemed to me the exact wrong way to go about garnering acceptance. In fact, to me it was a cop-out – a way of giving homophobia a free pass. I always wondered why school officials simply couldn't, or didn't have the will to, enforce their own policies designed to counter bullying and harassment.

As I found out on a recent assignment, not much has changed. To look good, and perhaps as an excuse to expand their bureaucratic fiefdoms, the Toronto school board has created all kinds of nice, politically correct anti-bullying policies and hired a long list of staff to tackle gender-based violence. It's all just window dressing. As I found out in 2014 with the sad case of fourteen-year-old Toronto student Mylissa Black – who was bullied relentlessly in her elementary school for four years to the point where she considered suicide while her principal and the superintendent turned a blind eye – it seems that far too many of the board's bureaucrats have done nothing but allow the problem to fester in their schools, even though carefully crafted anti-bullying policies are at their disposal. Also, what about some plain and common sense? How about displaying some tough love toward those students who bully aggressively and without remorse? It's a question of will, which teachers and their bosses do not seem to have: they would sooner sweep the problem under the rug for fear that any attempts to deal with violence might affect the public image of their schools or force them to deal with parents who might perceive it a problem that their kid is a bully. Miss Black was a case in point. Her parents repeatedly sought action from the school, but the principal, even though she had disciplinary tools she could have employed, like week-long suspensions, did not use them. Her inaction only enabled the students who victimized the young woman. That, in itself, is a sad statement. Not only are our public schools delivering a touchy-feely curriculum – particularly in math, literacy, and writing – that is leaving kids ill-prepared for college, university, and the workplace, but they have also chosen to take a back seat when it comes to meting out proper consequences for bad behaviour. As a consequence, the board has become enablers of the very abusive behaviour they have put policies in place to prevent.

AT TORONTO CITY HALL, officials and the politicians have become so decidedly focused on hiring visible minorities to show they run a "positive and progressive workplace" – a policy that seemed to ramp up during Mayor David Miller's time in office – that a reverse discrimination has developed. I've heard it over and over again that white males need not apply for management jobs at the city. Don't get me wrong. I believe everybody deserves a fair chance, regardless of their gender, race, or country of origin. But it is clear to me that in an attempt to bend over backwards to ensure that the right mix of visible minorities appears in every office at City Hall, adherence to standards, including a proper dress code, has been severely relaxed. This is political correctness at work – placing greater value on how things appear rather than what makes good old common sense.

I don't consider myself old-fashioned. However, I was constantly amazed by the number of female employees, even in management at City Hall, dressed like they had just left their night job on Jarvis Street, or were about to go to the gym or take out the trash. Managers showed up to meetings like they've never even heard of a jacket or tie. My goodness, it wasn't as if they weren't making enough to afford a suit or two. In my mind, it represents a complete lack of respect for the job. How can one have pride in one's job if there is no effort instilled to look like one comes to work ready to work? I also lost count of how many times I phoned City Hall offices and not for the life of me was able to understand the administrative assistant or clerk at the other end of the line – their command of the English language was so weak. Surely it isn't too much to expect people in those jobs to have a better command of English. One would think not, but try and say this in "polite" company and you risk being called a racist.

Nearly from the moment I walked into City Hall as the *Toronto Sun*'s columnist, I had trouble understanding the purpose of what were called "access and equity grants." This was a pot of money that was given every year to a variety of groups such as those from Afghan, Aboriginal, Asian, African, Somali, or Arab backgrounds or representing the LGBT population that would propose politically correct, touchy-feely projects intended to help stamp out racism and oppression. It came as no surprise to me when that pot nearly doubled to $750,000 per year during Mayor David Miller's two terms. How these groups were supposed to eliminate racism I was never quite sure. Let us consider that while the money was being spent, I would repeatedly hear that anti-Semitic acts of vandalism continued to rise in Toronto and other large Canadian cities. Perhaps it's because City Hall never gave grants to Jewish groups. Year after year, they were conspicuously absent from the list of groups and projects that were handed tax money. There was even a political correctness bordering on reverse discrimination when it came to doling out those anti-racism grants. Each and every year, an A-list of fuzzy-wuzzy visible minority causes would automatically be handed these grants without question, and with few checks and balances on whether they accomplished anything remotely related to their mandate and goals, if goals existed. Each time I would bring up the fact that these grants were poorly monitored and represented one of the worst examples of political correctness run amok, city officials would look at me like I was both crazy and heartless. "There she goes again . . ."

I still remember the day in 2005 when I turned up at a city-funded community safety conference that was supposed to address the escalating gun violence and drug and gang problems of that summer, labelled the "Summer of the Gun." Instead of witnessing any serious and practical discussion to address a very real issue that continues to affect the city, however, I came just in time to hear an Australian poet and faith healer break into song with a tune she said had the power to remove "barriers." The director of the Centre for Indigenous Education at the University of Melbourne told the 150 people who hung on to her every word to close their eyes while she sang, and to remember the "sacred" words she chanted in her native dialect. I couldn't believe what I was hearing, and seeing. All eyes in the room were firmly shut! It's not as if anyone could understand what she was shrieking, let alone remember it. No one sat there, as I did, wondering first of all what the hell this ridiculous gobbledygook had to do with gun violence and, more significantly, how much this woman was costing taxpayers. If the audience there thought her antics crazy, they certainly weren't showing it. Like a bunch of indoctrinated cultists, they were all caught up in the madness of that moment. As ridiculous as they were, the grants persisted because, like the audience watching the Australian drummer that June day, no bureaucrat or politician ever had the guts to say "Stop the madness" or to cancel the grants for fear he or she would be called inhumane, racist, and all kinds of other pejorative terms perpetuated by the limousine lefties at City Hall.

Aggressive panhandling was another untouchable subject in the city of Toronto. When the problem first became an issue under Mayor Mel Lastman, he claimed there was nothing he could do, even though the province's Safe Streets Act was already well in place. All he had to do was instruct the Toronto police to beef up enforcement. But he didn't have the guts to do so and the problem got worse. Obviously he was scared of how it would look politically if the cops were actually allowed to do their job and fine those who committed crimes, sometimes quite aggressively. When in 2006 a gutsy councillor and mayoralty candidate, Jane Pitfield, had the temerity to try to legislate an anti-panhandling bylaw – similar to one being used in Vancouver, Calgary, Winnipeg, Moncton, Fredericton, and Montreal – she was harassed and threatened to the point of nearly being terrorized by the anti-poverty activists. In the spring of 2006, members of the Toronto Disaster Relief Committee led by homelessness activist Cathy Crowe, a group I came to call the poverty pimps, would repeatedly show up to the city's homelessness advisory committee – headed by Ms. Pitfield – and try to hijack the proceedings by screaming and shouting insults at the councillor. They also made a show of attempting to oust Ms. Pitfield as co-chair. When that didn't work, they boycotted the committee's final two meetings. The NDPers on council – in particular former councillor and world-champion trougher Howard Moscoe – pandered to Ms. Crowe and her friends, and the idea of banning panhandling in Toronto quickly fell by the wayside. Instead, the Millerites put in place a feel-good, politically correct five-million-dollar-a-year plan, for which an army of social workers were hired to get to the root causes of problem panhandling and to try to cajole beggars off the streets. That plan exists to this day and now costs more than six-million dollars. Judging from the number of panhandlers on the streets of downtown Toronto and other points beyond the downtown core, the program has proven to be an exercise in futility – just as I expected it would be.

As I was to discover in the fall of 2013, the senior brass of TO2015 – the group engaged to organize the 2015 Pan Am Games – made an attempt to put in place their own peculiar brand of tolerance and inclusivity. It started in 2011, when former CEO Ian Troop (who was ousted in 2013 following my front-page exclusive on spending abuses by the entire TO2015 senior management team) announced with great fanfare that diversity would be adopted as a standard practice in the day-to-day business of the games. "All of our procedures and decision-making criteria will embrace diversity, from how we purchase goods and services to how we hire employees and recruit volunteers," Troop said at the time. Lo and behold, when various would-be suppliers went online to register with the games' database, they were required to declare whether theirs was a diverse business – meaning they had to report whether their business was 51 per cent owned and operated by women, visible minorities, Aboriginals, disabled people, or members of the LGBT population.

What in god's name does diversity have to with the business of selling, say, hotdogs, T-shirts, stuffed animals, bobble-heads, and soccer balls? After I took up one man's case (a white guy selling ribs), Pan Am officials, appropriately red-faced, relaxed their restrictions. But my goodness, what has Canada come to?

I have a number of theories on why political correctness – which most people claim to disdain – more often than not goes unchecked, but the media's underreporting of it is at the top of the list. Many of my colleagues are clearly more interested in being part of the in-crowd than in sticking their necks out and appearing politically incorrect if there is a price to pay from the Lib-left for doing so, as there so often is. After all, everybody wants to be invited to the Christmas party. For years at City Hall, many in the media gave David Miller a free ride, more often than not treating him like he was above reproach. Why? Because he was the exact antithesis of his successor, Rob Ford, and for that reason alone he was able to dupe the masses. He presented perfectly: full head of blond hair, tall, good-looking, articulate, smooth, Harvard-educated, and quick on his feet. He could answer the most difficult questions and sound like he really knew what he was talking about or wasn't avoiding the question altogether. It didn't matter that he was a weak leader who was bone lazy and who rarely, if ever, in his seven years in office had the intestinal fortitude to make the really hard decisions that a mayor of a big and changing city needs to make. The packaging was perfect, so much so that he used his hair and his appearance in his 2003 and 2006 campaign ads. "Same Great Hair, Same Great Mayor," read one of his campaign signs in 2006. I can only imagine what the reaction would have been if Jane Pitfield had used her good looks to sell herself in that same 2006 mayoralty race. But the lemmings who voted for Mr. Miller trusted him implicitly and without question. An attractive Harvard-educated leader would never lie, would he? He had to be good at what he did because, well, he looked good and went to a prestigious school. Because he presented well and could reduce an easily intimidated reporter to mush, most of my media colleagues lobbed softballs at him, letting me and a few other brave souls take the heat for asking tough questions. Because I have an MBA, I'd often ask him about his spending decisions or try to press him on contracts with his union friends. He'd never refuse to take my questions. But more often than not, he'd use his height to try to intimidate me. I'd get a standard terse reply before he'd turn his back on me. But before he did, I knew I had gotten to him whenever his face turned a shade of red. I constantly felt like a salmon swimming upstream trying to get at the truth. Nevertheless, someone had to call him out for what he was, and it wasn't going to be anyone at the *Toronto Star* or, god knows, *NOW* magazine.

There was another reason Mr. Miller was allowed to get off scot-free. He dedicated himself to politically correct causes. And what is more politically correct than the environment? To question the multi-millions of dollars he tossed into his eco-projects or his motives for doing so was one certain way not to get invited to a dinner party in the Annex, Margaret Atwood's neighbourhood and Toronto's version of New York's West Village. Like Al Gore, Mayor Miller was saving us from global warming, goddammit! There's no doubt in my mind that his soft landing as CEO of the World Wildlife Fund, where he would pull in upwards of $300,000 a year, was bought and paid for by taxpayers. It wasn't just the $120 million he cheekily took from the city's reserves to spend on green projects (instead of using it to pay down the city's debt or for transit infrastructure) around the same time that he imposed new land transfer, car, and garbage taxes on Torontonians. He also handed over more than a quarter million dollars of Toronto's tax money between 2008 and 2010 to subsidize an environmental office in London, England, while he was chair of the C40 group of cities (nothing more than a gabfest of city officials claiming to be concerned about global warming).

Mr. Miller's most visible show of eco-political correctness had to be the asinine plastic bag fee initiated to make it look like he was actually doing something for the environment. Because the city's taxing powers didn't extend to charging an environmental fee, he and his like-minded environmentalists on council passed a bylaw allowing all retail stores to charge consumers five cents (plus one cent GST) for each plastic bag, presumably to reduce the number of plastic bags that go into landfill. The big chains – Loblaws, Sobeys, Metro, Winners, and so on – were quick to embrace this scheme and to extend it to stores beyond Toronto's borders. And why not? It was an absolute cash windfall for them. While Mr. Miller and his NDP supporters in council made some weak overtures about requiring retailers to donate some of their proceeds to the environment, he knew from the outset the city never had the authority or the resources to enforce any of it. They also were unable to enforce the section of the bylaw that mandated all retail chains to provide a recycled paper bag alternative to customers. Instead, it became a race by retail chains to see who could outdo the others with designer cloth bags costing $1.99 or more – yet more cash for them. In some instances, the cloth bags were proven to contain toxins and deemed unhealthy for carrying foods. It was all window dressing – lazy policy from a lazy politician done up in the guise of saving the environment. Plastic bags were never the big concern. As we heard repeatedly from city and environmental experts, plastic bags accounted for a fraction of 1 per cent of the waste that actually goes to landfill in Ontario.

Heavy durable plastic packaging and take-out food containers are far more harmful to our waste stream. These were all facts available to our eco-loving, Harvard-educated mayor. But over the years he was in power, virtually none of the media bothered to call Mr. Miller on them. The *Toronto Star*'s writers and columnists rarely uttered a peep about Mr. Miller's self-indulgent and highly negligent use of public funds, until the 2009 garbage strike and his dying days in office. It was sad proof of the unconscionable media double standard.

AT QUEEN'S PARK, it was even worse. I arrived there in 2013 with a mandate to "shake things up," which is what I'd tried to do at City Hall. For ten years, most of the media – except for the *Toronto Sun* – had given Premier Dalton McGuinty a free ride as he repeatedly broke his promises not to raise taxes, imposing tax after tax and stumbling from one billion-dollar scandal to another. By the time I got there, Mr. McGuinty had skipped off to a cozy sinecure at Harvard (see a pattern?) with his $313,000 severance package, leaving a trail of cover-ups and a litany of costly messes in his wake – all the while claiming, like Sergeant Schultz in *Hogan's Heroes*, that he "knew na-sing and saw na-sing." His successor, the then unelected Kathleen Wynne, was no better. Clearly loving the perks of being the first woman of Ontario and the first lesbian premier, but in way over her head and loath to call an election, she spent her time in office denying any ties to Mr. McGuinty and also pleading total ignorance as the scandals continued to mount (even though she'd held successive cabinet posts in his regime and been his campaign co-chair in 2011). I often thought the media was afraid to take on Ms. Wynne out of fear of provoking the LGBT community. This I feel contributed immensely to her shocking majority win in June 2014, despite the fact that she was running a party steeped in scandals and ready to drive the province down the economic road to Greece. I often thought and continue to think that voters and the media give her a free pass because she is an out lesbian and Ontario's first lesbian premier. And this from a lesbian! Since she got elected, that free ride has continued, even as she puts the province deeper and deeper in debt, mucks around with Ontario's energy policy, gives entitled teachers and their powerful unions everything they want and more, and tries to manipulate public sentiment about anyone who dares oppose her lefty agenda.

Take those who have dared oppose her sex-ed curriculum, which introduces the subject of same-sex relationships in grade three and "sexting" in grade four. Some of the objectors were ultra-religious and included many of her own Muslim constituency. They were branded homophobic. I guess you could call me homophobic too since I happen to think grade three, or the age of eight, is too early to ram same-sex relationships down kids' throats. Whatever happened to letting kids be kids? Instead, with all the problems with bullying in schools, why not focus at that age on being respectful and tolerant of others, especially those who look different or may have a different point of view? Perhaps we might share those lessons with our very own lesbian premier since she doesn't appear to be very tolerant or respectful of those with points of view other than her own.

In return, there is very little I respect about Ms. Wynne. I'll concede she's cunning and she sure knows how to manipulate public sentiment. But I find her the most offensive kind of political operative – and I use the word *operative* deliberately. Aside from the damage she's already done and continues to do to the province, when it comes right down to it little matters to her but ensuring the Liberals win at all costs – whether it means selling out to whatever group will prop up her fortunes (can we say "teachers"?), or changing the channel from her own sorry record to pick fights with Ontario's doctors, Stephen Harper or the late Rob Ford or Patrick Brown, or shilling for Justin Trudeau in the October 2015 federal election (surely her time would have been better spent running the province). I was extremely upset in June 2015 when Ms. Wynne quietly slipped off to Washington – for some ridiculous series of meetings that made her sound important and plugged in – and took time to sit down with Valerie Jarrett, President Obama's senior advisor. Ms. Jarrett is a highly dangerous woman who has made no secret of her loathing for Israel and its prime minister, Benjamin Netanyahu. Yet there Ms. Wynne was, barely three weeks later, cozying up to Toronto's Jewish community when she was feted at a Words and Deeds dinner sponsored by the Centre for Israel and Jewish Affairs and the United Jewish Appeal. I didn't know who to be more disgusted with: Ms. Wynne for her hypocrisy or the well-resourced Jewish organizations for turning a blind eye to, or neglecting to properly investigate, the company our premier keeps. No doubt the media helped perpetuate this ignorance by failing to call her out for her visit to Ms. Jarrett. It got barely a mention, except by me on social media.

While she herself expects tolerance and respect for free speech, Ms. Wynne is a master at spinning the truth and at putting up roadblocks to those who try to dig beyond her party line – like me. When I was at Queen's Park, I would get a daily visit from one of her press secretaries – acting on the pre-text that they wanted to help me with whatever I needed, but really trying to discern what I was working on that could possibly embarrass their boss. I loved telling them I was just fine, thank you. I would contact them if I needed them. When I did seek out a comment on some story or other, it was always by e-mail – phone interviews were rarely given because I might throw a hard question at them – and the answers always arrived no earlier than 5 p.m. Clearly they thought the closer the answers came to my deadline, the less chance I would have to further question them. It was a well-crafted strategy by the premier's office to contain any perceived criticism of her policies. One afternoon, when I was working on a story about Ms. Wynne's wife and the one million dollars in consultant contracts she obtained with an agency that was supposed to be serving autistic children, Liberal godfather Greg Sorbara suddenly turned up at our office. My *Sun* colleague Antonella Artuso said she'd never before had a visit from him. Why this sudden appearance, then? We figured it was because he was trying to find out what I knew. But god bless Antonella. She spent so much time talking to Mr. Sorbara about growing tomato plants – deliberately diverting him from his intended conversation – that he completely lost track of his purpose for dropping by and left for a lunch appointment without getting anything out of me.

By the middle of 2015, it had become clear that the Wynne government – desperately trying to manage an eleven-billion-dollar deficit that had nowhere to go but up because they couldn't stop spending – had developed a lingo all of their own to try to seduce the masses into thinking they had their hands firmly on the tiller. My favourites were that promises they'd made were "stretch goals" and their contention that each deal they made – whether selling Ontario's Hydro One at a loss or inking a contract with the province's entitled teachers – had a net-zero fiscal impact on taxpayers. They tried to imply that the teachers' unions gave up something to get the 2.5 per cent raise handed to them over two years, which I can guarantee you did not happen. The unions have a history of giving up nothing, particularly with the Liberals in power. They must think we are all blooming idiots. How the hell can giving every teacher in the province a raise *not* cost hundreds of millions of dollars? I'll tell you where the money will come from: it will come out of classroom supplies, maintenance, and school operations. It is clear to me that Ms. Wynne couldn't care less how much she impoverishes the classroom or Ontario schools, as long as her teacher pals are happy.

Given the premier's almost obsessive efforts to keep a lid on any and all controversy (can we say "gas plant e-mails"?), I was not surprised in the slightest that the release of the behind-the-scenes documentary done on her by White Pine Pictures was blocked by her office for months and months. A somewhat watered-down version of *Premier: The Unscripted Kathleen Wynne* was finally shown in October of 2015. Despite the edits clearly at her direction, it still came across loud and clear who is really running the show in this province: her aggressive wife Jane Rounthwaite, whom Ms. Wynne trots everywhere. I know what Ms. Wynne is all about. She may be a lesbian, but I shudder to think that this kind of lesbian is a role model for other women – gay or straight – in politics.

Every time anyone cozies up to her or lauds her for being openly gay, I want to shout that she's the furthest thing from being open, respectful, tolerant, or empathetic of the poor, the old, and those who are suffering. Her last name is very appropriate. For Ms. Wynne it's all about winning and power, nothing more, nothing less.

CHAPTER FIVE

Unaffordable Housing and
Other Tales of Troughmeistering

In 2012, I was asked by the *Sun* to follow the money on the one-billion-dollar revitalization of the Regent Park social housing development in downtown Toronto. Billed as the most ambitious revitalization in Canada, all of the initial legwork on the six-phase project had been carried on for the previous six years under the direction of a CEO, a management team, and a board that ended up leaving in 2011 after serious purchasing and spending irregularities were revealed by Toronto's intrepid auditor general, Jeff Griffiths.

While tenants were living in squalor – having been told there was not nearly enough money to fix their often decrepit units – Toronto Community Housing Corporation (TCHC) brass enjoyed $50,000 Christmas parties attended by 800 staff, $6,000 "bonding" sessions in Muskoka, and $1,925 planning meetings at a Toronto spa, where they availed themselves of mani-pedis and other such services at taxpayer expense. Mr. Griffiths also highlighted purchasing irregularities in a $5-million sole-sourced contract with China for fixtures, flooring, toilets, sinks, and solar panels. But that was merely the tip of the iceberg. Through the diligent digging of Councillor Mike Del Grande, a chartered accountant by training, it was revealed that the same players were also entrusted with a $75-million handout from Mayor David Miller in 2009, which was supposed to help alleviate TCHC's $750-million backlog. But they promptly squandered $41.4 million of it on high-risk stock market investments, and it took the persistent digging of Mr. Del Grande to discover it two years later. The TCHC board had either not cared or had turned a blind eye to the high-stakes investment strategy. It wasn't just that the TCHC brass performed an act that was unacceptably risky, considering they are only supposed to invest their reserves in bonds or highly risk-averse equities. They also tried to bury the loss in their audited statements.

To make matters worse, the whistleblower – Mr. Del Grande – was berated by TCHC board member Paula Fletcher for having the temerity to read through the audited statements and ask questions on the losses. She stood up at council and called his questioning the "Spanish Inquisition," claiming dramatically that Mr. Del Grande had put TCHC officials "on the rack in the 1400s." Her ridiculous attempt at trying to silence him only proved the lengths she and her fellow board members, who'd also ignored the TCHC culture of entitlement, would go to cover their tracks.

No wonder. It was all so neat and cozy. It did not come as the least bit surprising to me – given what I'd observed about the leftist politicians on council and how they flushed public money down the drain on their self-serving pet agendas and on their own perks – that most of the brass overseeing these disgraceful and highly negligent acts were NDP supporters. Yet this was the very group that continually presented itself as champions of the downtrodden. It made me absolutely sick to realize that while those politicians, bureaucrats, and media types who aligned either with the far left or the left-of-centre Liberals politically made a great show of being the voice of the poor, it seems most couldn't have cared less how they treated these people. Let's start with NDPers Paula Fletcher and Olivia Chow, who were on the TCHC board during the David Miller era and clearly sat on their hands as the brass they were charged with overseeing took care of themselves and let tenants live in squalor. I saw CEO Derek Ballantyne driving into the City Hall garage in his late-model Audi wagon many times for one meeting or another, where he would – in an arrogant tone of voice – talk about his grandiose visions for TCHC while the repair backlog kept climbing and climbing to $750 million. That's not to criticize Mr. Ballantyne's choice of cars to drive, but I sized him up as one of those champagne socialists who would rarely, if ever, lower himself to leave his Rosedale office to mingle with Jane-Finch residents, and who saw the housing portfolio as merely a means to an end – his end being moving to yet another six-figure social housing job or making money as a consultant off the backs of the poor. None of this mattered to the NDP set, who lauded him for his great vision – so much so that he was handed the Jane Jacobs prize in 2009 by a group called Ideas that Matter. (I don't suppose it mattered to them either that Mr. Ballantyne wasn't doing a darn thing to improve the quality of life of his tenants by repairing their dilapidated homes – except to whine that all levels of government needed to cough up ever more money that could be squandered.)

Former councillor Adam Vaughan, a nasty journalist turned politician and another alleged champion of the down-trodden, was a prominent member of the NDP until 2015 when he ran for the federal Liberal Party under Justin Trudeau – hedging his bets that the Liberals would be more likely to win a majority and he'd end up with a cabinet post (they did, but he didn't). Mr. Vaughan is never one to miss an opportunity. Nevertheless, when Mr. Griffiths released his damning report on TCHC, Mr. Vaughan aimed his vitriol not at the housing officials who were taking care of themselves instead of their poor clients, but at Mr. Griffiths, for heaven's sake.

Right in lock-step was the left-wing media – the *Toronto Star* in particular – who made and continue to make it all too easy for these NDP supporters to get away with what they do. When Mr. Ballantyne left his sinecure at Build Toronto following the serious spending, investment, and procurement irregularities that occurred under his watch at TCHC (he had left TCHC for Build Toronto by the time Mr. Griffiths' report came to light), *Toronto Star* reporter Dave Rider started his story with "Celebrated until recently as a public housing 'genius,' Derek Ballantyne finds his reputation in tatters as the latest casualty of the Toronto Community Housing Corp. spending scandal." Mr. Rider seemed to imply that Mr. Ballantyne's reputation was in tatters because somebody else – most likely Rob Ford, considering it was the *Toronto Star* – created his problems. It probably didn't hurt that Mr. Ballantyne was by then keeping company with *Toronto Star* editorial writer

Kerry Gillespie, who had quoted Mr. Ballantyne in her stories about Regent Park ten years earlier.

Mr. Toronto Housing himself, *Toronto Star* columnist Joe Fiorito, a one-trick pony who spent much of his time finding the TCHC weeper of the week, depicted Dipper and long-time councillor Maria Augimeri as a heroine for wanting to stay on the housing authority board when then Mayor Rob Ford tried to clean house as one way to make changes after the spending scandal.

It has become clear to me over the years during which I've investigated these abuses that there is one common theme: the social housing agencies are run largely by the same group of industry insiders who, after messing up and treating themselves to the spoils at one non-profit agency, simply coast to the next cozy sinecure, ensuring they negotiate themselves contracts that provide extravagant severance clauses. At best they are dreamers who don't have the first clue how to operate a going concern in an efficient manner without a massive influx of public cash; at worst they are motivated by self-aggrandizement. Take as a prime example disgraced TCHC CEO Keiko Nakamura, who was forced out in 2011 for allowing the spending abuses revealed by Mr. Griffiths to occur under her watch. She walked away with a $320,000 severance package and promptly landed at Goodwill Industries, where she made $230,538 in salary and taxable benefits in 2014 – more than she'd made at TCHC before she left! In January 2016, Ms. Nakamura stood in front of the media crying the same tears I saw five years earlier at TCHC as she blamed the difficult retail landscape for forcing her suddenly to shut down sixteen Goodwill stores and ten donation centres, leaving

430 employees without jobs. A few weeks later, under a cloud of secrecy, Ms. Nakamura filed for bankruptcy.

With this culture of deceit and entitlement as a backdrop, my task on the Regent Park story was to trace the purchases of a series of condos in the first two high-rise buildings by members of the project's management team. The condo buyers in question included former TCHC CEO Derek Ballantyne and his partner Kerry Gillespie, then a member of the *Toronto Star* editorial board (who'd presumably met Mr. Ballantyne while covering the social housing beat a few years before); the well-entrenched developer Mitch Cohen of Daniels Corp. and some of his management team; and the long-time local councillor responsible for pushing through the heavily subsidized development, Pam McConnell. With the help of my dear friend real estate lawyer Martin Gladstone and a private investigator working with me on the story, I discovered through a search of sales records on file with the Ontario Land Registry Office that all of these insiders had bought in on the ground floor of an investment that had nowhere to go but up. Initial buyers are probably looking at increases of 30 per cent or more in value. Indeed, how could that not happen, given Toronto's ongoing housing boom? The fifteen-year gentrification of Canada's oldest and largest social housing project, located just east of Toronto's downtown core, aimed to transform it from an isolated community of decrepit war-torn houses and apartment blocks where drug dealers and crime was rampant to a mixed-use socialist Utopia. This Utopia would contain three thousand units of spanking-new upscale market-value condos, a bank and grocery store, a Tim Hortons, an aquatic complex, a park, and the Regent

Park Arts and Cultural Centre. The poor would be living cheek by jowl with the more upwardly mobile.

Or would they? Figuring where there's smoke there's fire, and knowing full well that the same players who left TCHC management and the board the previous year had their paw prints all over this project, I was not content to simply investigate the condo purchases alone. I realized very early on that my investigation would be an uphill battle. TCHC was a highly secretive organization, so secretive that even the names of employees were not listed either online or in any sort of publicly accessible place. This lack of transparency was deliberate and, sadly, it continues to this day. The pompous TCHC brass, most of them champagne socialists if there ever were such a thing, seemed not to believe for a minute that they had to be the slightest bit responsive or accountable to tenants, or to the public and the media, who for the most part let them get away with it. The TCHC brass exerted their power over the tenants, many of them down on their luck, vulnerable, and not terribly sophisticated about their rights. Most of the information about the Regent Park project – and it was extremely limited – was contained on the TCHC website or from Ms. McConnell herself in a series of highly sanitized, self-promotional press releases. Over three months, investigating the Regent Park deal became a crusade for me. I was determined to find out where the public dollars were going, if taxpayers were in fact getting the best value for their money, and who was truly being served by the development – the poor who were supposed to be recipients, or the more upwardly mobile.

Hampered by my inability to get around easily (I had broken my ankle just as I started on the assignment), I spent many long hours at my computer researching condo values and the sales history of the Regent Park condos from 2009 to 2012, and trying to trace the history of the development itself, the City's approval process, how the Daniels Corp. came to be involved, and Mitch Cohen's career in the affordable housing development business. Mr. Cohen called himself "the developer with a heart," which raised a big red flag. It felt like I was peeling away the layers of an onion, as one tidbit of information led to yet another. Unlike the *Toronto Star*, for example, which is well known for pouring tremendous resources (staff teams and big budgets) into its investigative projects to further its agenda or to win National Newspaper Awards, I was a team of one who had to be creative about doing research and about how I spent the paper's money on that research. To get a feel for what units would have been available to Ms. McConnell and other purchasers, I asked a real estate agent friend of mine to take me to see a few of the condos listed for sale in the same building where Ms. McConnell had purchased her prime south-facing 1,200-square-foot corner unit with its wraparound balcony from which she could wave to her loyal (and poor) subjects. Because I only had apartment numbers for the purchasers, I enlisted Martin Gladstone to help me obtain the title search documents from the Land Registry Office, plus the registered floor plans pinpointing where each condo would be located and its square footage, along with the parking spots assigned to each owner.

To try to discern whether the purchasers had a conflict of interest, I spent hours searching online city reports to trace the timing of Ms. McConnell's involvement advocating for the development in city council and how the various development companies for each Regent Park phase were structured.

Ms. McConnell never once raised the issue of conflict of interest when she advocated for the project, before, during, or after her purchase because she didn't think there was one. That is just how business seemed to be done at City Hall. I also discovered by reviewing the MPAC tax rolls that the developer's various companies, as well as Mr. Cohen and his chief lieutenants on the project, purchased a total of eighteen condos in three of the first market-value condo buildings. Yet when confronted in the final days before the stories appeared, Ms. McConnell admonished me for daring to ask her about the conflict or even suggesting there might be a perception of one. She behaved as if I was out to get her, claiming my questions were very "typical" of me (she was right on both counts!). The developer maintained that by purchasing so many suites they were just expressing "confidence" in the revitalization, as they did with other development projects – clearly not understanding or caring that this project was being built with one billion dollars in public money, tax, and development concessions, and that the rules were different. Mr. Cohen's front man on the project, Daniels Corp. VP Martin Blake, contradicted himself in a subsequent interview by saying that 100 per cent of the first four buildings were completely sold out. My review of sales data for the first two market-value condo buildings also showed that 10 per cent of them had flipped in the first year at prices up to 20 per cent higher than the original investment.

But what really incensed me was what happened with the intended residents. It became evident, the more I peeled away the layers of that onion, that the very real losers were the long-time inhabitants of Regent Park. This mixed-use development wasn't so mixed after all. Contrary to the spin from

Daniels Corp., TCHC, and the tight little circle of poverty pimps and activists who are quick to jump on the bandwagon whenever they smell opportunities to improve their own circumstances or their influence, the poor would not be living in the same buildings as the rich. Not at all. While Mr. Cohen and his top brass were busily snapping up their eighteen prime condos, knowing full well they were buying into an investment that would only go up in value, only twelve Regent Park tenants at the time of my investigation could even remotely afford to purchase into the market-value buildings – the TCHC and the developer having made them jump through hoops to do so. To this day, that has not changed. To make matters worse, City of Toronto housing officials were happily handing out second-mortgage money for first-time buyers making up to $81,000 per year, likely far beyond what any long-time Regent Park resident could ever hope to earn. The thirty-year loans from that publicly funded $6.5-million slush fund – ironically called the Toronto Affordable Housing Fund (no one knew about it until I found it quite by chance) – do not need to be repaid until the home is sold, and are forgivable if the owner stays in his or her condo for twenty years. No such fund was being offered to the poor at the time of my investigation. I discovered, after considerable digging, that 175 market-value condo buyers had been handed these second mortgages. Even Mr. Cohen's niece, Anna, had gotten herself a $25,340 second mortgage for her unit from the fund. When it comes to his own family, Mitch Cohen lives up to his own slogan about being the developer with a heart!

It seems the poor would not be living side by side in the very same buildings with the new inhabitants of the market-value buildings either. The affordable housing buildings were located on the periphery of Regent Park. But I realized it was far worse than that. Many of the residents were shipped like cattle out of Regent Park into new buildings as far as 1.5 kilometres away from the neighbourhood they'd called home for decades. Not particularly sophisticated about their legal rights, they were seduced by TCHC officials into believing they'd be returned to one of the very first units in the revitalized Regent Park. But unknown to them at the time, they signed away their right to return when they decided to move to the off-site units. The displaced residents, who were all subject to a lottery, were informed by letter that a new unit was available to them in the off-site buildings. The letter stated that if they refused to move they'd go to the bottom of the waiting list for a new unit. The very fine print revealed that if they opted for the new unit, then no other unit would be made available to them. But TCHC officials told them quite the opposite. They were damned if they did and damned if they didn't. Sadly, these long-time residents only discovered this once it was too late. Even worse, the displacement of the original inhabitants to buildings far, far away from the Regent Park footprint continues to this day, and only a select number of residents are being permitted to move back into the new units. So many residents of Muslim extraction are being permitted to jump the queue, over others who lived there before the redevelopment, that people have come to whisper – for fear of being labelled politically incorrect, or worse, racist – that there is such a large Muslim community living there that free public space has been set aside for their prayers and there's talk of creating a mosque on-site.

Like with most other stories I have chosen to pursue, the Regent Park investigation ended up being not just a matter of ruffling feathers and calling to account those in charge of a heavily subsidized housing project. I was absolutely incensed that the poor would be duped as they'd been and I wanted to help them. As a result of pressure from my articles, some of the women I featured living in what they called the "501 Adelaide Penitentiary" were moved to more suitable TCHC buildings at least closer to Regent Park. The series earned me a Sun Media investigative reporting award for my efforts, and former TCHC CEO Gene Jones would confide to me more than once – before he was ousted from the organization after twenty-two months for daring to clean house – that I'd shaken things up within the organization and ensured there was far more oversight on the project. (Sadly, once Mr. Jones left, TCHC, under his successor, Greg Spearn, quickly reverted to the troubled, secretive organization it had been – an organization that seemed to put the brass first and tenants last.)

Nevertheless, on the Regent Park file, I also exposed the so-called compassionate Lib-left for what they were: motivated by opportunism, not by a genuine desire to help the poor. I don't for one minute believe that all the players who bought into the new condos were showing good faith in the project, or confidence in the community, or as Pam McConnell claimed, a desire to live among the poor. They saw an investment opportunity and bought in while the getting was good. My findings did exact a personal price, however. With the apparent ties between the *Toronto Star* and Mr. Ballantyne extremely tight, especially given his relationship with Ms. Gillespie, most of the media coverage up until my series was effusive, over-the-top, and ridiculously one-sided. As seasoned as I am, I didn't realize until my findings were published the lengths the left in Toronto and their media apologists would go to attack my credibility and to protect the status quo and the old guard at TCHC. Daniels Corp. – used to a free pass from the media and to throwing their weight around – issued a press release two days after the initial stories appeared, attacking my professionalism. Their intent was also to downplay calls for an inquiry into the condo purchases. They accused the *Toronto Sun* (me) of "attempting to discredit" a public–private partnership "celebrated around the world" and of undermining the "incredible accomplishments" of local residents "who have worked tirelessly since 1995 to transform their community." It was truly a first to have virtually an entire press release written about my findings.

On it went throughout the week after my series appeared. I was vilified on blogs, targeted in columns, on radio shows, and on Twitter. The attacks on Twitter were very personal, so much so that my editor, Lorrie Goldstein, told me to stay off social media for the good of my health. Under some pressure, the TCHC board decided to call in former Ontario Superior Court chief justice Patrick LeSage to look at whether the condo purchases by the Daniels team and the TCHC execs were a conflict. In August, Mr. Justice LeSage ruled there was no conflict after TCHC spent $125,000 to have him arrive at that conclusion. He did point out that the optics of the purchases weren't good and that greater transparency was indeed required, but it didn't much matter by that point. I was glad to have helped bring the plight of the poor to light, despite the pushback I received from all the usual suspects.

It certainly wasn't the first or the last time the media and the Lib-left would gang up on me for having the audacity to suggest their record of advocating for the downtrodden, or students, or seniors, or the mentally challenged was less than stellar, and more often than not, non-existent.

Sadly, those same clucking apologists – led by the *Toronto Star* – managed to help run Gene Jones out of town after only twenty-two months at the helm of TCHC. The MBA grad had been brought in from Detroit with a solid background in social housing in a variety of major U.S. cities to clean house – to attack the waste and mismanagement, and to put together a plan to tackle the long-ignored over nine-hundred-million-dollar backlog in repairs. He took his job seriously, and unlike his pompous predecessors, treated the tenants as first-class citizens, addressing their concerns on their own turf. No other CEO had visited TCHC buildings regularly, as he did, and Jones's successor, Greg Spearn, is as arrogant as, and even more inexperienced in social housing than, those who ran the show in the past. Mr. Jones got the job done, but when he got too close to the underlying issues for comfort, his detractors conspired to push him out. I do not say this lightly. Mr. Jones was not at all familiar with the highly charged political landscape of TCHC and how far the politicians who had let TCHC become a cesspool under their watch would go to protect the status quo. He took the board seriously – most particularly board chairman Bud Purves – when they promised they'd have his back when he did what he needed to clean up the rot. But they didn't. It didn't matter that those before him had used precious money needed for repairs to hold pricey company bonding sessions, or that sole-sourced contracts were rampant, or that the same repairs were being done two and three times (with the full approval of TCHC managers), or that Mr. Jones had found money for repairs and was investigating six companies allegedly engaged in a kickback scheme. When leftist and highly political former Toronto ombudsman Fiona Crean – who seems to be forever preoccupied with protecting her job and promoting herself – put together a one-sided report about his dismissal of incompetent employees, that was all the detractors needed to show Mr. Jones the door. Mayor Rob Ford, under siege for his own addiction issues at the time, did nothing to stand up for Mr. Jones, who was brought in under his watch (but not hired by Mr. Ford as his detractors claimed). The *Toronto Star*, eager to erase the ties they wrongly suggested Mr. Jones had to Mayor Ford, and having their own connections to Mr. Ballantyne, created a maelstrom over Ms. Crean's report, and the lazy, left-wing media were only too happy to join in and gang up on Mr. Jones. It was a disgraceful way to treat a man with integrity. But exactly who did the TCHC board and their media apologists end up hurting? Why, the very vulnerable tenants for whom they purport to advocate. Within mere months, TCHC had reverted to the pre–Gene Jones days of treating tenants with disdain, little accountability, and an entrenched bureaucracy. Resident Bonnie Booth puts it this way: "A pall of silence fell over TCHC with the resignation of Gene Jones, the CEO I called 'the man of steel with a heart of gold.' Immediately the housing authority's headquarters became a fortress with the installation of a barrier at board meetings to separate residents from staff. The staff directory Mr. Jones had put online, disappeared from the TCHC website. Residents became dismayed again when no one listened to their concerns. Those who challenged the status quo, like me, had their e-mails blocked and privacy violated. A 'culture of fear' became palpable amongst those who feared for their jobs while daring to follow Mr. Jones' vision. Entitlement and a lack of integrity now permeate the top brass, who are desperately trying to undo everything positive Mr. Jones did."

Mr. Jones and I have kept in touch since he was driven out of Toronto. I very much enjoyed the day in early June 2015 when I turned up at a TCHC board meeting, just hours after my exclusive story had been published that he'd been hired as CEO of the Chicago Housing Authority, working under Mayor Rahm Emanuel. Tongues were indeed wagging at TCHC. The sore losers at the *Toronto Star*, seemingly incredulous that he'd landed on his feet in such a short time, refused to give him his due. In their follow-up on my story, they whined that a statement from Mr. Emanuel's office made no mention of the turmoil that surrounded Mr. Jones when he left Toronto, and claimed he'd be in charge of only half the number of units he'd overseen at TCHC. Mr. Jones was always classy after he left, and he often told me he really missed the tenants. But one thing he did wonder, being a black man, was whether there was an element of racism in the way he was treated by the left-wing media and his other detractors. I can't say for sure whether that was true, but wouldn't that just fit with what I've said about the Lib-left: they're inclusive and tolerant only when it is politically expedient for them to be so.

WHILE I CONSIDER MYSELF POLITICAL and reasonably politically astute, in my twenty-six years as a journalist at the *Toronto Sun*, I have never much liked covering the political sideshow, the "he said, she said" that comes with the day-to-day blood sport we mistake for debate in political arenas like the Toronto school board, City Hall, and Queen's Park. I feel a far greater sense of personal and professional satisfaction when I've been able to dig into the story behind the story, hold the feet of politicians or bureaucrats to the fire, and pursue fairness and social justice.

It didn't take long in my journalism career to figure out that a major stone needing to be overturned was at the Toronto school boards – both Catholic and public – where in the early 1990s board bureaucrats were spending money on their own perks while the boards struggled with tremendous deficits. There was the Catholic board's education director driving around in a Toyota Camry leased for him using board money that included a thousand-dollar buyback when the lease expired. There was the Scarborough board's education director who spent eleven thousand dollars to be part of then prime minister Jean Chretien's two-week mission to Asia. There was the director of the Toronto school board, who spent more than twelve thousand dollars on lunches, travel, and car expenses in 1992 – regularly frequenting the pricey Prince Arthur Garden in the former Park Plaza Hotel. I sought out anyone who was prepared to rock the education boat, and that is how I met Mike Del Grande in 1995. He was part of the group Sunshine Trustees, who tried, with considerable pushback, to shine a light on the highly secretive and unaccountable bureaucrats running the Catholic school board. Nothing was sacred to me while on the education beat. When the teachers' unions were poised to take the entire province out on an illegal strike in 1997 – over attempts by the Mike Harris government to rein in teacher pay and perks and bloated school boards (sound familiar?) – I did a piece outlining who the five union bosses were and what kind of pay and perks they earned. The *Toronto Sun* ran their pictures on its front page. The more militant teachers, a thin-skinned, whiny bunch even twenty years ago, never forgave me for that. When they struck illegally for two weeks in late October 1997 (a strike in which they failed to win any concessions from the government), I was criticized and attacked for daring to remind the public how self-serving the teachers' union leaders really are. Fast forward twenty years and it has gotten far worse, courtesy of more than a decade of Liberal premiers and education ministers pandering to the unions' every whim – in exchange, of course, for their support at election time. I found it absolutely disgraceful to hear Sam Hammond, the Grand Poobah of the Elementary Teachers Federation of Ontario (ETFO), pounding his chest at the union's annual meeting in August 2013 and declaring that if they were treated with "fairness and respect" there wouldn't be a repeat of the previous year – what they proudly called in their manifesto their year of "fighting for democratic rights." That year, not to be confused with 2015, was the year when they spent as much time as they could protesting and with-drawing any services they were supposed to provide (coaching or administering extracurricular activities, organizing school trips and holding parent-teacher interviews) as they did offering their barebones classroom instruction time, to let the public know how they felt about Dalton McGuinty's highly controversial Bill 115, passed in September 2012. That long-overdue legislation froze wages for some teachers, cut sick days, and finally put to rest the generous payouts for unused sick leave that were helping to bankrupt the province.

Although Bill 115 was repealed in January 2013, the imposed union contracts stood until Kathleen Wynne got into the act.

I'm not sure what Hammond had to whine about at that meeting in August 2013. Just months before, newly appointed premier Kathleen Wynne, knowing she'd have to face voters sooner rather than later, decided to give ETFO some extra TLC once she became leader. She reopened their collective agreement, handing them a nice little 2 per cent pay hike and grandfathering sick-leave payouts for teachers with ten years of service or more – about 60 per cent of ETFO membership. What was good for ETFO was good for all other Ontario teachers' unions, and before we knew it, Wynne's little dose of TLC cost taxpayers an extra five hundred million dollars. The Liberals, desperately in debt and with a deficit climbing every day, couldn't even stick to their guns on one very important issue. It was pathetic.

Fast forward to August 2015 and seemingly the same meeting with the same cast of militant elementary teachers. A now out of control Hammond didn't just tell them they would be fighting to "Heave Steve" – meaning Stephen Harper (what that has to do with education is certainly way beyond me). He also let his militant troops (and the media) know that they'd be back at it with a work-to-rule campaign the first day of school if they weren't treated with "fairness and respect." There's that "fairness and respect" comment again – which is really code for "Give us everything we want, and then some, or else we'll hold students ransom." I couldn't for the life of me figure out exactly what the teachers wanted. Certainly they wanted more money, but we already knew Ms. Wynne couldn't afford that – not that unaffordability ever stopped her. I realized that besides their desire to get paid more, what they were arguing for was so inane they'd lost all perspective on how the public perceived them. One big sticking point was Regulation 274, brought in by Mr. McGuinty, which forced school boards to hire teachers based on seniority and *not* their skills, talents, and fit with a particular school. The regulation so completely tied principals' hands that they were left with no choice but to hire incompetent teachers or the deadwood ahead of fresh, energetic, tech-savvy new graduates. It was absurd. But the unions clung on to the regulation because they wanted to protect the deadwood and were afraid young, enthusiastic, quality candidates would show up the incompetents.

It was a bit of an eye-opener to see the militant teachers come out of the woodwork in August 2015 when I simply dared to write about their pay, perks, and some of the special concessions they'd already won from the Liberal government under both Dalton McGuinty and Kathleen Wynne, and that they still wanted more, more, more. They attacked me on social media for days afterward, claiming I'd lied and that I hated teachers – the furthest thing from the truth. I simply think teachers are so insulated from what is happening in the private sector (mergers, layoffs, people being forced into contract or part-time work) that they sound like whiny, self-serving brats. I guess I had forgotten how childish and petulant they can be. If anything, they'd become more churlish in the eighteen years since I'd last covered teachers' unions. It has left me to wonder how much of a quality education kids are actually getting in the classroom, with their teachers so busy protesting about how hard done by they are and deciding whether they'll work to rule or not.

A big part of the problem – in addition to a union empowered by a Liberal government that panders to their every desire, judging from the contract deals struck with them in August 2015 – are the trustees who are selected and elected largely with union and NDP support. Fourteen of twenty-two, or two-thirds, of trustees on the TDSB owe their election win in October 2014 to their links with the NDP councillor located in their particular ward (for example, councillors Mike Layton and Joe Cressy ran on the same ticket as Muslim and Hezbollah supporter Ausma Malik) or to union financial and manpower assistance. Naturally the unions expect, actually demand, their quid pro quo. So it is not the least bit surprising that even as school enrolment has gone down in the Toronto board, the number of teachers has increased and that Toronto's lefty trustees fought vociferously in the spring of 2015 against selling off any of the 130 – yes, 130! – schools that are operating at 65 per cent capacity or less. Fewer schools would mean fewer teachers and the unions would never allow that. Never mind that maintaining these underutilized schools makes absolutely no economic sense!

WHEN I WAS SENT to City Hall in 1998, I made myself a promise that I would not allow myself to run with the pack, focusing instead on my own personal mission of demanding accountability and trying to help those who found themselves caught in red tape or bullied by either bureaucrats or politicians, many of whom were adept at abusing their power. I kept hearing the words of one of my *Toronto Sun* mentors, Bob MacDonald (the father of my good friend Moira), who never gave up on a story lead. I wanted to be just like the late Peter Worthington, one of the *Toronto Sun*'s founders, whom I admired for his tell-like-it-is style and tremendous work ethic. Both Mr. MacDonald and Mr. Worthington were old-time journalists who knew how to work a story and their sources, and who didn't back down from what they believed was right. I suspect they would be horrified by the number of dilettantes in the news business these days.

I gravitated toward those politicians I felt were truly there for the right reasons: Doug Holyday, Frances Nunziata, Mike Del Grande, Jane Pitfield, Cesar Palacio, Case Ootes, and yes, Rob Ford. Before long, I'd found my first cause: the plight of the homeless. It all started when, in 1999, I witnessed Jack Layton bring 450 homeless people, as well as assorted industry hangers-on, to council in an attempt to guilt councillors into declaring homelessness a national disaster. His message would have been music to the ears of anyone who actually wanted to help the homeless if the whole stunt wasn't really about getting his hands on more money for his pet agenda, something then mayor Mel Lastman was only too eager to comply with. Over the years, seeing that most councillors – bleeding hearts all – didn't have the intestinal fortitude to challenge the idea of endless money being thrown at what was considered a sacred cow at City Hall, I tried to inject a voice of reason into the homelessness debate. I did an investigative series on the high cost of the homeless in 2002, which pointed out that more than thirty-two thousand dollars was being spent per hard-core homeless person while they remained out on the street as a kind of testament to the so-called need for affordable housing. I pointed out the absurdity of keeping 112 Tent City squatters on contaminated Cherry Street land for four years – a move propped up by Mr. Layton and his wife, Olivia Chow, until the city's bureaucrats finally got the guts to evict them in September 2002. That decision, I believe, was made only because the *New York Times* had written about Tent City three months earlier and the politicians were shamed into doing something. I presented the face of residents who felt the streets in their downtown neighbourhoods were being hijacked by the homeless and drug dealers let out of shelters at 7 a.m. to wander wherever they pleased. I served as the voice for ratepayers whose councillors were ramming more homeless shelters into their neighbourhoods without consultation or any concern for the homeowners around the site being considered. With the support of Mr. Holyday, Ms. Pitfield, and Mr. Ootes, I advocated persistently for an anti-panhandling bylaw, a street census to count the homeless, and a program that would put the homeless in the many available private apartments using rent supplements instead of waiting for federal government funding to build not-so-affordable affordable housing units (costing upwards of $250,000 per unit). I was successful on the latter two issues, but despite two attempts by Mr. Ootes and Ms. Pitfield, council never had the guts to impose an anti-panhandling bylaw similar to the ones put in place in Vancouver, Calgary, Winnipeg, Moncton, Fredericton, and Montreal. Never mind that Toronto was the place where panhandlers were known to flock every summer, like Canada geese returning north. I never gave up exposing the huge amount of money that went to the homeless to support misguided and often useless initiatives that ostensibly made the lefties on council feel good at night but did little or nothing to tackle the problem and give the homeless a hand up – that is, get them on their feet and off the street.

As David Miller's term went on, I honed my skills as the go-to gal who could be trusted to keep off-the-record sources secret and who took up the causes of taxpayers who found themselves on the wrong side of the socialist regime's draconian policies or its sheer arrogance toward those who paid the city's bills. Who knew that trees would interest me so much, but I became very much incensed with the city's ridiculous private-tree bylaw, which allowed the city's tree police to dictate who was allowed to take down a tree and who was not. I soon discovered, not surprisingly, that the tree removal rules were applied very selectively. Developers regularly got the green light to take down the same trees that poor residents without money or the same kind of influence were forbidden to touch. I even brought the issue to the city ombudsman in 2009, but as I was to discover, Fiona Crean (big surprise!) proved to be far more interested in investigating issues that fulfilled her leftist agenda than in the bread-and-butter concerns of residents with City Hall red tape. I was not to know it at the time, but my intervention in what appeared to be an ongoing but little known problem at City Hall in 2008 – refunding money on a timely basis to those who overpaid for work done by the city's Water Division – earned me a campaign supporter when I ran the next year for MPP in St. Paul's. Property manager Gerry Kawaguchi did not live in St. Paul's, or in Toronto, for that matter, but as a thank you for helping to get him back the $5,106.54 he was owed for seven months, he turned up to help on my campaign – more than once. He wasn't the only one. In late February 2012, still hobbling around on my broken ankle, I met another whistle-blower at another coffee shop by the name of Cecilia Leung. The tiny thirty-five-year-old computer specialist had been fired a week before her wedding in May 2011 for trying to make the TTC's blue suits and chair Karen Stintz aware of the tremendous mismanagement, the inability to get projects done on time and on budget, and the misuse of tax dollars at this monolith. A few weeks after our meeting, Chief General Manager Gary Webster – the root of many problems – was turfed. Unfortunately, it was too late for Ms. Leung, who had been put through the wringer for daring to speak up and whose warnings have proven to be prophetic, particularly with respect to the tremendous cost overruns on the Spadina subway extension.

WHEN I LEFT CITY HALL for Queen's Park, I was determined to continue focusing on the vulnerable, deciding that health care and mental health services would become my newest crusade. I felt it was something that hadn't been well-covered at all by the media to that point. As at City Hall, but far worse, most journalists at Queen's Park were concerned with the daily sideshow and whatever they were fed by the three political parties. The PCs were doing an almost non-existent job of addressing what I called very basic bread-and-butter issues. That inability to connect with what really concerned voters would add to the party's devastating loss in the June 2014 general election. Kathleen Wynne and her gal pal health minister, Deb Matthews, made my job quite easy when they tried to quietly cut the number of diabetes strips available through OHIP to those diabetics who were not insulin-dependent, and to nickel-and-dime frail seniors who were covered by OHIP for physiotherapy services in clinics or in retirement homes. It started with the tale of Wayne Beatty, a then sixty-eight-year-old Welland man who had managed to keep his type 2 diabetes in check without the need for insulin by testing his blood sugar four to six times a day using those strips. With the Liberal cutbacks, he'd only be able to test himself once a day unless the Canada Pensioner forked out an extra $1,000 a year. The Liberals told me they would save $15 million to $25 million a year from this move – mere chicken feed when you consider the $1.1 billion they blew on the gas plant scandal and the $1 billion on eHealth. But besides that, the cut showed that Ms. Wynne and Ms. Matthews had absolutely no vision whatsoever. Did they need someone like Mr. Beatty to remind them that diabetes, left unchecked, could easily escalate into strokes, heart attacks, or blindness – all far more costly to treat than any amount they'd save on those measly strips? But the Liberals truly showed their meanness with the cuts to physiotherapy – a desperately needed service that helped keep frail seniors mobile and able to continue living independently either in their own homes or in retirement homes – and their decision to put in a quota system for cataract surgery. There were no greater underdogs – in my view – than vulnerable seniors who'd worked hard and paid taxes all their lives, only to find the Liberal government, under the aforementioned stewardship of Ms. Wynne and Ms. Matthews, prepared to virtually toss them out on an ice floe, hoping they'd quietly drift away.

Unluckily for the Liberal Gruesome Twosome, seniors were living far too long and were needing those services, the money for which had already been squandered not only on various fiascos of the past but on the Pan Am Games, green energy schemes, and contracts for Liberal insiders, including Ms. Wynne's wife, Jane Rounthwaite. I didn't know whether to laugh or cry when I visited a Toronto retirement home called St. Hilda's Towers in August 2013 and met two feisty centenarians, Ida Hall and Eva Altay, who'd been dependent on physiotherapy to keep them mobile. Ms. Hall, then on the verge of turning 105, proudly showed me the physio workout with two-pound weights she did three times weekly to keep from stiffening up, and which allowed her to get out of bed each morning. Eva Altay, who was just about to turn 102, credited the physio with getting her from wheelchair to walker to walking on her own again after she broke her hip doing tai chi the January before. When I turned up that Friday morning, there was a sign on the door of the retirement home's physiotherapy room indicating services would no longer be provided at the $12.20 billed per visit to OHIP, and that Ms. Matthews's friends at the Community Care Access Centres (CCACs) – stuffed with more middle managers than frontline service providers – would be taking over at $120 per visit. It would be two months before the CCAC would get their act together to assess these seniors and start providing services again. When the dust settled, seniors would be granted $312 per episode of care, meaning physiotherapists would make the same from a particular case whether they visited a senior three times or thirteen times. In most cases, three-times-weekly visits shrank to three visits over a period of months. Heaven forbid it should have mattered to Ms. Matthews that the change was poorly communicated and poorly managed, and that seniors were suffering. They were dispensable. The same appalling lack of vision and the penny-wise pound-foolish mentality of the Liberals applied in this case as well. Their tunnel vision has also been evident in the case of cataract surgery, which has been subject to cutbacks and a quota system – meaning that hospitals now have the funding to do just so many per year, and once that money dries up, prospective ophthalmology patients are put on a waiting list for six months. Does it ever dawn on Ms. Wynne and her health minister that seniors who are able to see are able to keep driving, live in their own homes, and remain independent? Does Ms. Wynne not think she'll get old some day? By offering these preventative services, the Ontario government might just avoid the drain of costly health care programs down the road. Isn't it far better to keep aging baby boomers active and living in their homes rather than forcing them to be a drain on the already over stretched hospital and chronic care systems?

As a journalist, I was able to tell the story of St. Catharines senior and retired educator Marian Walsh, who had three health crises in early 2013 and found herself thrown out of the hospital without proper home care – although she'd been "promised the moon" by her local CCAC. Remember those? They are the centres staffed with many of Ms. Matthews's friends that have middle managers positively tripping over each other shuffling paperwork and creating unnecessary red tape while the senior brass are making six-figure salaries. Ms. Walsh ended up getting through the challenging time by hiring her own help and virtually exhausting her private insurance benefits, including thousands of dollars of her savings. She also relied on neighbours to pitch in. As I pointed out in my column about Ms. Walsh, home care involving two nursing visits plus 7.5 personal support worker hours per week would cost the government a mere $4,400, but because of the growing demand and the Liberals' mismanagement of the budget, the average home care client in Ontario was being forced to wait a ridiculous nineteen days to see a personal support worker.

During my brief but very fruitful six months at Queen's Park, I also tackled the very sad situation at Kinark Family and Child Services, one of the largest agencies in Ontario providing desperately needed intensive behavioural intervention (IBI) therapy for severely autistic kids. Kinark actually serves as the money dispensary only, handing out funding for the IBI therapy provided by another agency. In September 2013, I wrote about three families in York Region who'd been informed – with no rationale or warning provided – that the funding was to be cut off for their sons, even though all of them had improved tremendously with the IBI therapy. Kinark's officials would never admit it, but the funding cut was to make way for other families on the waiting list. Meanwhile, as I dug more into Kinark and its controversial history, I inadvertently discovered that Jane Rounthwaite, Premier Kathleen Wynne's wife, had cashed in with more than one million dollars in contracts from Kinark, even filling in as Kinark's interim director of program services in 2010 and 2011. This was at the same time that the agency was picking and choosing the families who'd be lucky enough to receive funding for autism services. In late March of 2016 the province cut off funding for IBI therapy entirely for kids five years and older, proving once again they care little about the vulnerable.

It had become clear to my editors that while at Queen's Park I was far more interested in digging into stories of political and bureaucratic mismanagement and the mistreatment of taxpayers by the Liberal government than the news story of the day. I loved watching politicians squirm when I asked them the hard questions. But I was bored by the political theatre. I felt I could do much more for my readers by putting a human face on that mismanagement and mistreatment. My ongoing desire to scratch below the surface and my scoop on the obscene spending by the brass at the Pan Am Games in September 2013 – an investigative series that led to the firing of three senior executives including the CEO Ian Troop – got me reassigned full-time to investigative reporting. That subsequently brought paramedic Patrick Allen and Olympian "Mighty Mouse" Elaine Tanner out of the woodwork. Mr. Allen approached me a few days before he was fired in May 2014 for trying to keep costs down, believe it or not. He was also an unfortunate casualty of two bosses jockeying for power within the TO2015 organization. He risked his severance to blow the whistle on what had become a terribly mismanaged and dysfunctional organization. It was touch and go for at least two weeks whether he'd get his severance, but he finally did. I suspect the Pan Am officials decided to pay him what he was owed rather than have me make a hero of him in another story. Ms. Tanner, affectionately named "Mighty Mouse" because of her tiny stature, was at the tender age of seventeen the first Canadian woman to win an Olympic medal in swimming. In 1968, in Mexico City, she took home three medals from a single Olympic Games to add to the ten times she was called to the medals podium in the Pan Am and Commonwealth Games the year before.

But when she retired from competition at age eighteen, the Canadian sports world tossed her aside like a used-up piece of garbage. Mighty Mouse and I spoke after my Pan Am exposé appeared and we had an instant connection – two underdogs who'd come out on top after experiencing many obstacles in our lives. She was brave enough to relay her tale of being cast aside by the sports world and, after suffering from anorexia and depression, finding herself homeless on the streets of Vancouver in the 1980s. She also spoke about her disappointment with the system, which she feels has lost sight of the fact that the Olympics, or Pan Am Games, or Commonwealth Games are to celebrate athleticism and not a way to "feed a lot of elite people" who are "at the trough." I have no doubt her story was read by a good number of people in the competitive sports business the day it ran, and I was very proud of her for speaking up. She's started her own website called TeamUnderdog.ca to raise awareness of a variety of underdog stories in the areas of mental health, homelessness, water safety, animal safety, and even the story of a journalist who was threatened with legal action for writing an exposé on John Furlong, the former CEO of the Vancouver 2010 Olympics, pertaining to abuse allegations against him while he was a teacher in 1970. (The defamation suit and all legal action pertaining to Mr. Furlong was dismissed in the fall of 2015).

BY THE TIME I was putting the finishing touches on this chapter – about two years after I'd first taken on the investigative beat at the *Toronto Sun* – I'd managed to touch on municipal, provincial, and school board issues of mismanagement.

The more I wrote, the more my Twitter and Facebook messenger feed, as well as my e-mail inbox, filled to the brim with tips and possible stories. I saw a need and was happy to fill it. I'm nothing special, but let's face it, there are not many avenues out there, whether in government services or in the media, that legitimate whistle-blowers and the discontented can access to have their voices heard. We pat ourselves on the back plenty as Canadians for being there for those in need, but all too often those who pride themselves with caring and helping the most – government bureaucrats, the Lib-left, etc. – are in it to help only themselves and their various sanctimonious agendas. "We care," they say. Yes, they do care – about themselves only. Calling them out is the best job I could ever have, slings and arrows be damned!

CHAPTER SIX

Ford Nation

I t was during the Toronto budget debate in 2002 that I first got a sense of how much councillors, Mayor Mel Lastman, and even city staff treated Rob Ford's repeated attempts to trim the fat at City Hall as a big joke. The then thirty-two-year-old newbie councillor had felt, and quite rightly, that if taxpayers were going to be handed a 4.32 per cent property tax hike that year, councillors and bureaucrats should lead by example and tighten their own belts, even if just a little. By then, I'd been at City Hall for four years and had watched how self-indulgent the politicians could be. I had also observed how Toronto's amalgamation from six cities into one mega-city – instead of being a downsizing exercise as originally envisaged by Premier Mike Harris – had turned into an excuse to harmonize union wages, city services, and even councillors' own perks up to the rich levels enjoyed by the pampered downtowners and professional grant-getters in the old City of Toronto.

The savings Mr. Ford proposed that day were more symbolic than anything, and he knew it. They wouldn't have made a tremendous difference to City Hall's bottom line and they certainly wouldn't have left councillors feeling the pinch in the slightest. He wanted to cut the $100,000 worth of free food and drink served at council and committee meetings, and to trim per-councillor slush funds (office budgets that they use for self-promotional flyers, travel, and meals out, over and above the staff budgets and the free offices, equipment, and the like) from $53,100 to $35,000 per year. He also asked councillors and city staff to water their own plants so he could get rid of the $78,000 City Hall plant watering budget. Was the man mad?

It wasn't enough for councillors to vote down his ideas. They intended to humiliate him on that March day. Even the bureaucrats joined in the fray because councillors sent the message that it was acceptable to mock this man, his ideas, his intelligence, his weight, you name it. Beefy NDPer Howard Moscoe, best known during his thirty long years in office for only moving quickly when he spotted a free buffet, for his relentless efforts to increase his already generous pay, and for the mess he made of the TTC during his time as chairman, heaved himself out of his council seat with a derisive snort, and – bellowing to the crowd as he always did – asked if Ford expected the city's top boss, Shirley Hoy, to also clean the windows and the urinals. Councillors roared at his lame joke. But the die was cast.

It went on for years and years. Whenever Mr. Ford tried to inject some sanity into council decisions – whether they were related to the draconian tree bylaws of the David Miller regime, or some out-of-control leftist pet project, or council's obsession with speed-bumping the city to death – he often found himself the lone wolf and one of the few voices of reason. Whenever he got emotional about council's dependence on overspending and their complete disregard for balancing the books – saying things in the heat of the moment that were not couched in the phony political rhetoric used by his council colleagues – he was mocked and ostracized. Council's bullies treated him as nothing more than the punching bag they could use to divert attention from their ridiculous spending decisions, from their arrogant dismissal of taxpayer wants, and from their childish debates. While I would often cringe in those days at the clumsy way Mr. Ford expressed himself – he called Giorgio Mammoliti a "Gino Boy" and Gloria Lindsay Luby a "waste of skin," and claimed that "Orientals" work like dogs – I admired him for standing up to the bullies on council and sticking to his principles.

As I noted in the *Toronto Sun* in March 2002 – not realizing how prescient I was – one day Ford would have the last laugh. Some twelve years and many Rob Ford escapades later, I was certainly not laughing at what happened to our controversial former mayor – his crack cocaine smoking, his alcoholism, his crude outbursts, or how he himself derailed a fiscally sane and sound agenda. I despaired every time I thought of the Lib-left elitists taking delicious delight in the ruination of the fiscally conservative agenda and the return to good times at the taxpayer trough – though I'm not so sure this is the end of what we can call the backlash against the political arrogance and mismanagement, judging from the number of hard-core supporters Mr. Ford continued to have throughout all of his troubles and the massive outpouring from supporters at his funeral. Still, I am forever amused when a member of Toronto's chattering classes – including some of my colleagues in the media – continues to accuse me, even following his death, of enabling Mr Ford's addictions because I had the audacity (in their minds) to support him when he deserved supporting, and to call out his fellow councillors and the compliant media for stooping to a level of crudity, vindictiveness, and cruelty I've never ever seen in my eighteen years of covering politicians. If students behaved like this in grade school, they'd be reprimanded, disciplined, and sent home. The attitude was, either you were anti-Ford or you were pro-Ford. There was no in between or shades of grey, as is necessary in any democracy. The debate was extremely polarized, and I was often berated for daring to show the slightest bit of empathy given that he might have had a mental illness or for understanding why he was in denial about his alcoholism.

Of course, I had as little to do with enabling Mr. Ford's rise to power as I did with creating the circumstances that empowered his bid for mayor. It was arrogant Liberal and NDP politicians in Canada's largest city – such as Kyle Rae, Paula Fletcher, Sandra Bussin, Howard Moscoe, and Adam Vaughan – who spent with impunity, and seemed to care little about their constituents, and who actually created the environment in which a Rob Ford would not only resonate with the public but would become the rational choice for mayor. They were the enablers – the ones who empowered Mr. Ford, who, for all his warts, his penchant for inappropriate and sometimes bordering on racist discourse, and his personal issues, had his heart in the right place when it came to respecting taxpayers.

If anyone enabled Rob Ford to become mayor of Toronto in 2010, it was David Miller, with his arrogant disdain of anyone who dared question his self-righteous environmental agenda, and the unalienable fact that he tripled the city's debt and raised four new taxes over his seven years as mayor. If there was one final act that sealed the deal for Torontonians in paving the way for Ford Nation, it was the mayor's cowardly surrender to the unions' demands after forcing the city to endure a thirty-nine-day garbage strike in 2009.

Councillor Kyle Rae did his bit when he threw himself a twelve-thousand-dollar taxpayer-funded farewell party to himself at the Rosewater Supper Club. The entitlement was so entrenched and accepted at City Hall that the integrity commissioner – the same woman who helped bring Rob Ford down – refused to investigate Mr. Rae's abuse of taxpayer money or the fact that a long list of political guests, including George Smitherman, who was running for mayor at the time, turned up to lap up the free booze and hors d'oeuvres. Rob Ford would never have been caught dead at such a party. My editor at the time, Rob Granatstein, had such a friendly relationship with the councillor that I made a conscious decision not to turn up at the party to break the initial story, figuring Mr. Rae would feel well within his rights to throw a very public temper tantrum at me, as he had in other instances.

Paula Fletcher, a classic leftist bully, got Toronto tongues wagging for days when she publicly dressed down a citizen, John Smith, in 2010, for turning up at City Hall to provide feedback on the $9.2-billion operating budget. No doubt irate that he dared criticize the spending excesses of the Miller regime, she screamed at Mr. Smith to "come on down" and deliver his criticisms to her face, as if she were some schoolyard bully. Her rant was replayed and discussed on radio talk shows for days. It wasn't enough that Toronto residents had been taxed to death under the NDP regime of David Miller. Torontonians let it be known that they were simply fed up with the rude and overbearing Ms. Fletcher and some of her socialist compatriots – and this was yet another nail in the coffin of the leftist stranglehold on City Hall. There's no doubt in my mind that Adam Vaughan, novelist Margaret Atwood, Premier Kathleen Wynne, a long list of Red Tories, assorted other elitists, and the *Toronto Star* helped roll out a red carpet for Mr. Ford's victory in 2010 when they engaged in vicious fear mongering, intimidation, and attacks on his character for weeks and months before the election to prop up their chosen candidate, George Smitherman – the same deputy premier to Dalton McGuinty who had his paw prints all over the eHealth, Ornge, Samsung, and Green Energy Act spending fiascos. When integrity commissioner and David Miller hire Janet Leiper came up with the first of her numerous one-sided reports chiding Mr. Ford, then still a councillor, for his many alleged crimes against the socialist state, I watched with amazement how councillors took turns lining him up in front of a verbal firing squad. I kept thinking they just couldn't get it through their thick heads that by disparaging Mr. Ford, they were driving voters to support him. As the days drew closer to the October 2010 election, it didn't dawn on the self-perceived A-listers that their tricks weren't working – that Torontonians were plain tired of the corruption, the arrogance, the overspending on pet agendas, and the phony crocodile tears for the downtrodden. But more than anything, they were fed up with being treated as second-class citizens. The *Toronto Star* and its long list of past-their-prime columnists, thinking they ran the city, never did recover from Mr. Ford's win, and they set out to destroy him from the moment he took office. They finally succeeded when he succumbed to his aggressive cancer in March 2016, barely 46. Actually they tried for months before, but didn't get very far by spitting in the faces of a large constituency of voters who just happened not to read their newspaper or live in the Annex.

Fact is, no one was more surprised than me when council's "enfant terrible" decided in late March 2010 to run for mayor. It wasn't just that I thought him unpolished, far from diplomatic, and extremely limited in his fiscal and intellectual scope. But as the lone wolf on council who refused to even try to play nice with others, I wondered how he'd ever be able to coalesce such a dysfunctional council. While I knew he had balls and determination and his heart was in the right place, I figured him far more suited to the role of opposition critic, holding his colleagues' feet to the fire, than actually tackling the complex job of running a city. My hopes in the early days of the mayoralty race were pinned on Rocco Rossi, who I knew not only had the guts and integrity to make the tough changes needed to clean up City Hall, but had the right intellectual stuff to follow through on a vision that went well beyond saving a few hundred thousand dollars here and there by cutting free food for councillors and their office budgets. Mr. Rossi had the polish to bring together a highly dysfunctional council of competing interests without pandering to them. I saw him present a well-thought-out fiscal action plan and outside-the-box thinking on the gridlock problem, and to this day, I suspect he would have tackled the ongoing issues with construction in Toronto that never seems to be delivered on time or on budget. But it was not to be with Mr. Rossi. Regrettably, his message of change never did resonate with voters, who – so fed up with the constant onslaught of new taxes and fees imposed under the David Miller regime and the slick talk that had come from City Hall – really wanted a quick fix, a campaign plat-form delivered in sixty-second sound bites by a "regular guy."

I understood why Mr. Ford's message of stopping the "gravy train" quickly caught on with those disenfranchised by City Hall. I had watched the anger grow during the ten years prior to the 2010 election. People were already feeling disconnected from an amalgamated city government that had grown too big – too unwieldy, bloated, and beholden to the unions that worked there. The thirty-nine-day garbage strike in the summer of 2009 managed to bring that anger to a boil. When I decided to take a five-week leave from my job at the paper just after that strike and run for MPP in St. Paul's under newly selected PC leader Tim Hudak, I encountered the anger at the door while campaigning. In fact, I heard far more outrage about Mr. Miller's mishandling of the garbage strike than, unfortunately, then premier Dalton McGuinty.

At a time when most of the David Miller acolytes had lost touch with what they were there for and started believ-ing their own rhetoric about how important they were, Mr. Ford presented as the antithesis of the arrogant politi-cian – an Everyman who returned phone calls, gave out his home number to constituents, and connected with residents in their own neighbourhoods. To many disenfranchised vot-ers, Ford practised what he preached by not spending his tax-payer-funded office budget or jetting around the world. He told dirty jokes, was overweight and loud, liked football, and actually preferred hanging out at a suburban barbecue rather than the Giller Prize event. I still remember Denise telling me that when she had her issue with Councillor Michael Walker, who helped her neighbours to take away her widened drive-way in 2006, Mr. Ford was one of the few councillors who took the time to actually sit down and talk to her about it. That was his appeal in a nutshell.

As the months went on and Mr. Rossi's campaign did not gain much ground, I realized that Mr. Ford represented the best chance of shaking up the entitlement at City Hall and getting the city's fiscal fortunes back on track. My editors at the *Toronto Sun* agreed. I knew he had the determination to make the hard decisions; I just hoped that he would surround himself with strong councillors to make up for his many weaknesses, whether it was his inability to understand the hard numbers in the budget or to build bridges with all members of council. I suspected that life would never be dull with Rob Ford as mayor, but I certainly underestimated the sideshow that would emerge. I knew Mr. Ford would always be rough around the edges and boorish, and would say things that would send the elitists on council into histrionics. But to be honest, I didn't think much of their dramatics, considering that far too many of them had their moments too over the ten years I'd watched their every move. Adam Vaughan? His nastiness drove Mel Lastman to threaten to kill him. Shelley Carroll? The former bank teller drove the city's finances into freefall while pretending to know what she was talking about or making it up as she went along. If she didn't like what someone was saying at a committee – whether citizen or councillor – she'd pace around the room, heckle and mock, talk loudly, and break into her horsey laugh to try to distract and intimidate them. Ditto for Pam McConnell and Paula Fletcher. Gord Perks? He became well known for grilling residents who didn't share his view of the world, as if he considered himself a defence lawyer questioning a hostile witness in court. If Rob Ford's colleagues on council had anything in common, it was their complete lack of class and decorum and their constant mean-spirited bullying of anybody who dared criticize them or their agenda. True, he could get somewhat emotional, but if Mr. Ford had drinking or drug problems during those years as a councillor, he hid them well. Mike Del Grande and I both watched him for ten years and never saw any sign of alcohol or drug abuse.

I knew Mr. Ford's home life was unsettled and that he liked to drink, but I always thought it was his wife, Renata, who had the drug problem. Over dinner in 2010 with his campaign manager, Nick Kouvalis, and his communications advisor and now *Sun* editor-in-chief, Adrienne Batra, they hinted to me that they wished Mr. Ford had waited to get through his personal problems before running for mayor. They never elaborated, and I just assumed the comment was referencing his wife's drug issues. When I was provided the tape of Mr. Ford's fifty-two-minute conversation with a then thirty-year-old gay man by the name of Dieter Doneit-Henderson in June of that year – who was begging Mr. Ford to score him the extremely addictive painkiller OxyContin – I pushed the would-be mayor to tell his side of the story. The fact that Doneit-Henderson taped the conversation and subsequently gave the tape to the *Toronto Star*, and to *Xtra* and *fab* magazines, only made me suspicious of the whole thing. Still, I didn't think Mr. Ford showed terribly sound judgment in talking to a man I considered a nutcase and a drug addict, and certainly not in advising him to buy drugs off the street. But at the time it appeared that he was trying to do so to prove he was not homophobic. He told me during our interview that he didn't know any drug dealers and didn't know what OxyContin was. Perhaps Mr. Ford knew more about drug deals and OxyContin than he admitted at the time – given everything that came to light in 2013 – but I had no reason and certainly no evidence to disbelieve him. It seemed most voters sympathized with him, and a potential crisis was averted.

It was Labour Day of 2010 when the campaign to discredit Mr. Ford's mayoralty bid went into overdrive – in what would prove to be a dramatic foreshadowing of the vicious attempts to drive him from office. I'd learned that, about a month before the municipal election, Kathleen Wynne (functioning then as transportation minister in the pathetic, controversy-plagued Dalton McGuinty government) had sent an e-mail to her constituents using her office resources and raising fears about Rob Ford's style of governance. As she was later to prove in the 2014 provincial election, Ms. Wynne was and is adept at doing whatever it takes, even being confrontational or engaging in fear mongering, to win. She contended that Mr. Ford would not have the "best interests" of the city at heart, or compassion for the people who live in it. "I believe that he has a very small view of Toronto," she wrote. We all know, of course, that the Liberals have a lock on compassion, especially when they refuse to fund cancer drugs for dying moms or when they cancel OHIP-funded physiotherapy for frail seniors. But that is beside the point. This attempt by Ms. Wynne to change the channel from her own sorry record would become a pattern throughout Mr. Ford's time in office.

By the end of September, half-baked pseudo-Rastafarian (can we say "trustafarian"?) and perennial political candidate Sarah Thomson dropped out of the mayoral race, throwing what meagre support she had to the very man she'd labelled as a "completely irresponsible, corrupt boondoggle of a career politician." No, not Rob Ford but George Smitherman, a walking trunkful of personal baggage and, of course, a good chum of Kathleen Wynne. It seemed Ms. Thomson had experienced a sudden epiphany and thought Toronto would be "severely hurt" by a mayor like Mr. Ford. The "Anybody but Ford" movement gained momentum, propped up by the *Toronto Star*, the Women for George Smitherman, former mayors Art Eggleton and David Crombie, MP Carolyn Bennett, and most of the Liberal caucus at Queen's Park. Even officials of YWCA Toronto leapt into the fray, worried that their gravy train might end, and came out with a statement knocking Mr. Ford for his lack of vision and his history of poor-bashing. My goodness, this was war, man. There was no shortage of professional grant-getters, has-beens, and hacks prepared to hop on the George Smitherman bandwagon in their desperation to keep Toronto Liberal Red. But despite all of these groups' efforts to paint Mr. Ford as the bogeyman, the voters were angry with David Miller and they were not prepared to pretend Mr. Smitherman was their saviour. They saw through the Liberal propaganda and brought in Mr. Ford with a sweeping 47 per cent of the vote. I was sitting in a CBC-radio studio waiting to go on air when the election night results were confirmed. I watched the faces of those around me go white. I have to admit I enjoyed the upset, although I suspected even that night Mr. Ford's term would not be without a sideshow. I just never imagined how decidedly both Mr. Ford and his fiscally sound agenda would fall apart.

Mr. Ford had little more than a year of grace in office before the media and his detractors started to gang up on him in earnest. To this day, I suspect that this delay was because they didn't really believe at the outset he had the cojones to make good on his promises. When he started to make major and very lasting gains with the union contracts, with contracting out garbage, and with trimming what had been an unsustainable budget and a soaring debt under Mr. Miller, the knives came out. Their intent was to throw him off his game, and they proved to be adept at it. Before the wheels started to fall off the bus, Mr. Ford kept many of his campaign promises. He got rid of Mr. Miller's personal vehicle tax grab, contracted out cleaning at police stations, contracted out garbage pickup for all residential homes west of Yonge Street (to save eleven million dollars a year) and got ground-breaking contract deals with both CUPE 416 and 79 – ones that did away with the unions' "jobs for life" provisions without inciting a strike. Under the excellent stewardship of his deputy mayor Doug Holyday, the contract deals were made in the early spring when the unions couldn't use the hot weather and the threat of stinky garbage piling up – as it had in the thirty-nine-day strike in 2009 under Mr. Miller – as a bargaining chip. For the first time in all of my thirteen years at City Hall, council under Rob Ford and Doug Holyday not only had the guts to say no, but didn't allow the unions to manipulate the timing of the negotiations. This was a crucial factor in the negotiating process. Both Mel Lastman and David Miller had forever allowed the unions to set the agenda and back council against the wall.

In his early days in office, Mr. Ford put strong members of his inner circle on key files: Mr. Holyday on labour relations and Denzil Minnan-Wong on public works and the contracting out of garbage. And Mike Del Grande worked tirelessly as budget chief to balance the city's books. One of the mayor's biggest mistakes early on was that he was not adept at letting the public know about his accomplishments. He could have learned from his successor, John Tory, who even in his first hundred days in office seemed to hold a photo op or press opportunity daily. Mr. Tory's shameless self-promotion continues to this day. Mr. Ford's other big mistake was putting Karen Stintz in the position of TTC chair. As he was soon to learn, Ms. Stintz, a backstabbing opportunist, would renege on her promise to back his subway plan and would turn on him in a very public way. I'd warned the mayor's brother Doug, when he appointed Ms. Stintz in their first weeks in office, that I'd watched her, from the time she was elected in 2003, flip-flop many times in council, saying one thing on the council floor and then voting the exact opposite way. But these mistakes aside, the changes Mr. Ford achieved during his first eighteen months as mayor were long overdue. This is what made his fall from grace – the crack cocaine smoking, the binge drinking, the consorting with criminals, and the crude outbursts – so disheartening. He could have done so much to turn the city around. Or could he? I'm convinced to this day that the champagne socialists, the downtown elites, and the left-wing media (always led by the *Toronto Star*) would have never let him get too far without bringing him down. His control of the agenda was too good to be true, and is now a mere dream that quickly turned into a nightmare.

While I can't be sure of the exact moment the daggers were drawn, it was likely when that washed-up comedienne Mary Walsh of CBC's *This Hour Has 22 Minutes*, in a desperate attempt to resurrect her career, showed up dressed as her character Marg Delahunty at the mayor's home at 8 a.m. one Monday morning in October of 2011. When Mr. Ford called 9-1-1, not knowing who the heck she was and what her little game of sabotage was all about, Toronto's elitists laughed hysterically at his reaction to her visit. Never mind that she had no business showing up on his property, or that her stab at humour was terribly unfunny – the point was to make the mayor look pathetic. I can only imagine how the left would have reacted if a journalist critical of David Miller – me, for example – had turned up at his home one morning at 8 a.m. uninvited and dressed in a ridiculous Viking costume with a CBC camera in tow. The fact is, that would never happen.

By the spring of 2012 – eighteen months into the new mayor's mandate – the natives were growing restless. Mr. Ford had been too successful in his efforts to stop the gravy train, the unions had been kneecapped, and a series of reviews from accountancy consultant firm KPMG on how to really dig into the fat at City Hall were about to be released. The mayor had not been distracted by insults or persistent attacks by left-wing columnists, or by the tasteless photo-shopped picture of his head on a naked body on the front cover of *NOW* magazine. It was time to pull out the heavy artillery. The objectors turned to the most opportunistic, malleable, and easily flattered member of his so-called inner circle – Karen Stintz. With the help of Gary Webster, the chief general manager of the TTC, they convinced Ms. Stintz to flip-flop on her subway promise to the mayor and to start advocating, once again, for LRTs for Scarborough's Sheppard Avenue. I sat on a panel with her in March 2012, when she was jeered and booed by the Scarborough audience for claiming there was no money for a subway – even as long-time transit insider Gordon Chong sat beside her holding up a plan for how to fund it. Ms. Stintz would flip-flop so many times on subways versus LRTs for Scarborough in 2012 and 2013 that she single-handedly managed to delay the decision by at least a year or more. Although the mayor eventually got his Scarborough subway (now whittled down to one stop by his successor John Tory), Ms. Stintz, egged on by council's lefties, was the first to try to undermine and derail Mr. Ford's agenda. I wouldn't be the least bit surprised if at the time she was already thinking of running for mayor and needed to shore up the support of the usual suspects.

Then came an item at a council meeting in February that would be the first of many issues to distract the mayor from his agenda and one I suspect began his downward slide into alcohol and drug addiction. I'm sure no one in the media but me bothered to review the readily available tapes of that evening's session. Mr. Ford was encouraged by the Speaker in the chair at the time, John Parker – who was seen to follow Ms. Stintz around like a lovesick puppy and was not at all well-schooled in council proceedings – to not only stay in the council chamber but to speak about the Rob Ford Football Foundation and to vote on a ridiculous ruling by the David Miller–appointed integrity commissioner, Janet Leiper. Leiper, or Miss Manners, as I had come to call her for her single-minded focus on the so-called indiscretions of the Ford brothers (to the exclusion of anyone else on council) and her constant demands to exact apologies from them for what I deemed politically incorrect slights, had her nose out of joint because Mr. Ford, while a councillor, had inadvertently solicited donations to his football foundation on his councillor letterhead instead of using his personal note paper. She had ruled that he should repay the donors the $3,150 he'd collected, even though the donations had gone directly to his foundation serving under-privileged kids. Ms. Manners was dogged about trying to exact her pound of flesh from Mr. Ford, having written him six letters reminding him of that obligation even after he indicated the donors did not want the money returned. He repeatedly told her that they had made a donation to a great cause and they wanted the money to remain where it was. It was not that Mr. Ford couldn't afford the $3,150; but out of principle, he refused. It was later learned that Ms. Leiper's obsessive repayment demands – her very ruling that ended up dragging Ford through the courts – were well beyond her mandate. I always wondered why she gave such short shrift to the many other issues that were brought to her attention regarding the spending and code-of-conduct abuses by the rest of council – like the twelve-thousand-dollar taxpayer-funded farewell party Kyle Rae threw for himself, or the fact that Sandra Bussin left her office unattended for thirty days after losing the October 2010 election.

In any event, her ruling and Mr. Ford's decision to stay in council to vote, after being encouraged to do so, was the exact loophole Ms. Leiper's lawyer friend, the King of Champagne Socialists, Clayton Ruby, needed to launch a vexatious court case against the mayor under the Municipal Conflict of Interest Act. The plot was concocted by a professional protester, the highly irritating Adam Chaleff-Freudenthaler, who'd learned the art of being vindictive at the knee of Olivia Chow while serving on her Toronto Youth Cabinet, one of Ms. Chow's expensive pet projects in the days of Mel Lastman. Knowing full well that his actions would be interpreted as sour grapes, Mr. Chaleff-Freudenthaler solicited his milquetoast friend Paul Magder (not to be confused with the furrier) to be his front man on the lawsuit. Mr. Chaleff-Freudenthaler, who thought himself part of the political in-crowd, never got over the fact that David Miller was an abysmal failure, that someone like Mr. Ford had been voted into office, and that, as a consequence, his good councillor friend NDPer Joe Mihevc had been sidelined. Following me so far? To add to his woes, when Mr. Ford came to office, Mr. Chaleff-Freudenthaler was bounced from a seat on the library board – a move for which he never forgave the mayor. Anyway, if the shoe had been on the other foot, right-wing objectors would have been laughed out of court for wasting valuable time and resources on such a vexatious lawsuit, one announced with great fanfare by the pompous Mr. Ruby (who took on the case pro-bono). But somehow it all became perfectly acceptable for these combined forces to use the courts to try to get the mayor out of office. And in a surreal twist of fate, they very nearly did.

It was indeed telling how Ford's conflict of interest troubles became a cause célèbre for the *Toronto Star* from the time the lawsuit was first filed until Ford won his appeal, often bumping more important news from the paper's front pages. Just days before the mayor was due to go to court in November 2012, the *Star* published a story claiming Ford was to face a "high stakes public grilling" (from the great man Clayton Ruby himself) and provided a rundown on all the players involved in the lawsuit – as if this ridiculous court case was due the same consideration as the O.J. Simpson trial. The day after Ford lost his initial lawsuit (he subsequently won on appeal), the *Toronto Star* did a huge feature on the annoying Mr. Chaleff-Freudenthaler, breathlessly reporting that a mere twenty-seven-year-old had managed to bring the mayor down, as if he was the conquering hero. It was sickening.

At the same time that the mayor was dealing with this lawsuit, he was also forced to defend himself in a six-million-dollar libel suit brought forward by George Foulidis, the owner of the Boardwalk Café. In May 2010, I had blown the whistle on the sweet twenty-year sole-sourced deal handed to Mr. Foulidis – with considerable help from his councillor, Sandra Bussin – which gave him the exclusive rights to sell beverages, food, and trinkets along a five-kilometre stretch of beach in Toronto's east end. The contract, approved in a secret vote at a council meeting while several councillors were absent, was wrong for many reasons, not the least of which was that city officials failed to put it out for tender. Mr. Ford claimed in a *Toronto Sun* editorial board meeting two months before the 2010 election that the deal "stinks to high heaven." Mr. Ford was right about that. It sure did stink to high heaven. In return, Mr. Foulidis, a hot-headed Greek man who'd threatened me many times with libel chill and who eventually banned me from coming into his café (to interview him) by way of a lawyer's letter, hired Brian Schiller of Mr. Ruby's firm to sue Mr. Ford for allegedly damaging his reputation. It was what one might call a full-court press by the King of Champagne Socialists. Although the Foulidis lawsuit was eventually dismissed in 2012, Mr. Ford was dealing with the libel allegations at the very same time as his job hung in the balance over the municipal conflict of interest lawsuit. The mayor was spending more time in court across the way from City Hall than at City Hall – and his enemies had him just where they wanted him, distracted and unable to focus on his cost-cutting agenda.

But this was hardly the end of it. One May evening, Daniel Dale, a highly ambitious and passive-aggressive *Toronto Star* reporter, decided to check out a piece of property adjacent to the mayor's home that Mr. Ford was hoping to buy from the Toronto Region Conservation Authority. While peering over Mr. Ford's backyard fence with a cellphone camera in hand, the reporter was noticed by a neighbour, who called the mayor, thinking it was an intruder. When the mayor came out to see who it was, Mr. Dale got frightened and ran away, dropping his cellphone. Why didn't he behave in a professional manner and just knock on Mr. Ford's door? Or stand and face the music when caught? Because he would have realized what he was doing would be seen by many as an invasion of the mayor's privacy, particularly just after 7:30 p.m. This was yellow journalism at its finest. When Mr. Dale first started at City Hall, I thought him a fairly decent journalist. Inexperienced, but decent. But the brown noser quickly got co-opted by the *Star*'s editor-in-chief to do nothing but try to dig dirt on the mayor or his family and friends; he rarely covered anything else at City Hall during Mr. Ford's entire mayoralty. After the incident at the mayor's house, I lost all respect for him. He milked it for all its worth, even threatening to sue Mr. Ford for libel (and writing a self-serving column about it) when the mayor questioned Mr. Dale's intentions in peering over his fence in a Vision TV interview with Conrad Black. While Mr. Ford never actually said the word, Dale implied he was called a pedophile. His response became very personal and bordered on self-indulgent. My goodness, the first rule of journalism is to try to not become part of the story! Yet, for months his media colleagues continuously painted the wimpy Mr. Dale as the victim.

In late November 2012, Justice Charles Hackland, who heard the conflict of interest case, found that Mr. Ford was indeed guilty of breaking the municipal conflict of interest act and would need to step down from office within thirty days. The long list of characters at the *Toronto Star*, who'd long before ceased to have any objectivity on the mayor, were over the moon, promoting the weasel Mr. Chaleff-Freudenthaler on their front page the next day as a "hero" for bringing the mayor down. But Mr. Ford wasn't giving in that easily. He launched a judicial review so he could remain in office until an appeal was heard. Clayton Ruby and friends, who were becoming subject to public backlash from Ford supporters, agreed to a stay of the original judge's order. When a three-judge panel threw out Justice Hackland's ruling in late January 2013 and granted the mayor a stay of execution, there was no acknowledgement that a lawsuit over $3,150 in donations to a children's charity had cost the mayor personally $300,000 and taxpayers the expense of using up valuable court services, and been a general waste of the voting public's time. Still, what I found far more hideous and telling was that Janet Leiper, after being found by the appeal judges to have overstepped her authority under the City of Toronto Act for imposing the $3,150 financial sanction in the first place, never apologized. Not once. The integrity commissioner, who forced too many apologies to count out of the Ford brothers – and even chastised them for not being sincere enough in their apologies – never once conceded she'd overstepped her authority or made a mistake. I still get angry when I think about the piling on, the stalking of Mr. Ford's family, the obsessive witch hunts, and the almost daily and very personal attacks in the *Toronto Star* and other like-minded media that crossed over the line of objectivity and decency every time they licked their lips in delicious delight at the idea of beating up on this man.

Unfortunately, this was all just a dress rehearsal for the left's crowning achievement, which began, ostensibly, on May 22, 2013, the date when there was the first whiff of a video about Mr. Ford's crack cocaine smoking, reported first by the U.S. blog *Gawker* and subsequently by the *Toronto Star*. Within a heartbeat, the Toronto Catholic District School Board announced they were removing the mayor as coach of his beloved Don Bosco Eagles football team, a volunteer position he'd held for ten years. They also made it clear they would not allow him to coach at any school in the board. He gave his heart and soul to those football players. They were like his sons. I often wondered if he loved coaching more than being mayor. Either way, it was cruel. It proved how prepared even the school board brass were to kick a dog when he was down. Looking back at the tremendous pressures on the mayor and the horrible, vindictive way in which he was treated, I can only imagine how all of this ate away at him. I highly doubt many of the various and sundry media, politicians, and members of the public who laughed at, mocked, and turned their backs on him after he slid into his addictive state would have been able to handle the daily abuse he took without either quitting, having to take stress leave, or turning to a bottle or pills themselves. In fact, in early 2015, I revealed that more than 1,230 city employees were on long-term disability over stress issues (many of those with issues far more minor than those the mayor faced).

As of January 2013, after Mr. Ford won his appeal in the conflict of interest case, I hoped – a fantasy, I guess – that he would put the sideshow behind him and salvage the rest of his term. With the help of the strong councillors who were part of his inner circle – Mike Del Grande, Doug Holyday, Frances Nunziata, Cesar Palacio, and his brother Doug – he could even pick up where he left off, implementing his cost-cutting agenda. But it was too late. As February turned into March, Mr. Ford started turning up late for work and showing up at public events appearing inebriated. When, in March, perennial self-promoter and *Women's Post* publisher Sarah Thomson accused the mayor of groping her at a Canadian Jewish Political Action Committee event, I had a hard time believing it because, well, I had a hard time believing anything she said. I suspect he probably was inebriated that night, but as a real victim of not one – but two – assaults in my lifetime, I was incensed at what I saw as her shameless attempt to get publicity at the mayor's expense, IF he did indeed grope her. Sadly, his slide continued, and just before the long weekend in May, *Gawker* and the *Toronto Star* came forward with the story that they'd seen a video allegedly being shopped around by Somali drug dealers showing the mayor smoking crack cocaine with some pretty dodgy characters outside an apartment complex known to police on the western fringes of Toronto. Of course, Rob Ford denied smoking crack and the very existence of the video. But it was as if nothing else was going on in the world as far as the press were concerned. They ran and reran every salacious detail in what seemed like a twenty-four-hour loop. The circus continued right into the next week, when Mr. Ford and his chief of staff, Mark Towhey, had a tremendous falling out. Mr. Towhey tried to push the mayor to go into rehab, and the mayor, channelling his inner Amy Winehouse, said, no, no, no. Mr. Towhey was fired for his attempts to do the right thing, which was a real shame.

Former Toronto police chief Bill Blair – more often a politician (and a liberal one at that) than a champion of law and order – got immersed in the circus. Clearly upset at Mr. Ford's ongoing efforts to make him rein in his out-of-control spending on toys and overtime for the boys in blue, Blair spent a million dollars investigating Ford's drug ties, even engaging in costly air surveillance to do so. Throughout, Blair crossed the line many times with political comments about the investigation, and often tried to intimidate anyone who dared criticize him about the investigation or about his spending. When he was forced to hand the investigation over to the OPP, who subsequently found no grounds to charge the mayor with any drug offences, I never once heard any contrition or an apology out of the power-mad police chief either.

At the time, I refused to call Mr. Ford guilty without seeing the video or being provided solid proof that it existed. I wasn't in denial. I just wanted proof. Predictably, the very people who were out to crucify the mayor for a possible addiction were and are the same ones pushing harm-reduction programs, safe injection sites, and publicly funded safe crack kits for those with the same addictions. I surmised that addiction was only acceptable if one was the right kind of addict. It didn't matter that I wrote a column clearly stating that he'd lost my trust in early November of 2012 when he finally admitted to his crack cocaine smoking. I was quickly branded an enabler of the mayor's addictions for merely suggesting we rely on due process before assuming guilt. I wrote the column long after I'd left for Queen's Park and it wasn't my beat to be writing about him. Nor was I asked by my editors to do so. I wanted to do it because I felt I needed to state my feelings about the uncertain existence of the video and the mayor's need for professional help, after making it clear a few months before that I would not judge the situation until the video appeared.

I will never condone many of the things Mr. Ford did, or his hiding of his condition. I would have respected him far, far more if he'd been honest about his crack use and his binge drinking from the get-go, and about the stresses that led him to lose control. He most certainly should have sought professional help when Mr. Towhey suggested it instead of lying about it for months and pretending he was okay. He had a perfect reason to disappear and get his life in order. He could probably have salvaged the situation if he'd done so, and been returned for a second term. I said many, many times that, while I empathized with what drove him to drink and smoke crack, Rob Ford was his own worst enemy. He had come undone and he refused to admit it. Instead he spiralled out of control, embarrassing himself, his family, and the office of mayor many times. He repeatedly asked for trouble from the media when he said things that were crude or offensive – including homophobic and sexist comments – or he made a drunken public spectacle of himself and made a mockery of what was a serious addiction. I knew from my own dealings with him that he wasn't homophobic, but he just provoked the endless attempts by his detractors to paint him that way. I didn't really care much that he'd appeared on *Jimmy Kimmel Live!* or that he became known around the world, even in my Florida community, for his crack cocaine scandals and his outrageous behaviour. Even though it drove the left nuts – since they're very adept at manufacturing outrage – as far as I'm concerned, there is no bad publicity. I joked many times that he'd done what no other mayor had managed to do – that is, put Toronto on the map. Even jaded Americans seemed to be fascinated by his chutzpah. Despite David Miller's swanning around the world purporting to be the environmental guru to end all environmental gurus, he never managed to get much publicity at all for Toronto. Even during SARS, and with all the costly promotional attempts to draw tourism to Toronto – including his appearance on CNN – Mel Lastman was never subject matter for Jon Stewart.

What really troubled me was that the more Mr. Ford spiralled out of control – deluding himself into thinking he could keep his house in order – and the more he became the butt of every talk show joke, the more he played into the hands of his detractors. He completely lost sight of his agenda, particularly the fiscal one. The bureaucrats were free to do and spend what they wanted, and they took full advantage of the situation. By the late fall of 2013, when most of his supporters had deserted Mr. Ford and council had cruelly revoked most of his powers, giving them to that long-time Liberal teat-sucker and deputy mayor Norm Kelly, he wasn't even pretending to do what he'd been elected to do. It got even worse when more cellphone videos surfaced of Mr. Ford engaged in a late-night drunken, Jamaican-accented rant at a restaurant near his home, and in another drunken episode after the St. Patrick's Day Parade. I wanted him to get off the stage and get into rehab. By then I was exhausted with the nonsense and angry with him for letting down all those who'd relied on him to clean up City Hall, for giving the Lib-leftists all the fodder they needed to contend that the right wing couldn't run Toronto, and for feeding into the media sideshow that just wouldn't quit. As Mr. Kelly took over his role and started to enjoy the perks of office (including a car and driver, free junkets, and free meals), I knew all checks and balances were gone and it would just be a matter of time before council started spending with impunity from their office slush funds and the bureaucrats started taking liberties again to undo all the good Mr. Ford had done.

I always thought, given his weight, his poor eating habits, and his various addictions, Rob Ford would end up with a stroke or a heart attack. Who could have predicted that he'd be forced to drop out of the 2014 mayor's race after being diagnosed with a rare and aggressive form of malignant liposarcoma? The day the diagnosis was confirmed, I found myself reduced to tears because no human being, no one, deserved to be treated with such disrespect by the media, the public, and his fellow politicians.

No matter how much one might say that Rob Ford was his own worst enemy and that he brought on his own problems, I liked and even identified with him. Perhaps it was because I myself was bullied and treated as an outsider for many of my early years – or because I knew Mr. Ford's heart was in the right place about getting waste and mismanagement under control, he actually tried to do what he promised (unlike most politicians), and no one was prepared to let him do his job – that I forever felt protective towards him. I can truly say I would offer a stray dog far better treatment than the absolutely visceral disdain with which his many detractors treated him even after he passed away. Let's remember that Rob Ford was never charged with anything. Nor was he convicted of anything. The behaviour of Toronto's chattering classes hit a new low during his regime.

After a brave 18-month fight – with the same toughness he displayed as mayor and councillor – Rob Ford suc-
cumbed to a very aggressive and rare form of liposarcoma
on March 22, 2016 at the young age of 46. He left behind his
wife Renata and two children, Stephanie, 10, and Dougie, 7.
A few days before his death, when I heard he was in pallia-
tive care and it was just a matter of time, I wept uncontrolla-
bly. My tears were not just over the loss of a decent, generous
man, a grassroots politician this city has not seen in a long
time – who may have been deeply flawed and suffered with
addictions, but who had a good heart, the very best of intentions and who truly cared about the residents he served. But I
cried out of anger for the way he was bullied, and mocked for
his entire fifteen years at Toronto City Hall (as a councillor
and mayor) with the kind of vitriol and contempt I'd never
seen levelled at any politician and probably never will. He
could never catch a break from the left-wing media, his fellow politicians, Premier Kathleen Wynne and Toronto's elitists, who persecuted him with very personal attacks on his
appearance, his weight, his manner of speaking, and those
who forced him to defend himself against a long list of vexatious court cases and frivolous integrity complaints. When
he finally admitted to his addictions and was at his lowest,
they kicked him like a dog, stripped him of his powers, and
turned their backs on him in council. Even after he passed
away, there were those in the leftist media who didn't have
the class to allow a few hours pass by before they once again
beat up on him.

There's no doubt in my mind, watching the way he
was treated, that despite claiming to have very thick skin,
the stress of it all got to him – first manifesting itself in

drug-fuelled behaviour and then in the very aggressive cancer that eventually cost him his life. The left wanted him out of the picture and I say, with not the least bit of cynicism, that they got their wish.

Needless to say, I was disgusted when on the day of his funeral the very leftist councillors who'd terrorized him with delicious delight throughout his time as councillor and especially mayor, turned up to allegedly "pay their respects". It sickened me to see Shelley Carroll, Josh Matlow, Janet Davis, Paul Ainslie, and Pam McConnell huddle two pews in front of me and I found it near revolting to see the man who treated him with absolutely vile contempt, Adam Vaughan, parked in the front row of the church, in plain sight of the Ford family and the TV cameras, with Ms. Wynne right behind him. What about the lack of respect these hypocrites showed him in life? I can only conclude that these narcissists have no shame.

But Mr. Ford had the last laugh at his leftist detractors, even in death. When I left the church, the crowd that lined up to pay their last respects to a man labelled by Toronto's chattering classes as a racist and a homophobe, did not just number in the thousands. They were people of colour, visible minorities, immigrants, and the average ordinary working-class resident – people who'd been touched in some way by Mr. Ford's populist appeal and genuine concern for the little guy, who'd been helped by him, and who'd been disenfranchised by the very elitist politicians who made Rob Ford's life a living hell.

CHAPTER SEVEN

Politicians Give Democracy a Bad Name

I f I'd collected $10 for every council debate during my fifteen years at City Hall that dragged on for six, seven, eight hours – after which the already pre-ordained decision was reached – I'd be a very wealthy woman by now. It represented to me the most ridiculous caricature of democracy in action – foolish grandstanding by a long list of blowhard politicians to give the illusion that they were actually listening and coming to a collective decision when, more often than not, I knew that they'd already horse-traded behind the council chambers or had arrived at council knowing how they'd vote.

The politicians on Toronto city council were so dysfunctional that I often joked that they couldn't even run a lemonade stand if offered the opportunity to do so. Despite all their yammering that Rob Ford was divisive, rest assured that decorum did not suddenly return when he, their alleged archnemesis, Rob Ford, was sidelined. Take what happened during the very same month – May 2013 – that the beleaguered late mayor found himself facing allegations of smoking crack cocaine (allegations he subsequently confessed to five months later). Council quickly slipped into that same chaotic Barnum & Bailey routine I'd witnessed many times during my years as a City Hall columnist. Smelling blood and lacking direction from a mayor's office that was coming apart at the seams, the politicians felt they had even greater licence than normal to waste endless hours with petty bickering and nonsensical platitudes. It was a debate Mr. Ford and those who still supported him did not want to have because it was a waste of time. He had no interest in propping up the Ontario Liberal government of Kathleen Wynne with more taxes – this time for transit infrastructure – considering they'd thrown billions of dollars down the drain in the eHealth computerized health record and Ornge medical helicopter scandals, in addition to cancelling gas plants in Mississauga and Oakville to buy two seats in the 2011 election.

But council, in an act of defiance, voted to have a special meeting anyway, claiming democracy would not be served if they chose to refrain from debating the issue. Considering they made a great show of saying, as the ever insufferable then NDP councillor Adam Vaughan enjoyed repeating like a broken record, that councillors just did their work around the embattled mayor, this would have been a perfect opportunity to prove just that. Mr. Vaughan and his colleagues had their chance to show that council was not dysfunctional – that they could operate efficiently and effectively on an issue, with or without the mayor in charge. But it was and is just not in their DNA – or that of most politicians at any level – to do so.

Sadly, most councillors were not capable of recognizing they'd be perceived as bigger fools and ridiculous hypocrites if nothing came of the debate.

The irony was not lost on me that councillor Joe Mihevc – a career NDP politician – pronounced at the outset of what was to become a painful and highly irrelevant ten-hour debate that this was the "mature, adult conversation" they'd been meaning to have (on whether or not to raise more taxes) for a long time. I sometimes wonder if Mickey Mouse is his speech-writer, but that comment may be unfair to that lovable rodent. Mr. Mihevc is one of those insufferable NDP troughers who excuses everything he does – particularly his spending with impunity or the budget excesses for his pet projects such as the St. Clair dedicated streetcar line – as being for the "greater good." There's no doubt in my mind he rewarded those who supported him with city grants and ignored, or even punished, those who dared criticize him. Mr. Mihevc's almost incestuous relationship with Artscape – a not-for-profit organization that provides affordable housing for alleged starving artists courtesy of repeated funding from City Hall – comes to mind. Nevertheless, most days I ignored what he had to say because it was so predictable, and so outrageous.

But that day in May, I realized how completely out of touch politicians of his ilk were if they had the audacity to kick off a ten-hour debate – which produced nothing of substance – with such pap, and actually believe it. After councillors had yapped themselves silly in front of an audience of the usual unemployed or union suspects and left-wing, anti-Ford bloggers with various rings stuck in every orifice who regularly packed the public gallery of Toronto City Hall and enabled such grandstanding, they decided not to make a decision. I repeat, they made NO decision. They could have made a strong statement to the premier that Toronto's councillors were not prepared to do her dirty work and foist any new taxes on their residents until the province got its own house in order. Instead they copped out, leaving the tough decision to any other politician who might be prepared to take the heat at election time.

That's if such an animal exists. It was in fact business as usual that day. During my time watching this pack of misfits at City Hall, I found that whenever they could weasel out of a decision by deferring it for further study, they would, and Mayor John Tory has certainly continued that tradition. That was forever a given just before election time, unless, of course, the left wanted to hand their stakeholders a few special grants before they stepped down from office, as David Miller did to the arts community in the summer of 2010. Take the proposal by Robert Deluce, CEO of Porter Airlines, to expand services at the Billy Bishop City Centre Airport beyond the short-haul flights he offered with his Q400 aircraft to allow whisper jets to fly in there. The whisper jets would be able to handle flights to such destinations as Vancouver, Calgary, and Miami, and Mr. Deluce repeatedly said there was a demand for the same kind of service he was already offering but to more distant destinations. His had proven to be a very successful formula, despite former mayor David Miller's misguided environmentalist efforts to stop him in 2003. It was perfectly natural that he would want to expand the business to respond to market demand for longer-haul flights that would preclude the need for travellers to make their way to busy Pearson airport. But knowing there was strong opposition from a group calling itself NoJetsTO – one made up of the pampered

Toronto Island squatters and leftists purporting to be environmentalists, who could make councillors' lives miserable in the October 2014 election – those same councillors opted in April 2014 to send Mr. Deluce's expansion proposal back for further study (code for sending it to a dusty shelf somewhere). This was despite the fact that Mr. Deluce had provided the city with environmental and noise studies up the yin-yang. Heaven forbid these cowardly babies should have had to answer tough questions at the door during the 2014 election about the proposed expansion, or that they would have actually stuck their necks out to make a decision.

One only has to look at Toronto's pathetic subway system to find a perfect example of the years, never mind decades, of political foot-dragging, indecision, and petty infighting. For that alone, the politicians who've represented the Greater Toronto region for the past three decades should be absolutely ashamed of themselves. How any of them can visit cities like Vienna, Milan, Jerusalem, London, and Barcelona, to name just a few, without feeling embarrassed with our underground system is beyond me.

But this situation is no different than the ten-hour Toronto City council debate on transit taxes that produced nothing but a chamber full of hot air and considerable grandstanding. These are perfect examples of why I've lost complete respect for all but a few politicians of any political stripe. For years at City Hall, I heard the same ridiculous excuse for why decisions were deferred or weren't made at all. "Democracy is messy," those running the joint would say. Case Ootes, who bailed out Mel Lastman many times as his loyal deputy mayor, used that excuse in 1999 when former Tory MPP and long-time city councillor Doug Holyday first brought up the idea of downsizing council because there were too many politicians with competing interests eating up too much time talking and doing nothing. Mr. Ootes not only told me "democracy is a messy process" but added that every politician has a "right to be heard." For heaven's sake, did he really think we were all stupid? Let's be honest: Mr. Ootes and others didn't want to downsize council because it would put people like him out of a job. In 2003, when Mr. Holyday revisited the idea of cutting council from forty-four to twenty-two politicians – to be in sync with the provincial and federal ridings in Toronto – most of the seat-warming self-preservationists went berserk. Long-time councillor Norm Kelly – a failed real estate agent who repeatedly made it clear to all who would listen how enamoured he was with his self-professed brilliance and scholastic achievements – was most indignant with the prospect of losing his comfortable council seat. After all, he'd done so much for the taxpayer during his twenty-odd years in public office, or so he said. To Mr. Ootes's "democracy is messy" comment, Mr. Kelly added the proviso that it is also "productive." "We do a ton of business here and it's sad that it's not appreciated," he opined, his comments as cheesy as his delivery. "I think we've done a good job . . . I think pretty good policy flows from the congressional nature of this council." His words were more than prophetic considering that his fellow councillors decided in the winter of 2013 to strip the democratically elected Mr. Ford of many of his powers, even though he was never charged criminally, and put Mr. Kelly, then deputy mayor, in charge of city business – a move previously unheard of in city politics. While Mr. Ford was absolutely not to be defended for coming undone due to his crack cocaine and drinking issues, council proved that when it comes to him, democracy is both messy and undemocratic.

Premier Kathleen Wynne certainly didn't consider it an irony to be criticizing Mr. Ford's antics even while the OPP raided her office in search of deleted files related to the gas plant scandal, or as she continued to refuse to cough up the thousand e-mails that she herself may have written about the gas plant cancellations. She repeatedly denied she knew anything about the deliberate deletion of e-mails related to the gas plants on twenty-four computers in her own office just as she took over as premier in 2013. On the latter issue alone, Ms. Wynne proved she either didn't know – which I find hard to believe – or didn't care. Ms. Wynne outdid herself in April 2014 when she slapped a two-million-dollar defamation suit on then Ontario PC leader Tim Hudak and energy critic Lisa McLeod for daring to suggest she knew and possibly even ordered the criminal destruction of those e-mails. While her intent may have been to effect libel chill before the election, the premier showed herself to be childish and petulant. (A statement from the three parties in July 2015 said the lawsuit was "behind them," but we don't know whether it was dropped or settled, or how much Ms. Wynne cost taxpayers to muzzle her critics.)

Still, if most politicians are weak, arrogant, and lacking in moral fibre, the predominantly liberal media do not help matters by being entirely selective about whom they choose to target. Either out of laziness or because they have a short attention span coupled with their political leanings, they go out of their way to ignore, even avoid, any sort of follow-up or fallout on the plethora of controversial scandals that have plagued the Liberal government. Mr. McGuinty was the

Teflon Premier and Ms. Wynne has followed in his footsteps. In January 2014, when I took on an investigative role at the *Sun* and readers started inundating me with story tips, I realized how easy many of my media colleagues made it for the politicians and unaccountable public organizations. I would constantly hear from my tipsters how they contacted other media and heard nothing, absolutely nothing, back. The selective coverage was blatant during the terrible pre-Christmas ice storm of 2013 in the GTA, when ten to thirty millimetres of ice fell (the amount depending on the area), leaving roads blocked, trees down, and three hundred thousand residents without power for hours and days on end, some well beyond Christmas Day. Mr. Ford and Mr. Kelly jockeyed for position as to who would call the shots – egged on by the premier, who insisted she'd only deal with Mr. Kelly. Ms. Wynne, the Photo Op Queen with an election drawing near, appeared everywhere she could be seen to look like she was doing something. I'm surprised she didn't crawl up a hydro pole so the media could get pictures of her trying to fix the ice-laden downed lines herself. Some of Toronto's councillors behaved equally reprehensibly, trying to outdo each other in the martyr department. Jaye Robinson, who represents a North Toronto ward of upwardly mobile residents, claimed in one e-mail that she'd been up until four o'clock Christmas morning calling hydro officials to demand that power be restored in her ward, as if somehow the residents there were more entitled than others. My councillor, Josh Matlow, kept reminding us that he, too, was without power for days on end.

The public saw through all of this. But the media, as usual, didn't call out any of them for engaging in shameless grandstanding and politicking instead of concerning themselves with the needs of their constituents. They gave Ms. Wynne a free pass when she isolated Mr. Ford and criticized the democratically elected mayor for not calling a state of emergency to presumably get more help faster. A variety of emergency management experts later agreed that the situation was not life-threatening, that extra resources were already being provided to Toronto Hydro and Ontario's Hydro One, and that declaring a state of emergency would not have brought the power back on any faster. Still, that did not stop Mr. Ford's sharpest detractors on council from making political hay with the issue. But suddenly it all backfired on the chattering classes when Mr. Kelly, an award-winning teat sucker, couldn't help doing what he does best – abdicating responsibility. He slipped away to Tampa, Florida, over Christmas. It must have come as a surprise to Ms. Wynne, considering she'd indicated he was her go-to guy during the storm aftermath and cleanup. His constituents who were still without power weren't very amused either. Meanwhile, the real mayor spent day and night dealing with power outages, food shortages, and people in need over the holidays. After I exposed Mr. Kelly's little trip on Twitter, he was forced to fly back to Toronto, where he offered the media a story that he just went down to have Christmas dinner with an ailing sibling. In all my years covering this long-past-his-due-date trougher, I rarely witnessed him putting himself out for anyone but himself and his social convenor wife, Charlotte. The media never bothered to question Mr. Kelly's story or to chase down the ailing sibling. If that had been Mr. Ford, the *Toronto Star* would have sent a reporter and photographer down to Florida in a heartbeat.

This is why politicians give democracy a bad name. Democracy is not messy. The politicians are just adept at making a mess of it. I came to the sad realization as time went on during Mayor David Miller's reign that, save for a few exceptions, the right-wing members of council were absolutely ineffectual at forming any sort of credible opposition. They were lazy, egotistical, self-indulgent, and uninspiring. It was like herding a bunch of cats to get them to stand up to the many ridiculous measures Mr. Miller imposed on residents. I became the unofficial opposition at City Hall, using my columns or various radio talk shows to raise issues that received little attention by council's right wing or on which their follow-up was weak, at best.

Thank goodness I'm a runner. It has served me well throughout my career writing about politics and education, for there were many times when I found myself running down the halls or across a crowded council chamber looking to catch a bureaucrat or politician who was trying to avoid answering my questions. My best moves came just before I finished my investigative series in March 2012 on the aforementioned billion-dollar Regent Park revitalization. Before I could put the series to bed, I needed a comment from Councillor Pam McConnell, who'd represented the area for twenty-plus years and who had purchased a prime condo for $419,000 in the first gleaming glass building to go up on the revitalized lands.

Knowing full well that Ms. McConnell was not a fan – and that I would be slowed by the walking cast on my newly healed broken ankle – I ambushed her outside a committee meeting with my tape recorder and a videographer. When she tried to get by me and not answer questions, I planted my back against the committee room door and pushed it shut with my elbow. She was forced to answer whether she liked it or not, although her answer included berating me for daring to suggest she might have a conflict in the matter. As loyal as Ms. McConnell's NDP colleagues were to her interests – as evidenced by the complete silence at council on her conflicts – loyalty meant nothing to most of the right-of-centre politicians at City Hall. It was amazing to me long before the crack cocaine scandal and Rob Ford's drinking binges came to light – and the mayor was fighting conflict of interest allegations in court – how ready the rats in his very own inner circle were to desert the ship. Most noteworthy were Karen Stintz, Ana Bailão, and Paul Ainslie, who, despite being given plum posts in the Ford regime, wasted no time tarring and feathering him publicly and playing into the insatiable desire of his left-wing detractors to gang up on Mr. Ford on anything and everything. All of them were misfits and hypocrites. Ms. Bailão was picked up for driving at twice the legal alcohol limit after the Mayor's Ball for the Arts in October 2012. She hid her charges for months. I had to shame Mr. Ainslie on Twitter into confessing to *his* DUI in May 2013 after he'd lied to my *Toronto Sun* colleague the week before, saying he had never been stopped for being under the influence. And Ms. Stintz? Well, as TTC chair, as noted previously, she flip-flopped so many times between subways and LRTs on the Scarborough transit file, she can be thanked for delaying a decision by at least two years or more.

We can blame the politicians all we want, and they often deserve it in spades. But what about those of us who elect and re-elect them? I shudder to think about the fact that so many would-be young and not-so-young voters know more about how the Kardashians tick than they do about the political issues of the day. It makes me sick to think that long-time trougher Norm Kelly has gained notoriety not for his abuse of the taxpayer purse but for his Twitter exchanges with rappers. Perhaps past generations thought the same thing, but it is frightening to contemplate that these kinds of people are determining our future. I saw the same kind of wilful ignorance among voters in the federal election of 2015 which brought the man-child Justin Trudeau to power and most especially in Ontario's election of 2014, when a long list of unions, interested only in maintaining their lavish contracts and keeping in power the party who had bought their support (the Liberals), spent millions of dollars on attack ads to indoctrinate voters into thinking that PC leader Tim Hudak was ready to kill small dogs and babies, never mind his commitment to reduce the size of the unsustainable Ontario public service. Their ads worked. Granted, Mr. Hudak did little to help himself by not properly articulating how he'd lower the cost and size of government. But if anyone who voted for Ms. Wynne – anyone other than the union self-preservationists – had stopped to think about the fact that she'd already proven how little she cared about mounting debt, and that the great divide was steadily increasing between public and private sector wages, perhaps the outcome would have been different. It makes me wonder what exactly it takes to rouse most voters from their slumber, from their own self-indulgent lives or from a state of blissful ignorance to pay attention to what their government is doing to them or not doing for them. Such an awakening certainly did not happen in the provincial election of June 2014, and we will pay for it until 2018 and even beyond. But the pampered elitists certainly don't like that concept to be thrown in their faces. When I dared suggest on the morning after the June 12 election that the mojito-sipping Torontonians had been seduced and indoctrinated by touchy-feely messaging and union attack ads into putting Kathleen Wynne back into office – with a majority no less – my detractors went berserk, disparaging me for days afterward. I was told repeatedly that the "people have spoken" and they have kicked my "tea bagger" to the curb. I was accused of having "sour grapes"; of having "contempt" for the will of the people; of being a "sad, lonely woman" – nothing more than a "Shrew Ann" – who hates anyone who has more than me. The latter very personal comment has often been directed at me by those on the left, as if daring to criticize or see through their hypocrisy has earned me the distinction of having a sad, bitter life.

Then there's former Toronto mayor David Miller, whose bloated ego-driven, elitist, and highly autocratic reign deserves an entire library shelf of its own. It wasn't his carefully practised polished delivery and vanity that bothered me. Nor the fact that he nearly drove the city to bankruptcy; that is, after all, the NDP way of doing business. When it got down to it, what really disturbed me was how he abused his power, treating with contempt those who dared challenge him. He was a thin-skinned bully who was widely known to ostracize bureaucrats and sideline politicians for the most minimal of slights, even those politicians who were principled enough to vote against his tax increases. I kept wondering throughout his regime why he wasn't the dictator of some third-world country where everyone would bend and scrape to King David. Perhaps it was because of Mr. Miller that Barack Obama's messaging and the willingness of the U.S. population to jump on the bandwagon of hope irritated me more than it did the average Canadian. Mr. Obama's hopey-changey message that seduced voters was so eerily similar to the two campaigns of Mr. Miller – the same highly narcissistic would-be Emperor with No Clothes whom I'd watched in action at that point for five years. Like President Obama, and now our man-child Prime Minister, Mr. Miller was highly inexperienced in positions of leadership. In fact, during his time at City Hall before becoming mayor, he was known not to break a sweat on most files or take a leadership role on any committees. But he had the look and the smooth delivery that made voters feel hope and change was in the wind. Seeing through his phoniness, I couldn't understand why voters ate up his rhetoric. But they did. In May 2006, I stood in the crowded Steam Whistle Brewery off the Toronto lakefront, outnumbered by 450 fawning supporters, listening to Mr. Miller drone on for thirty minutes about how fiscally responsible he'd been in his first three years in office and how he'd kept his promises to make the city cleaner – with a City Hall free of backroom deals. Not one word of this was true, but the adoring supporters didn't care.

Mr. Miller informed us that, should he be re-elected that November, his focus would be on the Toronto of tomorrow. "My vision is of a city that is safe and strong . . . creative and clean . . . a city with opportunity for all . . . a city that leaves no one behind," he said. I questioned in print what I perceived as absolute airy-fairy pablum. Nevertheless, he was swept back into office for four more years – granted, with a much narrower majority. Most voters didn't wake up until 2009, when he put the city through an ugly thirty-nine-day garbage strike that accomplished nothing. It took the media and voters six long years to see through his empty promises. In the end, the only future Mr. Miller was concerned about was his own, as evidenced by his spending of ridiculous sums of public money on his green agenda to secure himself a soft landing at the World Wildlife Fund.

Other than during the few weeks I can grab in Florida each year, I watch President Obama mostly from north of the forty-ninth parallel. Like what I've read and seen of Mr. Obama in action, Mr. Miller knew exactly how to play to those media who fawned over him and how to sideline or freeze out those who dared question his policies. Mr. Miller, thankfully, was only responsible for a city of 2.5 million people with a nearly $12 billion budget and a $2.8 billion debt. Needless to say, President Obama's mishandling of a $3 trillion budget and nearly $17 trillion in debt and his pathetically weak foreign policies have been far, far more damaging, not simply to the U.S. but to the global economy as well. I had to laugh when I saw Mr. Obama trying to act tough with Vladimir Putin as the Russian autocrat invaded Crimea. Given Mr. Obama's weak-kneed approach to the nuclear threat in Iran, I suspect Mr. Putin considers the U.S. president is a joke. But it was the president's opponent in 2012, Mitt Romney, who had the last laugh. When Mr. Romney declared during the presidential debates that Russia represented the biggest threat to the U.S., as it endeavoured constantly to undermine America's influence on the world stage, Mr. Obama mocked his opponent. It's no joke that when the chips were down in the Ukraine, it was our former prime minister, Stephen Harper, who rushed there and condemned Mr. Putin for his actions – while Mr. Obama sat on his hands, or played another round of golf – or both, although he's reportedly not that proficient at the latter.

Sadly, what most politicians seem to share – no matter how far-reaching or limited their scope and how weak they are –

is an undying love for the image they see in the mirror. I was perhaps somewhat naive when I first got into the political game, thinking that those who are lucky enough to be elected – and considering it takes considerable money to do so – treat it truly as a public service. But I've discovered that, in fact, few go into the game because they really do want to change people's lives for the better. It doesn't matter what political party they affiliate with. Most politicians I've had the opportunity to observe over the past twenty years are driven completely by ego. Most are narcissists. Few have the guts to make the really hard decisions because that risks making them unpopular. Rarely do they stick to their principles, if they even have any, preferring to do what's politically expedient instead of what's right. It has come to the point where I consider many of them to be immoral.

Let's take as an example Mr. Obama's handling of the gay and lesbian file. He was the first black president of the United States, swept into power on that fuzzy-wuzzy mandate of change and hope. The world was his for the taking. He could have easily made a strong statement soon after being elected that he does not tolerate discrimination in marriage rights based on race or gender. His adoring fans, especially Oprah (who I believe is a closeted lesbian), would have cheered him on with reckless abandon. While individual states have the final say, Obama could have set the tone by saying enough is enough, that gays deserve to consummate their loving relationships in marriage – that it is disgraceful to think that gays are allowed to die for their country but not to wed each other. He could have used the example of his neighbours to the north – where same-sex marriage has been legalized since 2004 – to do what's right. When you think about it, considering he's a Democrat who clearly leans to the left, Mr. Obama should have been downright embarrassed at how much the so-called Land of the Free has trailed behind Canada on such a vital social policy issue. Aren't Democrats supposed to own files like these, to be champions of tolerance and respect? Instead, when asked what constituted marriage, Mr. Obama said it was a union between a man and a woman. Full stop.

Compare this to all the hullabaloo and supposition in the left-wing Canadian media that our former Conservative prime minister, Stephen Harper – whose early ties were with the right-wing Canadian Alliance movement – would reopen the debate on same-sex marriage laws when he came to power. Mr. Harper was shrewd and decisive enough to recognize that this ship had sailed. He made it clear that same-sex marriage was here to stay in Canada. End of story. Not so with Barack Obama. Instead of showing that he meant what he said about hope and change, Mr. Obama dithered on the issue throughout his entire first term, only choosing to make a statement on the eve of a Hollywood fundraiser for his re-election bid in May 2012 at the home of actor George Clooney. I suspect he may have been pressured into doing it, his handlers recognizing that it would become an excellent wedge issue to separate him from those in the far right of the Republican Party who believe – like Mr. Obama – that marriage should only be acknowledged between a man and a woman.

Instead of criticizing the president, the media apologists – the same ones who have painted all Republicans as anti-gay – let him off the hook, gushing in a downright embarrassing way that his comments were indicative of how far public opinion has shifted. Never mind that public opinion in Canada had shifted two decades earlier! Crowing that this was a clear sign of Mr. Obama's "strong leadership," the media even bought into his nonsense about this being a personal journey for him and that denial of same-sex marriage rights to some couples didn't make sense to his daughters. His daughters? No one saw it as ironic that Mr. Obama had to use his daughters as an excuse to take a stance he should have taken the moment he stepped into the Oval Office and that it ultimately ended up being the courts that decided to extend same-sex marriage rights throughout the U.S.

My wife, Denise, who is just as passionate as I am on the issue, asked Mr. Obama's former chief of staff, David Axelrod, about why his boss took so long to make a statement about same-sex marriage when we attended a Toronto speaking engagement he headlined in October 2013. When she dared to suggest that, according to his boss, it was perfectly okay for gays to fight and die for their country but not get married, Mr. Axelrod was quite taken aback by her chutzpah. He contended heatedly and arrogantly that if that was the way she saw it, that was her issue, and turned away from her to chat with someone who would not make him so uncomfortable.

But Mr. Obama is the epitome of your typical opportunistic politician – the kind who put their fingers to the wind and base their decisions on what will win them a popularity contest instead of on pure logic or common sense. It is sad to say this, but I've covered very few politicians who actually have the guts, the moral fibre, or the political will to stick to their principles. Aside from the handful at City Hall, our former prime minister, Mr. Harper, stands out, if only for his unwavering support of Israel alone, in spite of what we've seen from the dangerously milquetoast President Obama and the entirely ineffective and perhaps anti-Semitic United Nations.

GUTS ARE A RARITY in politics. I've seen evidence of cowardice far too many times. In early December 2011, I was invited to a public open house hosted by a new councillor, Mary-Margaret McMahon, representing a tony Toronto neighbourhood off of Lake Ontario called the Beaches to see proposed renovations to a café located on a prime piece of Toronto's waterfront. In a rare upset in the November 2010 election, Ms. McMahon had defeated long-time councillor Sandra Bussin, partly due to my revelations earlier that year about a questionable twenty-year sole-sourced lease deal with the café's owner, George Foulidis, that allowed him to essentially own all food and beverage rights and control the use of food and liquor by others, even those who wished to hold charity events, on this prime stretch of waterfront. Ms. McMahon invited me to the open house more than once, secretly hoping, I suspect, that I'd do the dirty work of keeping up the heat on him. But when I arrived, Mr. Foulidis and his brother very publicly tried to force me to leave. I stood my ground, refusing to leave the public meeting I was invited to attend, while capturing his threats on camera. The councillor took no action to diffuse the situation. She sat there watching like a scared mouse, doing and saying nothing. It was perfectly fine to invite me and to complain about Mr. Foulidis behind his back, but she was too weak to stand up to him in person.

Sadly, Toronto's most recent mayor, John Tory, has been as indecisive during his first 18 months in office as I predicted. He has made a great show of meeting and consulting with other big city mayors, he has held endless photo ops or press conferences virtually every day, and he has either deferred important decisions, like the contracting out of garbage east of Toronto's Yonge Street, or appointed panels to review the most controversial issues, instead of having the backbone to make the hard decisions himself. The one that drove me to near distraction was Tory's task force on Toronto Community Housing, named just after the city had done its own $119,000 review of the housing authority. When I exposed the fact in early March 2015 that top Toronto Community Housing Corporation officials had secretly voted themselves 20 per cent bonuses, Mr. Tory didn't have the balls to criticize either the magnitude of the bonuses or the lack of transparency in a public institution that serves the downtrodden. I suspected from that day forward that Mr. Tory would talk a good game but, as I'd worried since before he was elected, would forever be beholden to his many connections and wouldn't have the spine to make the really tough changes needed at City Hall. I continue to hope I'm proven wrong but so far I have not been.

As much as politicians constantly yap about vision, most have absolutely no long-term vision whatsoever. How could they? They operate on four-year time frames, forever focused on getting re-elected. Sticking their necks out and doing what's right could cost them votes in the next election. It was actually shocking to me how little voters paid attention to the antics of their councillors – allowing long-time troughers like Howard Moscoe, Joe Mihevc, Pam McConnell, and Kyle Rae to roll from one term to another with little, if any, opposition. (Mr. Rae actually ran unopposed in the 2000 election.) Any attempts by new blood to break through were invariably thwarted by name recognition and the ability of sitting councillors to use the perks of their offices to buy votes. They were able to use their expense budgets (at the time, fifty-three thousand dollars, on top of their salaries) to create fridge magnets, fancy calendars, or glossy newsletters full of pictures of them rubbing shoulders with their constituents or various A-listers at events like the Toronto International Film Festival, to which they all received free tickets. They could hold town hall meetings. They could push for publicly funded grants for the special interest groups most likely to help them on election campaigns. They could and would ensure that powerful unions – particularly the police and firefighters – not only endorsed them but actually erected signs for them and worked on their campaigns. The firefighters were renowned for holding their support over the heads of councillors, actually intimidating councillors into voting them sizable wage hikes to guarantee firefighter support at election time. Trouble is, it's extremely difficult to get lousy, incompetent politicians out, at all levels of government, because there are no term limits and none of them are prepared to vote to impose term limits (and put themselves out of a job). Politics is supposed to be a calling, but for most it has become a very lucrative career with fairly decent pay, good perks, a pension, and the potential to wield tremendous power over their constituency – and all on the taxpayers' dime. No wonder Rob Ford's support of the taxpayer resonated so deeply with disenchanted voters, even after his death.

As bad as the indecisiveness and lack of political will to make the tough decisions was at City Hall, it was far worse at Queen's Park. The only difference was the highly-practised Liberal machine that was adept at turning a sow's ear into a silk purse and spinning negatives into positives for the media. Ms. Wynne, far more NDP and union-friendly than Liberal in her leanings, was notorious, and continues to be so, for naming pricey panels and roundtables to consult and make it look like she was on top of issues – instead of actually making difficult decisions. By the time she'd been in office for ten months, there were more than forty consultation panels underway on everything from looking into whether Ontarians had an appetite to force restaurateurs to list calorie counts on their menus to a sixty-three-thousand-dollar panel put together – get this – to examine how her government could be more open and transparent. To make it seem like she was truly interested in actually hearing what Ontarians had to say – and that this was not another expensive exercise in futility – she would put a token confused-looking Progressive Conservative or two on each panel. The most ridiculous panel had to be the one on openness and accountability, which delivered its report on the same day news broke about possible criminal charges directed at Mr. McGuinty's chief of staff for essentially sneaking an outsider – the boyfriend of another member of McGuinty's team – into the premier's office in order to delete controversial e-mails related to the cancellation of two gas plants in Oakville and Mississauga.

At the federal and provincial levels, party discipline keeps politicians somewhat in check, if and only if the party's leader chooses to do the right thing. Mr. McGuinty governed with no scruples. He repeatedly promised he wouldn't raise taxes, only to do exactly that. He was so hungry to win at all costs that he had no problem throwing $1.1 billion down the drain on cancelling two gas-fired plants to save a few Liberal seats. He took his eye off the ball too many times to count, letting the bureaucrats at eHealth, charged with computerizing the medical records of all Ontarians, and those operating the Ornge air ambulance fritter millions of dollars away on bonuses, loans, unscrupulous perks, and expenses. There was no oversight. Little wonder he had such a pathetic, incompetent, and arrogant bunch in cabinet. Faced with increased heat and scrutiny, ministers like Dwight Duncan, George Smitherman, and Chris Bentley bailed while the getting was good. Mr. McGuinty prorogued the legislature to avoid being questioned, and subsequently quit, escaping to Harvard where heaven knows what he did to indoctrinate young minds about politics. There are no words to describe this obscene mismanagement of public money. He ought to be in prison.

Provincial PC leader Tim Hudak kept a stranglehold on his caucus through threats and intimidation, and by dangling critic portfolios over the heads of his MPPs – the one opportunity they had to establish a media profile for themselves. Party discipline is to be expected. But because he was a weak, uninspiring leader with almost no connection to voters, he created a team of mindless puppets, most of whom had very little of interest to say, despite the never-ending fodder offered up by the Liberal regime. One of the few firebrands in the caucus with an intellect and media savvy, Peter Shurman, was quickly sidelined when Mr. Hudak started to feel threatened by the well-liked and respected MPP. The cover story was that Mr. Shurman had found a loophole in MPP expense rules, allowing him to claim the rent for a Toronto apartment because his principal residence was in Niagara-on-the-Lake and he represented the riding of Thornhill. But the story behind the story was that Mr. Hudak and his inner circle, worried that Mr. Shurman might try to challenge his leadership, threw the loyal MPP under the bus after Mr. Hudak had approved the expense. In September 2013, when Mr. Shurman refused Mr. Hudak's request to pay back the money (some forty-eight thousand dollars), he was stripped of his finance critic duties and cast aside in the House. It was the equivalent of squashing a flea with a sledgehammer. In November 2013, Mr. Shurman gave up his Toronto apartment and moved full-time to his Niagara-on-the-Lake home, commuting back and forth to the legislature in Toronto. In early December, Mr. Hudak decided that his former finance critic was wrong, as well, to charge for his mileage to Toronto. By then, Mr. Shurman had had enough and resigned his seat effective December 2013. The Ontario Progressive Conservative caucus thus lost one of its few bright lights, leaving it with a team of barely mediocre yes-men and -women, many of them lazy and well past their due date.

And what about those transit taxes – the ones Toronto city councillors spent ten hours debating, only to make no decision? Premier Wynne went through the exercise of naming a panel in September 2013, headed by Liberal teat-sucker Anne Golden, who made nearly ninety thousand dollars for her consultative efforts. Golden spent three months with her busy-work, proclaiming three months later that gas and corporate taxes should be hiked sharply to pay for new transit infrastructure. But instead of making a decision, calling an election, and allowing Ontarians to determine whether they wanted dedicated transit taxes or increased gas taxes, Ms. Wynne played a cat-and-mouse game, always intimating that transit would need to be funded but never really conceding whether or not her intent was to raise taxes to do it. In 2014, perceiving she needed to buy NDP leader Andrea Horwath's loyalty on another budget, Ms. Wynne suddenly took the tax idea off the table entirely. After all the energy and political capital spent on promoting, debating, and pressuring the public to accept transit taxes, the premier took the cowardly way out. Of course she'd try to convince us that she did it to respect the democratic wishes of Ontarians. I would argue that her only interest was in saving her political skin. I hope this isn't so, but I am willing to bet those taxes will eventually find their way back on the table, seeing as Ms. Wynne won herself a majority government in June 2014. After all, she can say voters exercised their democratic rights and gave her a strong mandate. Going back on their promises never much matters for politicians in a democracy. It's a sad reality, but voters have come to expect it.

CHAPTER EIGHT

Not Your Typical Tory

During the heat of a policy convention in late September 2013 – after embattled leader Tim Hudak and his inner circle had fended off calls for a second leadership review or, should I say, had bullied his detractors into submission – Mr. Hudak stepped onto the main floor of the convention centre in London, Ontario, and tried to prove he was a man of the people.

He walked into the crowd, microphone in hand, lowering his voice to a level that made it seem like he was talking directly to each and every one of the eight hundred delegates assembled in the room.

He made a few self-deprecating comments in an effort to come across less stiffly than normal, and then offered to take unrehearsed and unplanned questions from the audience. It would have been a tremendous departure from the normally highly staged version of the man. Perhaps it would even have signalled he'd learned a few things from the attempt at an internal coup that had called for his head and become very public over the course of the two months prior to the September 2013 convention. I was ready to give him the benefit of the doubt that he'd heard the concerns of the party's grassroots about his inability to connect with voters and that he was really trying to bring a fresh face to the party.

That was until a Windsor delegate got up to ask him how he'd make himself and the party more winnable in the impending election. The question itself would have been perfect (and certainly appropriate) had the delegate not stuck his foot in his mouth by prefacing it with a highly misogynistic comment about NDP leader Andrea Horwath. The man said Ms. Horwath had earned herself the nickname "The Great Orange Pumpkin" down in Windsor. The name came about not just because she's NDP orange but also, according to him, because she'd "put on a little bit of weight." Now, you could criticize Ms. Horwath at the time for many things – especially her decision to prop up an unelected premier mired in scandals and spending abuses. But to attack her personal appearance was disgraceful. The delegate would never, ever have dared say the same thing about a man – and it made me sad to note that as many people in the audience that day laughed as booed. Mr. Hudak had a chance to address the comment head on, thus gaining some much-needed points, by pointedly telling the delegate and the crowd it was inappropriate, but the PC leader decided to ignore it entirely and to jump full throttle into how important it was to win seats in Toronto and the GTA to gain a majority, or at the very least a minority. The lack of response was cowardly of Mr. Hudak. It would have taken nothing to register his disapproval and would have gone a long way toward diffusing what became a story. But he didn't, and the irony of his suggesting to a room full of delegates – at least half of whom found the comment about Andrea Horwath amusing – that they've got to have what it takes to win seats in a cosmopolitan city like Toronto was not lost on me. He was just lucky that the comment was only made within the walls of the party's policy meeting and that none of the many reporters who attended, other than two of us from the *Toronto Sun*, bothered to mention it. At least the delegate had the good grace to resign from the party once I outed him in my column two days later. Hudak remained mum.

Sadly, the interchange was far too indicative of how the party's out-of-touch old guard felt. All Mr. Hudak's silence did was reinforce my belief that more than four years after I'd run for the Ontario Progressive Conservative Party in St. Paul's – the first by-election to occur with him as leader – both he and the party hadn't evolved one bit. Back in the summer of 2009, when the by-election was called, one could blame the fumbling on the part of Mr. Hudak's team at least partly on the chaos of a transition from one leader to another. After all, Mr. Hudak had won the leadership in June 2009, assumed office on July 1, and the by-election was called by the Liberals on August 19. He hadn't had much time to hire staff, let alone formulate a thorough policy platform. But after performing the full-court press to woo me – an openly gay and recently married Jewish lesbian – to run, Mr. Hudak and most of his team checked out. Half of his caucus – either too lazy to get off their duffs in mid-summer or, as I found out later, worried about being affiliated with a gay woman – didn't bother to show their faces even once to canvass with me. I was handed the B-team to run my campaign, including a campaign manager who took six days off to vacation during a thirty-five-day campaign. I learned after the campaign was over that the party had done some polling early on and discovered that while I might narrow the gap, I had no hope of winning St. Paul's, a traditionally Liberal midtown Toronto riding. Still, this would have been a perfect opportunity for Mr. Hudak to showcase himself as the new leader, particularly in St. Paul's, and to show that he wanted to get a better grasp of Toronto issues.

Make no mistake: I am not the least bit bitter. Running for office was a wonderfully insightful and rewarding experience. I learned a tremendous amount about operating a campaign, which only helped me as a political columnist. I went into the campaign knowing full well that St. Paul's is traditionally Liberal red – and hadn't been Tory blue since the Mike Harris days ten years prior – and that it would take nothing short of an open revolt by voters to win a seat in midtown Toronto. Voters were angry, but as I quickly discovered, they were livid with then mayor David Miller, not with the Teflon Premier, Dalton McGuinty. But I really hoped, perhaps naively, to educate the party from within about Toronto's hot-button issues with which I was so familiar, like gay rights, transit, homelessness, education and health care, our severely aging infrastructure, poverty, and crime. I even thought I could help the Progressive Conservatives to reach out to more women and new immigrant communities, who traditionally vote Liberal, particularly because the Liberals are adept at wooing voters with their touchy-feely words of hope and promise. I also hoped a candidate like me would dispel the image of the Tories under Mike Harris. I thought Mike Harris was right for the times. I admired his tenacity and the courageous way he endeavoured to rein in the bloated education and health care systems, despite the long list of professional protesters, and the forever disgruntled teachers unions who feverishly worked to derail his agenda. Even amalgamating Toronto made perfect sense. One Toronto government should have, by rights, exacted tremendous economies of scale – if there had been the political will to make it work. But unfortunately, there was not. As I've discovered, most bureaucrats and all but a few politicians are not hard-wired to be efficient, or effective.

Mr. Harris and his insiders were right for the late 1990s. But much has changed since then, and one big problem with the PC Party of Ontario is that the same cabal of well-past-their-prime insiders, eyeing tremendous business opportunities if the party should come to power again, have hung around. To put it bluntly, for these operatives, it's not at all about doing what's right for the party's fortunes but about doing what's right for themselves. This is what sickens me about politics, no matter which party is involved. The people who actually go into politics to perform a true public service have become few and far between. As we saw with Kathleen Wynne's majority win in June 2014, making promises and unapologetically breaking them and squandering billions of dollars on scandals seems to have become the new standard among Ontario voters, who were content as long as Ms. Wynne put on her understanding face, pretended to sympathize with their pain, and embraced their needs with lofty visions that she will never have the money to keep.

In the summer of 2009 the *Toronto Sun* gave me a six-week leave of absence so I could run in the provincial by-election. And "run" was the operative word. I knocked on 6,500 doors, pounded the pavement up to 14 hours a day, and wore out three pairs of shoes on the hustings. My days were a whirl-wind of early-morning glad handing at subway stops, visits to seniors' homes, and speaking engagements, as well as morning, afternoon, and evening canvasses. On a good day, I figured I hit 250 doorsteps. While many Tory MPPs didn't bother to show their faces on a single canvass throughout the 35 days, Mr. Hudak's predecessor and now Toronto mayor John Tory and a dozen city councillors more than made up for their apathy. Mr. Tory not only came out several times but e-mailed me messages throughout the campaign to keep up my spirits. His interest was very much appreciated and is something I'll never forget. Peter Shurman, then a fairly new MPP, joined me in canvassing as well, which turned out to be the beginning of a wonderful friendship and a true kinship when it comes to thinking what direction the PC Party of Ontario should take.

Former Toronto deputy mayor Doug Holyday, who lost his MPP seat in the Liberal rout of June 2014, helped me fend off an angry beer-drinking voter who shouted at us that Mike Harris had "raped and pillaged the province for eight years." Councillor Frances Nunziata marched, all five feet of herself, into a nunnery, regaling the sisters about what a devout Catholic she was. Anything to score more votes! Ms. Nunziata didn't mention that I was gay. Good thing. The sister in charge blessed me as we left. Rob Ford, then a councillor and not yet Toronto's most controversial mayor, taught me how to get my signs on even traditional Liberal and NDP lawns. Denise, who joined me on a canvass whenever I called to say I missed her, quickly earned the reputation of being feistier and more persuasive at the doors than me. Her specialty was to knock on doors of houses with Liberal signs on their lawns to try to convince them that voting Liberal by rote wasn't really the way to deal with the issues of the day. She talked up my background as a political journalist and got to be known as "the closer."

The amalgamated city's first mayor, Mel Lastman, who once told me in a fit of pique (after I'd criticized his spending in a column) that I didn't "love Toronto," spent a morning with me canvassing in Forest Hill village. He also gave me an idea for a press conference on the HST just before voting day – which I gladly used, especially considering my team wasn't all that creative with their campaign tactics. Assessing what would entice voters during the sleepy final days of summer was particularly where the party missed the boat. My handlers instructed me to focus on Premier McGuinty's proposed HST, which had been announced in the budget delivered in March of that year. Since that combined tax was not due to come into effect until July 2010, this by-election was to be treated as a kind of referendum on the combined tax and proposed exemptions from the tax – or so the PC Party thought. The HST issue dominated the literature my campaign team dropped at the doors. The PC Party caucus office schooled me extensively on the Tory party line about the HST and strongly suggested I stick to that platform.

But they misread urban voters and had no clue how to connect with them, much as they did in the election of 2014, when they stuck almost obsessively to their narrow focus on jobs and only jobs. I was not given any advice on how to deal with the constant questions I got at the doors about why the provincial Tories were not in sync with their federal counterparts – since their federal colleagues were the ones urging every province to combine the GST and their provincial sales taxes into one. So I started winging it, creating my own script about the fact that Mr. McGuinty did not take into consideration possible exemptions to the HST on home heating oil and other services that would impact vulnerable Ontario residents.

But the Tim Hudak team truly showed their ignorance about Toronto issues when they made no mention in their briefings about the thirty-nine-day acrimonious garbage strike to which Mayor David Miller and the CUPE thugs had subjected the city. That strike was settled a mere two weeks before the writ was dropped for the St. Paul's by-election. What an excellent opportunity that would have been to capitalize on the stranglehold unions have on taxpayers in this province and how self-serving they are – considering, as the CUPE strike showed, how prepared all union bosses were to bring down an economy in order to maintain their unaffordable perks and runaway salaries. As was proven five years later in the election of 2014, the greedy, entitled unions are willing to do anything and say anything – including spending gazillions of dollars on attack ads – to fulfill their demands, even though those demands have driven and will continue to drive the province down the road of deep debt toward an economic situation like that of Greece or Detroit. And Ms. Wynne was and is prepared to pander to their demands. When it became obvious that St. Paul's residents wanted to talk garbage strike, the fallout for the city, and how much David Miller had let them down, again I improvised with my own script. I told people at the doors that I was Mr. Miller's staunchest critic and, more often than not, they responded that, for that reason alone, I'd get their vote. Whatever worked! My campaign team, not understanding that my name recognition might carry weight even in traditional NDP polls, declared that certain pockets of the riding were the "badlands" and it was not worth wasting my time canvassing there. But I insisted that I try, choosing to cover streets in the far western edges of the riding and to canvass the shops along St. Clair, which had been hard hit by the seven-year construction of the grossly over budget hundred-million-dollar-plus dedicated streetcar line. I surprised everyone by nabbing Tory blue sign locations in the midst of a sea of NDP orange and winning at least one poll in this traditionally NDP area. Unfortunately there were those intransigents who'd always voted Liberal and would do so to their dying days, no matter how much the party took advantage of them. While out campaigning with me one Friday evening, my dear *Sun* colleague Zen Ruryk asked one forty-something voter, out of frustration, why he would support the Liberals and what specifically they had done for him or Toronto lately. I laughed when the man couldn't answer Zen's question. One ninety-year-old lady told me when I knocked on her door that while I seemed like a nice, intelligent woman, she'd always voted Liberal and wasn't about to change for me.

As hard as I fought to woo voters in this traditionally Liberal riding, I never rid myself of the feeling that Tim Hudak was merely going through the motions, dropping into the campaign for a few cameo appearances. It was noticed by the media, too, and by those friends and family who came out to support me. I realized about halfway through the campaign that, other than providing me with a minimal amount of resources to run my riding office and some media training to get through the one and only televised all-candidates debate – my Liberal opponent, Eric Hoskins, ended up being a no show – I was really on my own. I could have died when the PCs had Mr. Shurman show up at the Queen's Park media gallery with someone dressed as a giant chicken, suggesting Dr. Hoskins was a chicken for not participating in the debate. I didn't need shtick, I needed party support. Mr. Shurman says he's lived to regret being involved in that little photo opportunity. Nevertheless, I can't complain about the amount of media attention I received, including features in the *Globe and Mail*, the *National Post*, and my own paper, of course. Even the *Toronto Star* gave me considerable exposure, which was not just due to my position with the *Toronto Sun* but because those in the media, particularly on the left, were curious about why a newly married out Jewish lesbian would run for Tim Hudak and the Tory party.

With little more than a week to go before election day, when the final push should have been on, I found myself arguing with party brass who wanted to pull staff resources and potential canvassers from my campaign to have them work on the annual volunteer appreciation BBQ. Whether they'd lost their last shred of common sense or had given up, I wasn't prepared to throw in the towel, knocking on my very last door at 9 p.m. the night before voting day. Fact is, I was all the more inspired in the last few days when I discovered that the allegedly tolerant Liberals had issued three different attack pieces on me, pulling quotes out of context from my City Hall columns to imply I was heartless, didn't believe in human rights, and was as right wing as they come. That suggested they were a tad worried. My wife thought the Liberal Party took my clout and name recognition far more seriously than the PCs did. The Liberals spent a lot on advertising for Eric Hoskins, including bus shelter after bus shelter sporting his huge head. They even advertised in the *Canadian Jewish News*, since the September 17 by-election turned out to be a day before the Jewish New Year. Seeing that, Denise paid for and put in her own ad in the same paper.

But the Liberals need not have worried. Sadly, only 33 per cent of eligible voters exercised their franchise, and only 15 per cent of voters in Forest Hill – where I'd won the sign war by a country mile – took a break from their personal trainers to vote. Mr. Hudak showed his true colours on election night when he arrived at our house, a bottle of wine in hand, and sat stiffly on our couch pecking on his BlackBerry until CP24 declared twenty minutes after the polls closed that I'd lost. As he stood up, ready to depart for my "victory party" and concession speech, I crumpled into our friend Karen Basian's arms sobbing out of sheer emotion and tiredness after a hard-fought thirty-five days. Ms. Basian remembers to this day how detached Mr. Hudak was, as if he was following a script that dictated he should be at my house and that this was enough. When I arrived at the victory party and saw my dad, I fell into his arms still full of emotion – a picture that was featured in the *Toronto Star* the next day.

I might run again someday for the PC Party of Ontario, maybe even for leader, but certainly not until the party is prepared to look deep within itself and realize that the face of conservatism in Ontario has changed. I'm beginning to wonder if that will ever happen and whether the party truly has a death wish. I had hoped the results on election night of June 2014 – when Mr. Hudak was completely shut out in Toronto and his jobs message barely resonated around the entire province – would inspire positive change, but considering the motley crew of people who threw their names into the 2015 leadership race, I sincerely have my doubts. Ontario's PC Party has an uphill battle to dispel the myths that the

Lib-left are only too happy to perpetuate – that "conservative" stands for intolerant and homophobic. Yet the new breed of conservatives includes openly gay people like me and a cross-section of visible minorities. We represent a diverse, kinder, and gentler face of conservatism, without abandoning our core values and the fiscal positions we have supported from the very beginning. Unless the Ontario party's old guard is prepared to call it a day and make way for those who both embrace and establish a connection with these groups, and to show that the party has evolved – as members of the federal party under Stephen Harper did so adeptly – they will not make inroads into Ontario's urban centres, particularly Toronto. It's as plain as that. New PC leader Patrick Brown and his team claim the old guard is gone, but the jury is still out on this assertion given that Mr. Brown has yet to enunciate any policy positions, having stuck to mere pablum during the leadership race of spring 2015, and pretty much since.

WHO WOULD HAVE THOUGHT that the federal Conservatives would actually emerge as global leaders in gay rights? This was due largely to the unstoppable efforts of former foreign affairs minister John Baird, who, sadly for gays and for Israel, stepped down to take a job in the private sector in March 2015. Under Stephen Harper, the Tories made it clear that same-sex marriage is the law and the discussion is over. Mr. Harper put it to a vote in his early days in a minority government situation and did not touch the issue after that. Early in 2012, the Tories also rushed to close a loophole in the Liberal same-sex marriage legislation to make all gay marriages legal – even those performed on non-citizens from countries where gay marriage is not recognized.

But it was the activism on gay rights beyond Canada's borders that established the federal Tories as a far more inclusive party than their provincial counterparts. I was immensely proud of Mr. Baird when he publicly blasted Russia and its leader, Vladimir Putin, in August 2013 for the country's hateful anti-gay law after the foreign minister had worked behind the scenes to try to persuade Mr. Putin not to put the law in place in the run-up to the 2014 Olympic Winter Games in Sochi. I certainly didn't see Barack Obama opening his mouth in the slightest to Mr. Putin on anything, let alone the gay rights issue. But there's another little secret few in the left-wing media will admit about the federal Conservatives. There are hundreds of openly gay Conservatives in this country and they are starting to make a statement because of three trailblazers: Fred Litwin, Roy Eappen, and Jamie Ellerton. Mr. Litwin, proudly gay and right of centre, is the founder of the Ottawa-based Free Thinking Film Society. Dr. Eappen is an endocrinologist and conservative blogger, originally from India and now living in Montreal.

Mr. Ellerton joined the federal and provincial Conservative parties in 2004 and officially came out as a gay Tory in 2005. He was legislative and executive assistant to Jason Kenney from 2005 to 2010 and executive assistant and communications advisor to Mr. Hudak from September 2010 to December 2011. He now has his own communications consulting firm. He says it was in 2011 that he, Mr. Litwin, and Dr. Eappen decided gay Conservatism needed to have a visible presence at the federal party's June convention. They were tired of the left thinking they had ownership of the gay agenda. They created the Fabulous Blue Tent, a party hosted by gay Conservatives at an Ottawa hotel, to which all convention delegates were welcome. The pink and blue invitation said the party was to be hosted "by Dorothy and her sisters" (a tongue-in-cheek reference to gay men). Mr. Ellerton said the event was attended by a "wide swath" of delegates, from very socially conservative staffers and very staunch Catholics to those assumed to be more gay-positive. Senators Nancy Ruth and Linda Frum fully supported the endeavour and Mr. Baird gave money for the event. Urban Conservatives said it was about time – that at long last the party was starting to reflect diversity. Those who attended from smaller towns and cities, like Red Deer or Swift Current – not exactly hotbeds of visible gay culture – got a rare chance to interact with "fabulous" rank-and-file members, as Ellerton put it. Not surprisingly, the online left-of-centre blogs tried to make light of the event, writing about how oxymoronic it was that "self-hating people were getting together." But Mr. Litwin, Dr. Eappen, and Mr. Ellerton followed up the Ottawa fete with a second Fabulous Blue Tent party in Calgary in 2013. This time, the colourful pink and blue invitation actually invited people to "come out" to celebrate with "gay Conservatives and friends." "We were blown away with how successful the second one was," says Ellerton, noting they actually had to turn people away in Calgary because of capacity issues. Slowly but surely the narrative is changing thanks to Mr. Litwin, Dr. Eappen, and Mr. Ellerton. It remains an uphill battle, however. The LGBT Tory contingent, under the able leadership of Torontonian Benjamin Dichter, had to embarrass the parade organizers to be allowed to march in Ottawa's Capital Pride Parade in August 2015, after the NDP and the Liberals – playing politics due to the newly called federal election – tried to find a way to exclude them.

THERE'S NO DOUBT in my mind that federal gay Conservatives have made great strides toward showing the true face of the party – that it is more representative of the general population than the media cares to concede – and have succeeded in changing the public perception that it is just a party of old, white men who resist change. Provincially, however, the party is not even close to achieving this goal. Mr. Ellerton, who has worked on both the federal and provincial scenes, feels the provincial PCs will have a hard time being elected if they stick to their traditional principles and retreat back to their immediate support base. "It's too easy to throw red meat to the base," he says. The party needs to set forth with an "urban agenda" to keep the money coming in and to win a majority. Mr. Ellerton feels the party's message has to be more populist to attract LGBT and ethnic voters – not to mention to appeal to women and Millennials (those born between 1980 and the early 2000s). This is exactly what former MPP Peter Shurman and I tried to tell Mr. Hudak and his team before the 2011 election in Ontario, after spending eight months putting together proposed urban policies as co-chairs of the Toronto Policy Advisory Committee. We proposed transit ideas and suggested a review of the City of Toronto Act and the size of council. We provided ideas on how to tackle mental health, crime, and homeless issues, and how to fund desperately needed new infrastructure. I'd even hoped, knowing it was a long shot, that the Ontario Progressive Conservatives would have a strong showing with a float in

Toronto's Pride Parade. But the PC Party did not use one word of what we'd proposed in their 2011 campaign manifesto, paradoxically called *Changebook*. If it had not been for lawyer Pamela Taylor, a director of the Toronto Centre PC Riding Association, the party would have had no presence in the Pride Parade that year. Caucus members and PC staffers who are gay or lesbian are for the most part closeted. In recent years, Mr. Hudak attended one Pride Week event each year. No one was suggesting he turn up everywhere he could possibly be seen, as Ms. Wynne did during Pride Week 2013, making like she was the Queen Lesbian of Ontario. However, sadly, there is no one working from within at the provincial level to change the perception of the Ontario party like Mr. Baird, Mr. Ellerton, Dr. Eappen, and Mr. Litwin did in Ottawa. To his credit, new PC leader Patrick Brown showed up to march with a strong LGBT Tory contingent of sixty people, including me, in Toronto's Pride Parade in June 2015. I don't know if that will translate into good social policy. But he knew it would make a positive political statement if he did show.

It will be a real shame if the Ontario PCs don't evolve before the next election. By continuing to cling to their old insular ways, they not only play into but perpetuate the Lib-left mythology that paints the PC Party as not much more open and inclusive than the Tea Party south of the border. The face of the party has changed to some extent – and Mr. Brown tried to embrace ethnic minorities during his run for leader – but it still has a long way to go. A few token visible minorities and women were lured to run in Toronto ridings in the June 2014 election to make the team appear diverse and open-minded – not that the party did the slightest thing to support them. Regrettably, the Ontario Progressive

Conservative Party still acts and looks like a white men's club run by a bunch of misogynists.

In the June 2014 election, Mr. Ellerton, inspired by our conversation about how to make the provincial Tories more urban-centric, bravely signed up to run in the very strongly NDP riding of Parkdale–High Park. He told me he felt he had to "walk the talk." I was also thrilled to see Justine Deluce, a young, hip real estate professional, sign up to run against Eric Hoskins in St. Paul's. Former Ontario Taxpayers Federation president Kevin Gaudet – an articulate, smart urban professional – took his second stab at a provincial seat in the riding of Pickering–Scarborough East. Paramedic and single mom Roberta Scott tried her hand in the left-of-left riding of Trinity-Spadina. But Mr. Ellerton's concerns proved to be prophetic. Even though the face of PC candidates had changed in Toronto, Mr. Hudak and his inner circle let them down badly in the June 2014 election, when the PCs were practically decimated by the Liberals under Kathleen Wynne. The PCs did not win a single seat in Toronto, and Doug Holyday, one of the few politicians around who sticks to his principles, lost the Etobicoke-Lakeshore seat he'd won in an August 2013 by-election. It was Mr. Hudak's race to lose and he did just that. After all, how many parties, other than the Liberals, can lurch from one costly scandal to the next, mismanage virtually every file and project they oversee (including the Pan Am Games, the true cost of which we will likely never know), be under more than one criminal investigation by the OPP, destroy the evidence pertaining to the gas plants scandal, and *still* get a majority from voters? There are no two ways about it: Mr. Hudak and his advisors fumbled badly. Why? Because they didn't have a clue about how to connect with urban voters, or about what issues would resonate with them.

I could have predicted the election result a summer earlier, during my six-month sojourn at Queen's Park, when I could see that the party's focus was single-mindedly on the economy and jobs. Of course, the economy is important and the fact that the Liberals had racked up an eleven-billion-dollar deficit with no plan in place to reduce it is beyond scary. But unlike me, most Ontarians' eyes glaze over when confronted with numbers, even big debt and deficit numbers. Far too many voters, particularly pampered Torontonians, are wilfully ignorant, if not witless, and don't want to hear the stark realities. The message has to be distilled into very simple talking points such as Rob Ford's successful "Stop the Gravy Train" message in his 2010 municipal campaign. I told PC insiders that Mr. Hudak needed to focus more on bread-and-butter issues. If voters were not prepared to absorb the deficit, debt, and job messages, I advised, then speak to them where it really hurts – by condensing key health care, education, or energy issues into concise sound bites. Wait times for home care, cuts to physiotherapy, the quota system for cataract surgery, the smart meter disaster, and the reopening of teachers' union agreements to buy labour peace: there was certainly no shortage of areas where the Liberals were vulnerable. In frustration over the opposition's inability to articulate these basic concerns, I set about doing it myself on the health care front, interpreting for my readers how many nurses, home care visits, hospital stays, and physiotherapy sessions the $1.1 billion wasted on moving two gas plants would have bought. I also tackled transportation, taking a hard look at how many kilometres of subway the billions of dollars squandered on eHealth, Ornge, and the Pan Am Games could have built. How many of us in the GTA haven't been trapped in gridlock or crammed into a bursting at the seams subway car? How many of us in Toronto and throughout the province don't have a health care horror story or two to tell? These are places where the Hudak Tories completely missed the boat.

When Mr. Hudak's jobs platform came out at the start of the June 2014 election campaign, I just knew he was throwing gas on a fire. I was impressed with his decision not to sugarcoat the true state of Ontario's economy or make costly promises he could not keep simply to buy votes as the Liberals did. But his platform of reducing a hundred thousand jobs in the broader public service quickly got derailed because he didn't and couldn't articulate properly that this would be done through attrition – by not replacing the 5 per cent of civil servants who retire annually – and by getting rid of useless agencies with too many middle managers, like Drive Clean and the Local Health Integration Networks. He should have been reiterating day after day that no one on the front lines would lose their jobs, and that his ideas were directly out of Liberal consultant Don Drummond's well-articulated 2012 report. He should have been saying over and over again, until we got tired of hearing it, that he intended to build a responsive and responsible Ontario without the waste and mismanagement. Why didn't he back the unions into a corner by stating right out of the gate that, for the good of Ontario's fiscal health, already well-paid teachers, OPP officers, and other public sector workers could afford wage freezes in their next three-year contract? He should have published their salaries and embarrassed them. Why didn't he compare the great divide between private and public sector wages – study after study has shown that public sector wages are on average 14 per cent higher – and keep hammering home the idea that the private sector can't keep propping up the lavish public sector contracts? All of these were missed opportunities. I grew increasingly frustrated as I watched the entitled unions take control of the message because the Hudak Tories let them. Surely to goodness the Ontario PCs had to have known there would be pushback from the union-controlled Working Families Coalition as there had been in the last three provincial elections. Surely they had to have anticipated that the unions were prepared to spend millions of dollars on attack ads to indoctrinate low-information voters. The Hudak Tories just sat back and let it happen. I grew so frustrated with the misleading messaging from a long list of unions – and with Mr. Hudak's inability to clearly state his intentions – that I tried to expose the unions, their incestuous ties to the Liberals, and the money they spent on attack ads in the last week of the campaign. Judging by how well my stories resonated, I suspect that had the Tories been able to confront them head-on sooner instead of losing complete control of the message, the outcome of the June 2014 election might have been different.

SADLY, I CALLED IT in September 2013 when I said before and after that policy conference in London, Ontario, that Mr. Hudak needed to step down for the good of the party. Many party insiders agreed with me, but Mr. Hudak and his inner circle made sure all dissenters – especially Mr. Shurman – were sidelined. My voice got drowned out by those in the party – like former party president Ken Zeise – who felt Mr. Hudak needed to have a second chance, even though he'd already badly blown the 2011 election. I lost count of how many times Mr. Zeise blathered on about process and party protocol as the excuse for allowing the ineffectual leadership to continue. It was as if they had a death wish and didn't much care that they did. Mr. Hudak and his inner circle – and the party insiders who refused to see the writing on the wall – cost this province four more years of corruption and fiscal torture. When Mr. Hudak indicated his intentions to resign as leader the night of the June 2014 election, all I could think was that he was one election too late. I knew then, and am convinced to this day, that while the Liberals will do anything to win at all costs, the Progressive Conservative Party of Ontario doesn't have the slightest clue what it takes to win.

CHAPTER NINE

Loathing on the Left

Within hours of my "Coming Out" column in the *Toronto Sun* on Pride Day 2007, my inbox filled up with e-mails of support. One of the first came from then Ontario Progressive Conservative leader and now Toronto mayor John Tory, a good friend (until I dared to criticize his record as mayor). Written in the wee hours of that Sunday morning (when Mr. Tory is known to start his day), his words about my courage and my setting of an example were truly genuine and are ones I still remember. If I was the slightest bit shaky about what I'd done, that quickly disappeared over the next few days when the e-mails, calls, and words of encouragement from readers, *Sun* colleagues, right-wing politicians, bureaucrats from City Hall, and even gays still in the closet kept coming and coming. Nearly 99 per cent of the feedback was positive, heartfelt, and uplifting.

Readers who admitted to growing up in homophobic families wrote me tales of learning as adults that some of their dear friends were gay. They thanked me for presenting a positive role model. Others, who had no clue I was a lesbian until I wrote that column, told me they didn't care whether I was gay or straight, black or white – they just loved reading my tell-it-like-it-is columns. I'd come out so publicly not only to set the record "straight" but to challenge stereotypes. I wanted to educate my readers that gay people can come from every walk of life. They can even be outspoken Jewish, right-wing, fiscal conservatives. I wasn't looking for praise or pity. I wanted to make the point that the left doesn't own the gay agenda.

As the days went by, there was silence from left-wing councillors, and especially from Mayor David Miller. Not that I expected everyone to acknowledge my coming out, and obviously I understood that I was not the left's cup of tea, but even council's gay advocate, and my councillor at the time, Kyle Rae, acted like it never happened. That silence was broken when in the City Hall cafeteria I ran into Paula Fletcher a few days after my column appeared. Taking in the stylish leather jacket I happened to be sporting that day, she asked me if I was dressed in my "dyke suit." By then, I'd watched Ms. Fletcher and her fellow leftist councillors long enough to know that what they lacked in class, they made up for in nastiness. Perhaps the behaviour was payback for my refusal to fawn over Mayor Miller – like the rest of the media – and for generally being a pain in the ass on behalf of my readers. But I thought, I guess rather naively, that when it came to something so deeply personal, they'd put our political differences aside to embrace someone who might help further such an important cause. I remember calling the comment classless and Ms. Fletcher subsequently pretending it was simply a lighthearted joke.

She was hardly the only person from City Hall who mocked my very public coming out. A few months later, I learned from a councillor that when he tried to suggest to Kyle Rae, the Grand Poobah of All That Is Gay, that it was great what I had done so very publicly, Mr. Rae apparently retorted that while I may be a lesbian, I'm a "bad" lesbian. If being a bad lesbian constitutes calling the likes of Kyle Rae out on his expenditures as a councillor, or daring to ask him tough questions about whether he's pushing through deals for developers that were well beyond city density and planning rules, then yes, I'm a bad lesbian. To be a "good" lesbian in the eyes of Mr. Rae, I'm guessing one had to bend and scrape, fawn over him, be malleable, and turn a blind eye to his tight ties with developers. Mr. Rae was the epitome of the "do as I say, not as I do" liberal thinker. I'd regularly see him heave himself out of his council seat to express mock hysteria at some alleged slight, or homophobic remark, by one or more of his supposedly intolerant council colleagues. He didn't see the irony, or hypocrisy, in his puerile cheap shots and hissy fits at alleged "bad" lesbians, such as myself.

City's Hall Lib-left didn't evolve much in the two years between my public coming out and my marriage to Denise. When my colleagues in the City Hall press gallery kindly threw me a party a few days before I left to get married, neither the mayor nor one left-of-centre councillor, except for Shelley Carroll, were gracious enough to come down from their second-floor offices to wish me well. Even Mike Del Grande, who as a devout Catholic doesn't condone same-sex marriage, made sure to drop by with a card and a gift. I also wrote a column to run the day Denise and I got married, lauding the NDP for fighting to give gay people in Canada the right to marry. Again I received many wonderful e-mails – one of the most memorable coming from an Orthodox rabbi. He said that while same-sex marriage wasn't recognized by religious Jews like himself, he wanted us to know that he was thrilled that Denise and I were building a loving Jewish home together and that we weren't missing out on being married by a rabbi under a chuppah. In stark contrast, there was almost no reaction to that column from the left at City Hall or my left-wing critics. I certainly did not lose any sleep over the left's silence, and again, I'm not so presumptuous as to take real offence to it, but I was starting to feel like a Canadian version of Condoleezza Rice, whose appointment as the first black female secretary of state in U.S. history received almost no reaction from the left. Truth be told, all of this is sadly predictable. It says a lot about the character, or lack thereof, of the liberals. It wasn't just that they actually believed themselves well within their rights to behave with such small-mindedness because I'd been "mean" to them in print – to reiterate, I had held their feet to the fire – or had been an alleged "bad" lesbian for having the balls to do my job. It was also because I challenged their clearly narrow-minded view of the world.

Who said one cannot be a fiscal conservative or support a right-of-centre political stance and be openly gay? Well, in fact, it's the narrow of mind, those who should be ashamed of themselves for trying to pigeonhole a group into a singular stereotype. I've actually had people on Twitter – which is dominated mostly by the Lib-left – claim that right-of-centre gays are for the most part self-loathing. Really? A story told to me not too long ago by a friend of mine, Harvey Brownstone, who also happened to be the first openly gay man appointed to a judgeship in Toronto, proved how firmly held the stereotype can be. The family court judge, who also presides at some criminal hearings, was having dinner with a group of Toronto lesbians, self-identifying leftists as it turns out, and he happened to mention that he and I had grown up together in Hamilton and had recently reconnected. He also mentioned, seemingly to their horror, that I was out and very public about it. They argued with him, saying I couldn't be out and right-wing too. He invited them to read the columns in which I talk very publicly about being married to Denise. To this day, I'm guessing they have not taken a look at what I wrote about coming out or getting married, or at the very least would never admit they were wrong. The point is that it's as if the two ideas are mutually exclusive. But the bottom line is that I always have and always will agree that gays can be conservatives, or even Scientologists for that matter.

The Lib-leftists have convinced themselves they are tolerant, inclusive champions of diversity, advocates for the downtrodden and the poor, and paragons of open-mindedness. The truth is, at least in my experience, they are close-minded, intolerant, petulant, and prone to stereotyping. If they are challenged with facts, they will invariably go on the offence, often resorting to cheap, personal attacks. All too many Lib-leftists I've encountered and written about see absolutely no irony in the fact that while they purport to want to champion the downtrodden, and forever make a great show of supposedly doing so, leftist politicians, do-gooders, and assorted poverty industry activists are not only the first to line up at the public trough but have spent years sucking it dry. They're masters at recycling: if they do a terrible job, or get their hands caught in the cookie jar at one non-profit organization, they always seem to land unscathed at another. Keiko Nakamura, who allowed spending abuses to occur under her watch at

Toronto Community Housing Corporation and was eventually pushed out with a $320,000 severance for her incompetence, found a soft landing at Goodwill Industries, making initially $215,000 a year and then $230,000 in 2014. In early 2016, she managed to run that organization into the ground too. It defies logic. Yet most of them don't like the idea of their comfortably thin view of the world being upset, and heaven forbid one should go after the entitlements of those working in the social housing and poverty industries or for non-profit organizations, or should try to untangle their stranglehold on our public sector institutions and agencies. I liken them to a bunch of cockroaches, as they have tremendous staying power. Far too many of the Lib-leftists are adept at organizing, bullying, and knifing anyone in the back or front who dares stand in their way.

Those on the Lib-left are very selectively tolerant, selective in their inclusiveness, and, as I discovered when I came out, selective about those toward whom they direct any generosity of spirit. People who march to their political drum beat – muttering all the phony rhetoric they expect to hear – are tolerated, even set on a pedestal, despite their obvious flaws and very public blunders. Openly gay former Ontario Liberal cabinet minister George Smitherman is a perfect example of someone who has constantly received special treatment by the media and his fellow politicians. After allowing the eHealth nightmare to unfold under his watch, turning a blind eye to the spending abuses by the CEO of Ornge, appearing to mock seniors who suffer from incontinence by proposing a photo opportunity in adult diapers, and selling Ontario's energy future down the road by secretly inking a deal with Samsung (to create a multi-billion-dollar wind turbine facility), Mr. Smitherman actually thought he had what it took to be mayor of Toronto in 2010. And why not? The Lib-left sheep, led by their mouthpiece the *Toronto Star*, saw nothing wrong with the fact that he was a bad politician, had a whole closet full of baggage, and, in my estimation, was not known for being a particularly kind human being. In fact, he earned himself the nickname "Furious George."

I can only imagine, if I'd called him a "bad" gay man or pressed the case that Mr. Smitherman had been addicted to party drugs before running for politics – in the same way the media obsessed about Rob Ford's drinking and crack cocaine use – how his apologists would have squealed in self-righteous indignation. True, he has shown the courage to be true to himself by being out. But let's face it, like far too many politicians, Mr. Smitherman is a narcissist. He had already proven during his time at Queen's Park that he didn't give a hoot about providing services to those truly in need. If he had, he wouldn't have allowed billions of dollars that could have been used on health care for an aging demographic to be squandered on eHealth and other government fiascos, without giving it a second thought. If Mr. Smitherman had had the slightest bit of remorse over his failings as a provincial politician, he would have never thought himself worthy of running for Toronto mayor, or more accurately, worthy of rescuing Toronto from the fiscal morass left behind by David Miller, another narcissist.

But without the slightest bit of guilt and more than a touch of brazenness, this guy thought he was the man to put Toronto back on a solid footing. That fact alone was disturbing enough to me and many others. It was even more shocking to me how throughout 2010 the Lib-leftists and even a gaggle of Red Tories circled the wagons. Reinventing history, they painted this guy as a saint, as someone who was open-minded, had a heart, and should be given nothing short of a medal for his desire to turn the city around post–Mr. Miller. What about all the money he'd squandered in his succession of cabinet posts, helping to leave Ontario mired in debt, and the fact that he was part of a Liberal government that saw no issue with nickeling and diming seniors and the vulnerable to cut costs? These "minor details" were conveniently swept under the rug. Rob Ford, as sweaty and socially awkward as he was, truly wanted to get the city's debt under control so there would be more services for the people who most needed them. Unlike Mr. Smitherman, he walked the talk, never taking trips at the taxpayer's expense or using his office budget, and he made it his mission to get Toronto back on a solid financial footing while still finding ways to save tax money. Though Mr. Ford came across as bumbling, inarticulate, and extremely rough around the edges, his heart was in the right place. He wanted to undo the fiscal damage foisted on taxpayers by his predecessor, who seemed to care only about the image he saw in the mirror. Joining forces in a desperate attempt to fend off Rob Ford's growing popularity in the polls and to win at all costs in 2010, the Lib-left were persistent about painting Mr. Smitherman's opponent as homophobic, inarticulate, heartless, mean-spirited, and just plain bad for the city. And that was on a good day.

Led by the *Toronto Star*, the Keep Rob Ford Away From the Mayor's Chair forces were feverish in their efforts. In my many years of covering provincial and municipal elections, I'd never seen anything like it (that is, until the 2014 provincial election). Kathleen Wynne, then a cabinet minister, joined in the fray, using her taxpayer-funded office resources to try to indoctrinate her constituents with a nasty back-to-school e-mail about Mr. Ford in the fall of 2010. While claiming that Mr. Smitherman, a fellow gay, has the "heart, the experience and the energy" to represent her constituents well at City Hall, Ms. Wynne said that Toronto would not "grow and prosper" nor did Rob Ford have the best interests of the city at heart, or compassion for the people who live in it. A conservative would not have "compassion" for the people who live in it. I always love those overused lines because they are like maple syrup for the masses and Ms. Wynne has used them very well. The words were so sickeningly mind-numbing, she and her Liberal pals hoped they would lull voters into a peaceful slumber. The Lib-left has a lock on compassion and the conservatives are heartless. We hear it at every level of government.

If I was handed a loonie for every time the word *heartless* was used about me, I'd be a multi-millionaire by now. Why? Is it because I actually want precious government resources to go to the programs and people for which they are intended instead of being used to feather the nests of bureaucrats and politicians or put toward building political fiefdoms within governments and agencies? Or because I supported conservatives like Rob Ford, who wouldn't throw money at any special interest group with their hand out or a tall tale to tell? Or because those conservatives have had the cojones to say no to the unions and special interest groups that are slowly but surely crippling to the point of bankruptcy Toronto's and Ontario's economies? More often than not, the lack of resources for basic services is not due to lack of funds. Instead, the funds that come in to governments are squandered before they get to the front lines. If people stopped to think beyond the vitriolic hyperbole and the stereotyping of conservatives, they'd realize that during the regime of one premier (Dalton McGuinty) and deputy premier (Mr. Smitherman), Ontario was turned from a have into a have-not province, forcing it to beg for handouts from its federal counterparts. Ontario's debt doubled from $139 billion to $273 billion over the ten years Mr. McGuinty was in power, and tens of thousands of manufacturing jobs left the province for locations with less oppressive tax regimes. Because Premier McGuinty and his at first unelected successor, Ms. Wynne, were incapable of reining in spending, Moody's, a major global credit rating agency, downgraded Ontario's credit rating in mid-2012. It was downgraded again by the New York–based Fitch Ratings from AA to AA – in December of 2014 out of concern for Ontario's $12.5-billion deficit and the weak prospects of the province to balance its books by 2017–18 as finance minister Charles Sousa has ridiculously promised (a target he will never, ever meet.) To use Ms. Wynne's own words, there were indeed certain sectors of the economy that did "grow and prosper" under the NDP leadership at City Hall and under Premier Dalton McGuinty: public servants and employees belonging to powerful unions, like the firefighters, police, and teachers of Ontario. The very politicians who constantly scream "equality" have made it quite clear to the residents of Ontario that some are "more equal" than others. Tough love, it appears, need not be applied to those union members – teachers, firefighters, police, and other members of the labour movement – who will continue to prop up these politicians.

When Kathleen Wynne took over from Mr. McGuinty, she and her BFF in cabinet, the highly incompetent health minister Deb Matthews – desperate to offset the money wasted on all the Liberal scandals and pricey union deals – set about cutting services to vulnerable seniors and kids, the very two groups who were supposed to be at the top of the Liberal priority list. Never mind compassion. These were desperate times, folks. The number of diabetes strips covered under OHIP – the strips being a surefire, inexpensive way for non-insulin–dependent diabetics to monitor their blood sugar to prevent escalation of their disease – was quietly reduced in the early summer of 2013. After all, the money must come from somewhere.

In 2010, the self-proclaimed movers and shakers in the media and a long list of political hacks and has-beens all jumped into the fray to try to get their man George Smitherman into the Toronto mayor's office. It was war. The Liberal machine worked overtime with smear tactics, endorsements from any politician, no matter how long they'd been out of the spotlight, and a string of polls that were so far off in their predictions, it all became quite laughable. The Lib-leftists were so busy patting each other on the back and convincing themselves that they were the only ones with the heart to do what was right for Toronto, they grossly underestimated the groundswell of resistance from Toronto residents who saw through all of this. In 2010, for the first time in a long time, voters realized that the only real thing the Lib-left cared about, other than their own entitlements, was winning. In October, a silent majority came out of the closet and voted for Rob Ford. If the smear tactics and the obsessive bullying during the campaign and throughout Rob Ford's entire four-year term has been any proof, the Lib-left really has no heart.

If the Lib-left had an official mouthpiece, it would most definitely be the *Toronto Star*. After I'd left City Hall for Queen's Park in June 2013, I was able to watch the Rob Ford saga more from the sidelines instead of being caught up in the middle of the chaos. Believe me, the City Hall reporters at the *Toronto Star* deserve credit for their doggedness and for unmasking Rob Ford's addictions and nefarious links with the crime world – although frankly, if the crack video had fallen into our laps and the *Toronto Sun* had the same resources to put toward shadowing Rob Ford as they did, I can guarantee we would have had the story – no, stories – far sooner. Still, the so-called "people's paper" – the paper that brags about protecting the downtrodden – wasn't content to rest on the laurels it secured for revealing the mayor's addiction to alcohol and use of crack cocaine. I watched as a long list of columnists lost all sense of decorum, professionalism, and class by repeatedly kicking the dog when he was down – calling him every nasty name in the book, from monster and cockroach to vulgarian, homophobe, racist, misogynist, and on and on. If I'd ever, ever used even one tenth of those names for David Miller or George Smitherman, I would have been hung out to dry by my media colleagues. I wondered how many of these reporters and columnists could truly look in the mirror and claim not to have baggage of their own, including addictions to drugs or alcohol. But they never let up on the feeding frenzy. I saw formerly well-respected members of my profession sink to an unfathomable new low.

The Lib-left are good at using people for their own ends, but they rarely give credit where it is due. Perhaps one of the most egregious examples of this was when controversial pro-Palestinian and anti-Israel agitators John Greyson and Tarek Loubani found themselves in prison in Egypt for fifty days in 2013. It was Conservative foreign affairs minister John Baird who was instrumental in getting them out of prison – even though it was an uphill battle for him, considering the two changed their story more than once about why they ended up in the midst of a highly charged protest in Cairo's Ramses Square in mid-August of that year. On the October 2013 day they were freed, those close to Mr. Baird recall that while on holidays in Boston and Provincetown, the foreign affairs minister was "all over" the issue with his deputies and Canada's ambassador to Egypt. He also ensured Egypt's ambassador to Canada was in on the discussions. Before the day the prisoners were released, Mr. Baird reportedly gave up other arrangements to attend a dinner of the foreign ministers of the Gulf States to lobby the Egyptian minister.

Mr. Baird and his Conservative colleagues engaged in quiet behind-the-scenes diplomacy to secure the two agitators' release. The left-wing media would have you believe that it was the photo opportunities of celebrities like Sarah Polley, Naomi Klein, Michael Ondaatje, Stephen Lewis, and Atom Egoyan that got them out of prison. In a May 2014 article in *Toronto Life*, Mr. Greyson, painted as the hero despite his outrageous anti-Israel rhetoric and his suspected ties to Hamas, didn't have the class to acknowledge the work of the Conservative government to secure his release from an extremely dangerous situation that could have ended in his death.

There's no doubt this was because it wasn't his leftist pals and assorted Israel haters who saved his skinny butt, but a Conservative government – and one that is pro-Israel, yet. How to rationalize that? I can only imagine what would have happened if Mr. Greyson's captors had learned he is gay. He would have been condemned to death after a two-minute trial, as hundreds have been in Egypt.

The Lib-left not only does a remarkable job of reinventing history and deluding themselves into thinking they have a copyright on compassion, I've also discovered through much of my work championing the rights of the underdog that they really don't much care about the downtrodden at all – except to use them to prop up their political and funding fortunes, or for shameless photo opportunities. That quickly became apparent to me in 2002, when I spent six weeks studying the amount of money that had been poured into the homelessness file since Mel Lastman had become mayor and Jack Layton had anointed himself patron saint of the homeless. Mr. Lastman, of course, had been embarrassed during the 1997 mayoralty campaign by his comment that there were no homeless people in North York – a day before a woman was found dead behind a north Toronto gas station. Mr. Layton, never one to miss an opportunity to prop up his pet agendas, capitalized on Mr. Lastman's guilt by urging council to vote to declare homelessness a national disaster in October 1998 – as 450 of Mr. Layton's noisy friends, assorted homelessness activists, and ten TV cameras looked on. It was theatre of the absurd at its finest. The motion meant nothing. All it did was set up the homeless, who were trotted out for the cameras, to think payday (more shelter beds and more affordable housing) was around the corner. Still, that declaration, together with Liberal Anne Golden's three-hundred-page, six-hundred-thousand-dollar tome – representing a year's worth of study of the downtrodden at Mr. Lastman's request – did open up the municipal-funding floodgates.

The file was ripe for abuse and it was abused – turning homelessness into a growth industry at City Hall. The number of city staff, particularly managers assigned to homelessness, grew every year. The poverty pimps swooped in for their piece of the pie. And as is predictable, very little of that funding ever reached the homeless, in particular those wanting desperately to break the cycle of dependence.

There are many poverty pimps in Toronto masquerading as activists. I was convinced that these so-called activists never wanted to cure homelessness. Make no mistake: if they did, they'd find themselves out of a job or without a political agenda. No group was more notorious for shameless grandstanding and for using the poor for often violent and dodgy photo opportunities than the Ontario Coalition Against Poverty (OCAP) and its leader John Clarke. Mr. Clarke, formerly from London, England, and who became a factory worker when he immigrated to Canada in the 1980s, founded OCAP in 1989 after joining the ranks of the unemployed. Professional protesting has since become his full-time job and Mr. Clarke takes it very seriously. After earning their notoriety for engaging in an extremely violent protest on the lawn of Queen's Park in 2000, the OCAP leader and his hangers-on – many seemingly suffering from mental issues – would disrupt business at City Hall repeatedly to make some point or other, mostly related to getting more money for the homelessness agenda. They were loud and threatening, and more often than not their protests would be accompanied by a strong police presence. They thrived on being escorted out of City Hall by security or, in the worst cases, dragged off in handcuffs. It was all a sideshow for them. Whatever point they were trying to make – and I'm not sure they had any goal other than getting their faces on the six o'clock news – got lost in the hysteria surrounding their protest. The protesters – and certainly not the plight of the homeless and disenfranchised – became the news. During her years at City Hall, failed mayoralty candidate and professional public teat-sucker Olivia Chow regularly used OCAP to prop up her agenda. Ms. Chow showed up to the 2000 Queen's Park protest on her bike and tried to direct Toronto police to back off from arresting the OCAP protesters. Problem was, as a city councillor and a member of the Police Services Board at the time, she was not within her rights to do that. Shortly afterward, she was forced to resign from the Police Services Board over her gross error in judgment. Ms. Chow also sponsored a media event at City Hall in 2005 during which the poverty pimps made it clear they were encouraging welfare recipients to exploit a loophole that would allow them to collect an extra $250 per month in special diet benefits, whether they were eligible for the benefits or not.

Street health nurse Cathy Crowe, head of the now defunct Toronto Disaster Relief Committee (TDRC), was another one who created a career for herself on the backs of the homeless. In she would swoop to the city's homelessness advisory committee meetings like a queen bee, declaring to all who would listen that four billion dollars should be provided annually by the federal government and the provinces to build affordable housing and to fund other supports for the homeless. Ms. Crowe and her friends, propped up by *Toronto Star* coverage and by federal funding from the Liberal government of the day, showed their true colours very quickly; they had absolutely no interest in getting their homeless pawns off the streets. They vehemently opposed a homeless street count in 2006, no doubt because the count would, and did, end up confirming that there are far fewer hard-core homeless people living on the streets of Toronto than they'd ever admit. When in the spring of 2006 homeless committee chairman Jane Pitfield dared propose a quality of life bylaw – similar to that operating in many cities across Canada – to ban pesky panhandling in Toronto, Ms. Crowe and her homelessness industry pals went berserk. They ranted, raved, heckled, and tried to bully Ms. Pitfield, a right-of-centre councillor, into resigning as chair for daring to show leadership in tackling a controversial problem. Ms. Pitfield never did step down, and eventually Ms. Crowe decided to boycott the committee, hoping Mayor David Miller and the rest of council would back her. That didn't happen. But I will always remember that sideshow in 2006 for what it said about the poverty activists. Their activism appeared to have less to do with compassion than about keeping themselves employed and in the spotlight.

This truth was reinforced big time when Ms. Crowe won the *Toronto Star*–operated Atkinson Charitable Foundation's Economic Justice Award of one hundred thousand dollars per year for five and a half years to further her work on the homelessness cause. I'm not sure what she did with the award money. I do know that she produced a book, *Dying for a Home*, which Ms. Crowe says went into a second printing quite quickly and "was received well." She says that she shared the royalties she received with those featured in the book. She certainly didn't help the TDRC stay afloat in 2012, when it was forced to shut its doors due to financial problems. In both 2010 and 2011, Ms. Crowe ran for the NDP, vying for the provincial seat in Toronto Centre – Rosedale, but she did not win.

In the fall of 2013, Crowe landed a plum two-year position at Ryerson University as Distinguished Visiting Practitioner in the Department of Politics and Public Administration – to work, as she put it, on issues related to social justice. Her work included helping to set up a summer program called the Jack Layton School for Social Activists.

The following is written with no disrespect to Mr. Layton, who was extremely charming and personable. I admired his passion and his determination to get his agenda through city council. He put the federal NDP on the map, no question. I always found Mr. Layton far more affable than his wife, Olivia Chow, during the years I covered his comings and goings at City Hall. But, for heaven's sake, he was hardly a saint. He was just a man with a mission, much of which was not accomplished. Mr. Layton was flawed just like everyone else. He was a narcissist like every other politician. Like all of his NDP counterparts, he was a master of hypocrisy. Nicknamed "Bicycle Jack Layton," he would often ride his bike (for show) to City Hall with a city limo trailing him – costing eighty dollars per ride and spewing heaven knows how many greenhouse gases – to carry his paperwork. I'm not kidding. The limo carried his paperwork. I will not forget how he trotted out the homeless – many of them with mental health issues – before the camera to make some point or other. In the year 2000, when Mel Lastman and his supporters on council tried to get approval for the controversial million-dollar deal to send Toronto's garbage by rail to a willing host – the abandoned Adams Mine in Kirkland Lake – Mr. Layton brought in a council chamber full of professional protesters and used every trick in the book to stall the vote on the deal for four long days. In the end, the deal never went through because of

issues with the contract, and he and his ragtag group of pro-testers were only too happy to allow Toronto's garbage to be shipped by truck along Highway 401 to Michigan. That deci-sion made absolutely no sense to me: sending four hundred trucks a day down Highway 401 through London, St. Thomas, and Woodstock was supposedly much safer in Mr. Layton's opinion than shipping the garbage by rail up north to a will-ing host.

Even the letter Mr. Layton wrote from his deathbed to inspire Canadians was classic Jack Layton – one intended to manipulate public sentiment. To this day, it continues to evoke that fuzzy-wuzzy feeling of hope and the mistaken impression that the NDP are the ones who are there to act for the most vulnerable. It's all smoke and mirrors. Still, the outpouring of emotion in the days following Mr. Layton's death and leading up to his state funeral was so over-the-top, I wanted to shout from the green rooftops at City Hall to the many people inscribing sentiments in chalk on the stone wall below, "Get a grip!" I'd never seen so many people (several there simply to be part of the action) in need of a "group hug" over a politician's death in all my years covering politics. If I'd said anything remotely as politically incorrect as this back in 2011, I would have been branded a heretic. I expect I still will.

By now, it should be obvious that I don't have much use for public sector unions or their political supporters – mostly because they are greedy and out of touch with reality, and many of them are still living in the 1960s. But even I was sur-prised with the game of brinksmanship played between the entitled teachers' unions and the Wynne government in the summer and early fall of 2015 – dressed in the guise of concern for students and the quality of teaching delivered in

the classroom. It would have been laughable, had students not been caught in the middle. The teachers' unions actually thought they could dupe us into believing it was all about kids and not about their entitlements. As for Ms. Wynne, we already knew the leopard was not prepared to change her spots, despite her faux attempt at outrage about the teachers' unions' demands and her even phonier concern for the province's finances. My goodness, she'd already been bought and paid for by the teachers in the 2014 election. She wasn't about to let her benefactors down, no matter how it would affect the province's bottom line.

And so I've come to realize that those on the Lib-left are far more adept at manufacturing outrage and compassion – when it suits their political purpose, of course – than at actually using their outrage and self-righteousness to fuel action. It is little wonder public disenchantment with government and politicians is at such at an all-time high, and that people are convinced more than ever that their votes do not matter.

CHAPTER TEN

It's All About Me

As I headed out on the city's third homeless street count on a chilly April evening in 2013, my editors asked me if I would tweet about my experiences with a live feed planned on the *Toronto Sun* website. Even though I'd signed an agreement with the city's homelessness officials to respect the confidentiality of the street people we would encounter, I was assured by those same officials that I was perfectly safe tweeting about what I observed as my census team and I walked the streets we'd been assigned during the almost three hours we spent outside trying to track down the homeless. We were sent to the Bloor and Ossington area of Toronto – not exactly a part of town where the hard-core street people tended to gravitate, simply because the services they would normally access aren't there. Still, it took only a matter of minutes once I started my tweets – pretty innocuous and intentionally funny ones about the people we were required to stop who clearly weren't homeless – before the Twitter-sphere went berserk. They questioned my motives, suggesting nastily that I was just trying to prey on the homeless and take advantage of them for another column in which I would denigrate them as I always had.

Not that that was true. If my Twitter critics had bothered to read any of my columns on the homeless, they would have observed quite a different perspective. However, the response was par for the course. Over the years, it has become obvious the Lib-left prefer to remain ignorant about my position; otherwise, they'd have no reason to attack. Or, because many of them have a vested interest in keeping the industry thriving, it suited them to make it seem like I didn't care about the homeless. In fact, my columns had always questioned the amount of money poured into the homelessness cause, which, instead of being used to help break the cycle of dependence and give the homeless a hand up, went toward propping up an ever ballooning poverty industry.

Throughout the evening of the count, my critics called me a heartless opportunist and a variety of other unflattering names. As they tweeted from their warm homes, pubs, or wherever they were, I was actually out on a somewhat chilly spring evening growing more exhausted as each hour went by, walking the talk. I don't recall any of them indicating they were actually participating in the count. Perhaps my participation challenged their view of me as a heartless bitch. But they were definitely incensed that I was out there that night. Actually, it was the second time I'd volunteered to count the homeless. From 2002, when I spent several weeks investigating how much was being spent on Toronto's street people, it became a crusade of mine to question whether the millions of dollars allocated by council were going to those who needed it most, or to a growing industry of self-professed do-gooders and activists. In June 2002, I travelled to New York with then councillor Doug Holyday to see for myself what Mayor Rudy Giuliani had done to get the homeless off the streets of his city. At the time, the New York City Department of Homeless Services had just begun a count of the homeless living on the streets of selected areas of Manhattan, and was planning to expand the census to all of Manhattan the following year. The agency figured, quite rightly, that if they didn't know the extent of the problem, they couldn't fix it properly. I came back to Toronto pushing for a similar street census in our city. But when the NDP councillors – most particularly Olivia Chow and Joe Mihevc – and the poverty activists got their hands on the idea, they managed to drag their feet for four years, using every excuse they could think of to delay the count. They knew it would turn up far fewer serious street people than the grossly inflated numbers they regularly used to justify more cash for a cause that was already spending on average $32,631 per hard-core street person per year. Indeed the first baseline census in 2006 showed that instead of the 15,000 homeless Jack Layton estimated to be living on Toronto's streets, there were a mere 818 outside on April 19 of that year. Believing I had a certain stake in the street count, I decided to serve as a volunteer in 2009 and 2013 to see for myself how the survey was being conducted and exactly who was sleeping on the streets.

It confounded and incensed me that instead of applying tough love and forcing the homeless off the streets into shelters, the poverty activists were perfectly content to leave

Toronto's street people lying where they found them – as a testament to the federal and provincial governments' alleged refusal to properly fund affordable housing. The perennial mantra of the Lib-left is that if only the federal government would sink millions and billions of dollars into building more affordable housing units, there wouldn't be any more homeless on the streets. They still yap about the same thing today, fourteen years later. But as I soon discovered, affordable housing was darn unaffordable to build. It was beyond incomprehensible that the leftists would advocate for the construction of housing costing upwards of $300,000 or more per unit when there were and still are plenty of private apartments available in the city that could house street people at a fraction of the cost using rent supplements. There'd even be money left over to provide the homeless with proper counselling for whatever demons kept them on the street – whether it was alcohol, drugs, or mental issues. As the years went on and I heard the same story over and over again, I came to realize that the homelessness activists didn't truly want to end homelessness.

I got a sense of déjà vu about invading the alleged territory of the Lib-left on a bitterly cold January night during the hellish winter of 2014. This time I was not doing a street count but a tour of the city's streets and shelters to see how the homeless were coping, and I ran into leftist Toronto councillor Janet Davis. She made it clear she was not at all happy to see me. I did not encounter Ms. Davis, an avowed CUPE supporter who comes across as bitter and humourless at the best of times, outside on the streets in the bitter temperatures, where I had been for a few hours. I ran into her at the warming centre located in the lobby of one of the city-owned facilities, my last stop of the night. She was so put out by my presence, she complained to the city workers that I was bothering some of the homeless there that night by attempting to speak to them. Ms. Davis left after a quick tour, having not spoken to a single person in the centre – except me, of course.

THE LIBERALS CLEVERLY TRIED to play on the stereotype of me as a heartless bitch in the only all-candidates debate during my 2009 bid for MPP. They planted Karen Mock, the national director of the League of Human Rights, in the audience to pepper me with questions about my alleged newspaper attacks on the homeless. Ms. Mock, who had a vested interest in helping out given that she wanted to run for the Liberals herself (later vying unsuccessfully for a federal seat in Thornhill during the 2011 election), was only too happy to plant seeds of doubt in the minds of those in the audience.

After all, what a perfect counterbalance that would make me to my Liberal opponent Eric Hoskins – a doctor with perfectly coiffed hair and years of involvement as president of War Child Canada, a humanitarian organization that reached out to children in war zones. In his literature, the Liberals used all the right buzz words: "compassionate," "honest," "committed," "industrious," "renowned humanitarian," and – get this – "loving husband." Given that I'd married Denise just two months prior to the election, I've always wondered if that last label was meant to target those in the more ethnic reaches of the riding who didn't believe in same-sex marriage. Here I thought the Liberals were tolerant and inclusive! Still, Dr. Hoskins was portrayed as Dudley Do-Right, leaving the implication that I was Snidely Whiplash. I'm surprised he didn't have one of those sparkles one sees on TV ads, emanating from his front teeth whenever he smiled.

That night, the Liberal Machine hoped no one would notice that Dr. Do-Right couldn't answer a single question without referring like a programmed robot to a briefing book nearly two inches thick – complete with tabs denoting each issue – while I spoke from the heart I allegedly did not have. I even dealt with the attempts to portray me as unfeeling toward the homeless by addressing my critics head-on. Thankfully, one of my opponents in the debate called out Dr. Hoskins for not being able to answer a single question without consulting his thick briefing book.

A few weeks later, and mere days before the election, Dr. Do-Right skipped the only televised debate for our riding. Whether he was poised to win or not, to me his absence represented the height of arrogance and disrespect for voters. But of course, such disregard has become a Liberal trademark and his arrogance has only gotten worse as Liberal health minister.

The most amusing act just before voting day was the Liberal attempt to smear me in a series of flyers dropped in voters' doors. I was flattered that my opponents considered me enough of a threat to go to those lengths. But the funny thing was, many voters would have agreed with the quotes they pulled out of my columns, even though they were taken completely out of context. Under a heading claiming that for over fifteen years, "Sue-Ann Levy has been complaining about everything and everyone," they included this quote: "The TTC is inefficient and the management ranks bloated." Considering that I'd spent time on St. Clair West hearing from store owners who had barely hung on during the TTC's mishandling of the dedicated streetcar line construction – which went 100 per cent over budget – I'm not sure, if I were my opposition, that I would have used that particular quote.

The Liberals also included this one from a column I wrote about the city's decaying infrastructure, unkempt parks, and litter issues: "The fact is, I'm not the least bit proud to show off my city." From a column on David Miller's fiscal ineptitude, they included this comment: "It would be better if the province wouldn't agree to bail this city out yet again." It was hilarious. I ran for office mere days after the thirty-nine-day garbage strike ended – the strike that Mr. Miller put the entire city through for no reason. I heard the anger toward the mayor at virtually every single door during the campaign. In the Liberals' crude attempt to paint me as unfeeling, negative, unkind, and of course hard-hearted – in other words, the antithesis of their Liberal Golden Boy – they likely made more voters than they intended realize I was thinking just like them.

I'VE COME TO BELIEVE that when I stir things up or express provocative opinions, I'm often saying what is really on the minds of other people who don't have the forum or the ability to say it the way they see it. I've always accepted that I have to expect some pushback for my strong opinions. That doesn't bother me. Over my years as an outspoken political columnist, I've grown an extremely thick skin. The reaction of my critics is invariably visceral and personal. And when these detractors become personal, they resort to the usual stereotypes and lies about someone who is politically right of centre.

For instance, in May 2013, when word first came that a Rob Ford crack cocaine video existed, most people in the media and Toronto's chattering classes and talk show hosts were prepared to try to convict the mayor right on the spot. That was the start of what became a non-stop feeding frenzy. I was still prepared at that point to cut Mr. Ford some slack because the video had yet to surface. Besides, I put that latest round of harassment in the context of a witch hunt by the media (led by the *Toronto Star*) and Lib-left that had started virtually the day the mayor was elected to office in 2010, simply because he was right of centre, overweight, and at times inarticulate. It was like nothing I'd ever seen having covered three mayors during my fifteen years at City Hall.

For having the audacity not to rush to judgment and become part of the media pack that beat up on Mr. Ford with glee, I was practically eviscerated on social media. I was called the mayor's secretary, lackey, and apologist, a moron and hack. Apparently one was either with the Lib-left media or against them. And it got worse over the following months, when I dared to suggest to the supposedly "tolerant" left that they were being rather, well, intolerant and cruel toward the mayor, who clearly had serious addiction issues and was spiralling out of control. The word "enabler" was quickly added to their list of names for me. It became so ridiculous that I started to joke on social media and various other forums that yes, I'd personally bought Mr. Ford's crack cocaine and his forty-ouncers. The delicious delight with which so many people were prepared to mock and pile on Mr. Ford showed the true colours of both the supposedly tolerant Lib-left and far too many in the liberal media. I wondered if their over-the-top reaction stemmed from their need to belong to the so-called in crowd or to make themselves feel better about their own (perhaps insignificant or even dysfunctional) lives. I was shocked when I heard even rather rotund members of the media mocking Mr. Ford's weight. Perhaps I responded more strongly than others because such comments reminded me of those days in the schoolyard when I was chased and bullied, having been perceived as vulnerable and an outsider.

Premier Kathleen Wynne – facing a long list of messes of her own, from the gas plant scandal to deleted e-mails about that scandal, to her decision to capitulate to the powerful teachers' unions in one of her first vote-buying exercises – tried to divert attention from her own sorry government by ex-communicating Mr. Ford from meetings with the province, including any efforts to bring the city back from the terrible ice storm of the winter of 2013. I knew it was all political grandstanding on Ms. Wynne's part. But nevertheless I found it shameless and bordering on cruel that Ontario's first lesbian premier, who expects everyone to accept her, would dare to rush to judge a man who obviously had serious personal issues. I couldn't imagine not showing him any compassion.

The hypocrisy seemed pretty clear to me. But when I said on CP24's *Stephen LeDrew Live* that Ms. Wynne gave lesbians a bad name, the Twitterverse lit up. Sure it was a provocative statement. But I truly felt, as a fellow lesbian – and especially as someone who'd lived closeted for twenty years – that we needed to show some empathy towards Mr. Ford. Besides, unlike Ms. Wynne's corrupt government, Mr. Ford had not thrown precious tax dollars down the drain on scandals or handouts to his supporters. Quite the contrary. His personal problems didn't directly impact on taxpayers. In fact, I often joked that if he managed to accomplish everything he did while dealing with these personal issues, imagine what he could have done without them.

Nevertheless, that day and in the days that followed, yet another new name for me was added to the Lib-left repertoire on social media – that of self-loathing lesbian who was/ is a disgrace to the LGBT community. This made absolutely no sense. I'd lived in the closet for twenty years and finally had the guts to come out and write a column about who I really was. I had no problem calling Denise my wife, unlike Ms. Wynne, who while legally married to Jane Rounthwaite for years, still publicly calls her a partner – a move I suspect is simply an exercise to pander to her more religious voters. So, really, who is the self-loathing lesbian? Or perhaps the self-serving lesbian? That lie continued as I dared to counter the constant accusations that Mr. Ford was a homophobe. When he found out I was getting married to Denise, he wished us well, and whenever he saw her publicly he embraced her with a real fondness. That's not what I'd call homophobic behaviour. True, he stubbornly refused to participate in the Pride Parade, and that made it easy for his critics to target him. If I'd been in his shoes, I would have made it my business to turn up to at least one parade. But understanding nuance was never Rob Ford's forte. Nor was keeping his feet out of his mouth. I did not, however, ever believe he was a homophobe.

But so it goes. I've heard it all on social media, in the comment boards under my columns (which were discontinued in the fall of 2015 because the attacks got so personal toward controversial writers like me), from the left-wing fringe media and from bloggers. Many deliver their often bordering on obscene insults anonymously, which is a statement in itself. There is most assuredly a boldness that comes with anonymity. I've been called a Canadian version of Sarah Palin, Ann Coulter, and Glenn Beck; a hack with no integrity (that one is a favourite among my critics); and even a member of the Tea Party, although that makes absolutely no sense considering I'm an out lesbian. The most predictable and frequent insults from my detractors on social media, of course, contend I'm a "has-been" or "hack" or "hag" who works for that "tabloid paper," the latter words dripping with the supposed elitism that comes with proudly admitting one does not read the *Toronto Sun* or follow one of its controversial columnists, as tired as that sentiment has become. It's been so funny to watch my detractors squirm when I pointed out that they were the first to rush onto the comment boards and now to Twitter to try to discredit what I've written and to endeavour to gang up on me when I write a controversial column or post a similar Twitter remark. The immediacy of Twitter and Facebook and people's increased reliance on the Internet to not only disseminate news but to exchange feedback in the past half-dozen years has certainly boosted the ease of cyberbullying, and of doing so anonymously. I don't want to sound like a dinosaur, but I remember a time in my journalism career when people actually picked up the phone and delivered their criticism in a fairly civil exchange. Sure, some were heated at the outset, but at least I was afforded the opportunity to properly defend myself. Social media and the conducting of interchanges by e-mail can so easily misconstrue meaning and often escalate hostility because of the lack of a direct interface.

POLITICIANS ARE A VASTLY DIFFERENT ANIMAL. Unlike my social media and e-mail detractors, they prefer to tell me what they think of me in a public forum. Not always to my face, mind you, but when they think I can't respond. I have been singled out by thin-skinned politicians in the middle of meetings – for doing my job – so many times I've lost count. When I wrote about the high salaries paid to Toronto school bureaucrats in 1995, trustee Fiona Nelson, a long-time NDPer, whispered angrily at a meeting the day the story appeared that it was all "lies, lies, lies." That, of course, made it into my follow-up story. In 2013 and 2014, former Ontario premier and Pan Am Games chair David Peterson accused me of a variation on the same theme. When I wrote about the scandalous items being expensed by the senior executive team (all earning $300,000 or more) – anything from lavish team dinners overseas to $1.89 cups of Starbucks tea – Mr. Peterson suggested angrily that he knew "what journalists like to do." He never completed that thought, which also made it into my story, but I suspect he meant I like to make things up. He actually used those words when I contacted him for a story on a TO2015 insider who blew the whistle on the dysfunctional Pan Am organization, saying I was not only "making things up" but needed to find better sources who told me the truth. I had a good laugh at the latter comment, considering he'd hitched his wagon to the most corrupt Liberal government in recent memory and Mr. Peterson's sister-in-law, Deb Matthews, was I believed the most incompetent health minister I'd ever encountered (except for, perhaps, George Smitherman). I suspect the Pan Am Games will end up being as big a Liberal spending scandal as Ornge or eHealth, if the truth of what is spent ever actually gets out and is not buried in the bowels of various provincial ministries.

I was constantly being accused of something by councillors while covering Toronto City Hall for fifteen years.

Long-time midtown councillor Anne Johnston once claimed I earned too much money – during a debate on raising councillor salaries, which I vehemently opposed – because she felt I wore nice suits. Howard Moscoe named a "Levy levy" in my honour in 2001, when I dared attack council's cult of spending on free food and other perks. Mr. Moscoe, never one to miss a free buffet, free trips, or free tickets, and who would never dream of trimming his own personal fat, felt quite comfortable letting me know if I'd put on some weight. Norm Kelly, a perennial porker known to use campaign donations to treat himself to dinners with his wife, Charlotte, at his favourite fancy steak house, did the same. I often wondered if either of these two over-the-hill troughers would dare make the same comment to a man, whether a fellow councillor or a journalist.

I was even blamed in my early days at City Hall for the death of a limo driver because he was so distraught after my stories had embarrassed councillors into cancelling the costly and unnecessary limo service, which Toronto's auditor general had pointed out was costing taxpayers eighty dollars per ride. The accusations were completely over-the-top, considering none of these limo drivers ever lost their jobs. They just got reassigned to other city departments. But the most memorable phone message I ever got was from former Toronto councillor Sandra Bussin, who represented the Beaches area of the city. One night, after my colleague Zen Ruryk and I had exposed how the councillors had used their fifty-three-thousand-dollar expense accounts – and Ms. Bussin had been found to charge a bunny suit to her expenses – she called me in a panic. She said that, because of our stories, she'd been guilted into buying a late dinner (following a meeting) at a cheap Chinese restaurant in what she portrayed as a bad neighbourhood. When she'd pulled up in her late model BMW, a man had come up to her car and pounded on the window, scaring her – and this was all my fault. Her premise was that because I'd called her out on her expenses, she was afraid to spend too much on a meal she would be charging to her office budget.

One of the most laughable comments came in the spring of 2014, from the former chair of the Toronto and Region Conservation Authority (TRCA), Gerri Lynn O'Connor. Ms. O'Connor, the long-time mayor of Uxbridge, was clearly not accustomed to the pushback that came when I revealed that the conservation authority she'd been overseeing (for what seemed like forever) had been operating like an unaccountable fiefdom. When I disclosed in a series of articles in April 2014 that the perennially cash-strapped publicly funded TRCA owned 118 homes being rented to favoured friends and TRCA employees at below market rents and that its CEO was double-dipping (he retired with a full pension and then was hired back on contract), Ms. O'Connor's reaction bordered on frantic. She and her board weren't used to being put under the spotlight. The day after the stories appeared, she called to reprimand me like I was a first-year reporter with a small-town weekly, informing me I was "ruining people's lives." That really meant I was ruining their comfortable little social club at TRCA. Then she hung up on me. (She subsequently apologized after I phoned her back, told her she was being unprofessional, and explained that I was a seasoned journalist who was simply doing my job.) But that wasn't the end of the matter. In an e-mail response to a constituent who'd read my stories (which the constituent forwarded to me), Ms. O'Connor claimed she only read the *Globe and Mail* and, because of that, had no knowledge of what exactly I'd written about the TRCA. Just who was she kidding? Still, I laughed when I saw her e-mail response, not just because her intent was a cheap putdown of the *Toronto Sun* but because it once again amazed me how unprofessional and utterly classless politicians could be.

I'VE BEEN THREATENED by union bosses, too. In the spring of 2009, a few minutes before I was due to go on air with him, the late Brian Cochrane, head of CUPE 416, advised me that he knew where I lived – likely to try to intimidate me for advocating that garbage collection done by his union brothers and sisters be contracted out. Without skipping a beat, I asked him if that meant my garbage would be picked up quicker. Right after the interview, when I told Denise what happened, she said I should have gone on air and repeated what he'd said. I've been followed by the Toronto cops, who were trying to catch me in a DUI offence for daring to criticize their salary increase or former chief Bill Blair's refusal to trim his budget. This time, heeding Denise's advice, I went on the radio and called them out. It has never happened since.

When I write about entitled unions having extravagant contracts, wages, and benefits that outstrip any comparable jobs in the private sector, I'm pegged as a "grotesque enemy of working people." It apparently doesn't matter that I, too, am a working person who belongs to a union. My union, however, is part of a company that must compete in an embattled private sector industry. We are not a monopoly, and those of us still working for what is now Post Media all have the war wounds to prove what happens when a segment of the economy is in trouble. My point has always been that taxpayers working in the private sector can't continue to prop up out-of-this world union contracts. At the provincial level, surreal levels of union wages and benefits that outstrip inflation have created massive deficits and removed all hope of balancing the books, I would predict, in this decade. We've seen examples in Detroit, California, and Greece of what happens when unions and their contracts take precedence over a city or country's ability to afford the cost of such contracts. Public sector workers, for the most part insulated from job losses and enjoying the luxury of generous benefits, are able to work a shorter week and are retiring more than a year earlier than their private sector counterparts. And who props up these expensive contracts? Private sector workers, of course. But for daring to point out those simple facts, I'm branded a union-hater.

The prize for how far a union will go to protect its own interests and tell untruths about me resoundingly goes to the Toronto Professional Fire Fighters' Association (TPFFA). Over the years, I've pointed out many times what a terrific job the TPFFA does to indoctrinate easily intimidated councillors and the public – all to maintain their bloated contracts and benefits. I've got to hand it to them: they are masters at playing what I call the "fear and loathing" card, implying repeatedly that if they are forced to trim their ranks *in the slightest*, the entire city of Toronto will go up in flames. It just burns them that I understand how they manipulate public sentiment. From as far back as Toronto's amalgamation days in 1998, when six cities were melded into one and a long list of city departments were told to streamline their operations, Toronto's fire services escaped unscathed. Even though all six fire services were combined into one, they didn't cut one staffer or one penny of their budget. Without a second thought, in 2001 they took sixty-four firefighters off the front lines to provide glorified chauffeurs for the district chiefs at a cost of four million dollars, all the while crying that they needed fifty-five more firefighters to man trucks that were out of service. Common sense never matters when these kinds of moves are made. After the firefighters threw a temper tantrum for getting less than the boys in blue, David Miller generously gave them the same retention bonuses awarded to the police in 2000 to stem the tide of departures to police forces outside Toronto. There was just one small hitch: the firefighters did not have a retention problem. So why did they get their way? The answer is simple. They lobbied – meaning they in fact threatened – councillors. No increases for the firefighters, no support from their union in the next election.

In October 2007, when I had the nerve to break the story of a 9.66 per cent wage hike for firefighters voted on virtually in secret on June 20 of that year, their union tried to silence me by taking me to the Ontario Press Council. The deal was one of those council agenda items we call "hidden in plain sight" – on the agenda with the vaguest description possible and buried among mounds of paperwork. It was also voted on at 8 p.m., when those in favour of it knew the media would no longer be monitoring council. It was in the best interests of David Miller and his leftist supporters to keep the vote hush-hush if they were to have any hope of getting their new land transfer and personal vehicle taxes through council later that year. I only found out about it because I thought it was curious that rows and rows of firefighters – always dressed in some sort of T-shirt that made a statement – attended the October council meeting at which the taxes were debated and approved. I soon realized their presence and support were quid pro quo for their lucrative contract deal. The firefighters really had a problem with the headline on the column that broke the story: "City Hall's Secret Hose Job." But I took the heat for daring even to suggest that it was City Hall's best-kept secret, and the Ontario Press Council, in yet another decision that proved they were far more political than relevant, forced the *Toronto Sun* to run a correction claiming it was not in fact a secret deal.

The firefighters dined out for months and months on that success, claiming the one person in the media who hated firefighters had been silenced. Not that I hated them. They even cooked up a story saying that the reason I was so hard on them (and had an alleged soft spot for paramedics) was because my partner (Denise) was a paramedic. Not that she is. That myth circulated for a couple of years. It didn't dawn on them at the time that my criticism was all based in fact. The number of fires they fought per year was down to less than 10 per cent and the medical calls they'd taken on to reinvent themselves were up to almost 60 per cent of their responses. The tiered-response approach – meaning that police, ambulance, and fire all showed up to many 911 calls – was and is no longer affordable. In many cities in the U.S., the fire and ambulance services are combined. Yet here in Toronto we were still building separate stations for each service (sometimes on the same corner) and enriching the firefighter contracts, often to the exclusion of the paramedics. It made, and continues to make, no sense to me.

I wasn't silenced, however – to the firefighters' chagrin. In the summer of 2011, after Rob Ford came to power and the fire department was busy trying to counter a consultants' report that recommended the paramedics and fire be amalgamated, I wrote a column that had them fired up for days. As I ventured by the Yorkville fire hall around ten o'clock on a Saturday evening, I noticed a couple of beefy firefighters posing for a picture with a bunch of beauties in skin-tight, glittery dresses – during what turned out to be a bachelorette party. I wrote about that, daring to suggest that perhaps they're not so under-resourced after all if they have time to pose for pretty pictures. The nasty e-mails flooded in for days. After all, how dare I criticize those fire gods! I was accused of being jealous, of being a home-wrecker (by a wife whose husband had posed for the picture), of hating firefighters and having no empathy for the terribly difficult work they do, of being married to a paramedic (that was said over and over again), and many other offences too obscene to repeat. When a firefighter dug up a photo of me posing in a fire truck at a street party during my 2009 election campaign – one of those pictures I didn't remember taking and have since regretted – I was accused of being opportunistic for days and days. Evidently, it didn't strike them as ironic that they seemed to have a lot of time on their hands to find my picture and to send me attack e-mails, thus reinforcing what I'd been trying to say.

In addition to continuing to insist that Denise is a paramedic (I repeat, she isn't), the firefighters are convinced that I hate them and they have perpetuated that lie for years. It doesn't matter that I have no reason to hate them and have said so repeatedly. I simply loathe the way the fire gods manipulate public sentiment to get what they want in the way of unaffordable pay increases when common sense (and the facts) should dictate that they be forced to cut back like every other city department has (except for the police, the other sacred cow).

I hate the way politicians so easily cower in the face of their demands, more concerned about support and votes than balancing the books. I'm also not too fond of the way they've tried to gag and intimidate me for merely stating what is fact, and how they expect reporters only to write puff pieces about the latest five-alarm fire they battled (heroically, of course) on a cold night. I recognize that firefighting can be a dangerous job. But they get paid handsomely for it and only work seven days a month (on twenty-four-hour shifts). There is forever a long list of people who want to do the job if they don't.

NOT ONLY DO I WORK for "that tabloid" that seems to constantly fire up the masses – and not only have I loved every minute of my twenty-six years digging up the dirt – but evidently my loyalty is purchased at a bargain-basement price. My Lib-left detractors were still dining out years later, on a one-sided story penned by my then *Toronto Star* colleague Robyn Doolittle when she first came to the paper's City Hall bureau in 2010. She wrote that Rob Ford, then a councillor, donated one thousand dollars to my campaign for MPP a year earlier. To this day, I believe she deliberately did not get a comment from me so she could leave the implication out there that the donation bought my loyalty. After all the favours I saw being exchanged, the kickbacks quietly handed to certain downtown councillors by developers, and the public money spent by councillors on junkets to far-flung lands, I regularly joked after the story appeared that I sure went cheaply. But let's look at the reality of what occurred and how absolutely ludicrous the contentions were. During the thirty-five days of my by-election campaign, I was completely consumed with cramming as much canvassing and as many media interviews and speaking engagements into my fourteen-hour days as humanly possible. I had no idea who had contributed to my campaign until long after it was over, when I sat down to write my thank-you notes. And when the mayoralty campaign got into full swing a few months later, I made it quite clear that I supported Rocco Rossi for mayor. That continued well into the campaign until it became obvious that Mr. Rossi's message wasn't resonating and the only hope of cleaning up the waste at City Hall was to support Rob Ford's fiscal agenda. But my detractors have never let the real facts get in the way of their consistent efforts to discredit me.

What my critics should realize by now – whether it be those politicians whose feet I hold to the fire or those who read my writing – is that I don't run with the pack. I have a commonsensical view of the world and am not seduced by fuzzy-wuzzy words of hope or change, or as one of my good friends calls it, "social speak." I'm talking about platitudes that make lazy, pampered voters feel warm and happy but actually mean nothing and don't address the real issues of debt, corruption, or the absolutely immoral way many politicians and their union friends operate these days. I see politicians and bureaucrats for who they are. I am not interested in being friends with them, or the firefighters, or the union heads, or the cops, or the bloggers. I am not there to mouth whatever they feed to me. I am interested in championing the interests of those betrayed or treated unfairly by the system. I have a passion for social justice and am obsessive about tax money being used wisely. I keep on hoping my crusading might just embarrass the odd public service or politician into doing what's right. I am doing my job, hopefully the way it should be done. I am a reporter, not a repeater. If that makes me a "complainer about everyone and everything," as a Liberal attack piece contended during my 2009 campaign for MPP, perhaps that's because the truth really does hurt.

CHAPTER ELEVEN

The Neighbourhood Bully

If ever there was a tale of political correctness gone mad, of bureaucrats and politicians succumbing to the intimidation and bullying of a very vocal and hateful minority, it was the campaign to fight Queers Against Israeli Apartheid (QuAIA) from marching in Toronto's Pride Parade. Six years and many difficult uphill battles later, the Israel haters finally called it a day in the spring of 2015, after being virtually sidelined in the World Pride Parade in Toronto in 2014. Left almost to the end of the line in the five-hour parade, QuAIA's motley group of no more than a dozen anti-Israel protesters found that many of the spectators were already leaving for home by the time they started to wend their way along the parade route. They'd run out of steam and had become ridiculous and irrelevant, viciously attacking the only gay-friendly liberal democracy in the Middle East. It was just deserts for a group that had absolutely no business being in the parade in the first place. Fuelled by John Greyson and other gay filmmakers – who used this cause largely as an attempt to promote themselves and their government-subsidized commercially unsuccessful "niche" films – the presence of this group managed to polarize the gay community and put an unpleasant taint for years on what is supposed to be a celebration of gay rights and freedoms in Toronto.

In many ways, the presence of this radical, fringe group in the parade, and the inability of Pride's leaders to deal with it, caused Pride Toronto to lose its way. With QuAIA participating, the parade organizers couldn't consider the event mainstream or strictly educational, even though a long list of advertisers cozied up to them, knowing full well that the gay community had money to spend. But nor could it be deemed political as long as there was a conspicuous absence of any group marching against countries where gays are either thrown in jail, brutally murdered, or against the many instances of intolerance south of the border.

Only Israel was singled out for the entire six years, which led all of us fighting this cause to conclude that this was simply an exercise in Israel-bashing. It's not that Israel hasn't forever been the underdog. Tiny Israel, a mere twenty-two thousand square kilometres from north to south and east to west, with an estimated 2014 population of eight million people, is a miracle born from the desert, sandwiched between countries that can all be considered vicious enemies. Never mind talk of peace or a two-state solution. The Jewish homeland will never survive in a truly peaceful state as long as most of the Arab countries that surround it really want to see it annihilated, bombed into the sea. The entire landscape has changed in recent years, with a number of extremist factions – ISIS, the Iranian nuclear program, Hamas, Hezbollah, and a corrupt PLO – within a hair's breadth of Israel's borders.

When Denise and I arrived in Israel in late August 2014, two days after a truce had been declared in the fifty-day conflict with Hamas in Gaza – during which even the Tel Aviv airport was targeted and some southern towns encountered a constant barrage of up to one hundred Hamas rockets per day – we were surprised by the resilience of the Israeli people. Tel Aviv's beaches, cafés, shops, and buses were teeming with people, and the Israelis we spoke with told us resoundingly that they just wanted to live in peace. Still, they felt very much alone and battle-weary. While they believed that Prime Minister Stephen Harper had their backs, no one could say one nice thing about President Barack Obama, who, like the mainstream media, couldn't seem to grasp the concept that Israel had every right to protect itself from the rockets – which were all launched at civilian areas – with its state-of-the-art Iron Dome technology. And as we would soon learn from a very outspoken Arab journalist living in Jerusalem, the mainstream and international media embedded in Gaza – CNN, the BBC, and even Canada's own TV broadcasters – were all under the gun of Hamas and were being told to report the party line or risk being thrown out. "They did Israel a great injustice," said the journalist, a stringer with the *Jerusalem Post* and a variety of North American and European news outlets.

The one-sided media coverage of any and all conflicts between Israel and its Arab neighbours is a given. The persistent ganging up on Israel by the United Nations and a variety of European countries is nothing new. But the disturbing thing is the rise in anti-Semitism masquerading as concern for the Palestinians and the completely false claims that Israel is an apartheid state similar to what once existed in South Africa. Neo-Nazis are less to be feared by Jews these days than the fringe left, who've become useful idiots for the Arab contingent. They first made their presence known on university campuses across Canada ten or so years ago with Israeli Apartheid Week (IAW), and I've watched that movement grow, enabled and fuelled by weak-kneed university presidents and senior university officials who use the "freedom of speech and discourse" card as the reason not to clamp down on this veiled attack on the Jewish state and the Jews.

That very same excuse became the mantra of the weak-willed bureaucrats at City Hall, who were easily intimidated by QuAIA and their supporters. These same bureaucrats, while forever horrified by the idea that tolerance and inclusivity might not be extended to other visible minorities, especially Muslims, seemed to feel that somehow it was perfectly fine to delegitimize Israel and the Jews. Is it any wonder that the Boycott, Divestment and Sanctions (BDS) movement – a far more egregious campaign started in 2005 by pro-Palestinian groups to attack and isolate Israel – has gathered steam globally? Once the door was opened with Israeli Apartheid Week, and universities turned a blind eye to the ramifications of this week's events, the Israel haters were emboldened. One sad part of this is the pressure that has been successfully applied by BDS activists to musicians and other artists and to university lecturers, urging them not to fulfill concerts or other engagements in Israel. If artists don't back down, they continue to be intimidated and ridiculed. In a *Toronto Life* article in 2014, Mr. Greyson announced quite proudly, after nearly losing his life in an Egyptian jail the year before, that he intended to have a QuAIA float in Toronto's Pride Parade that would mock actress Scarlett Johansson for daring to stand up to the pressure exerted on her to quit her role as ambassador for the West Bank company SodaStream, which, ironically, employed 950 Palestinians and Israeli Arabs. (Mr. Greyson never followed through with that float, but his arrogance and his ignorance were still shocking.) The Palestinians working at SodaStream made the same wages and got the same benefits as Israelis – and took home nearly five times the income any Palestinian could earn in Ramallah. SodaStream officials would not admit that pressure from the BDS movement was a factor, but they decided to consolidate operations at a new plant in the south of Israel and phased out the West Bank factory at the end of 2015, putting five hundred Palestinians out of work.

As much as many of those associated with the Israeli apartheid and BDS movements will repeatedly deny they are anti-Semites, there is usually no other way to describe them. That goes as well for the Jews who, for some reason – whether out of a need to belong, or guilt, or the fact that they really loathe being Jewish – have become part of these movements. I've come to call them "useful idiots" or "Judiots" for the left and for Islamic terrorists everywhere.

It was in spring 2009 – as we were busily putting together our wedding celebrations – that Denise and I first heard about QuAIA marching in Toronto's Pride Parade. At that point, we had already travelled together as a couple to Israel twice and found ourselves sharing a passionate commitment to and protectiveness toward our Jewish homeland. Denise has family living just outside Tel Aviv, and her parents are well known in

Toronto for championing and donating extensively to a wide variety of Israeli causes. We knew little about QuAIA in the summer of 2009, but we agreed to march in the parade with a Jewish and pro-Israel LGBT group called Kulanu (Hebrew for "all of us") that was very passionately run by Justine Apple. For Ms. Apple, who was used to helming mostly social activities and events tied to the Jewish holidays, this step into a heated political arena was perhaps a baptism by fire. But she handled all of it adeptly. Although both Denise and I had never before considered marching in the parade, we wanted to be part of a strong pro-Israel presence to offset the lies we felt were being perpetuated by the fringe group of anti-Israel protesters. It was at that parade that Toronto lawyer Martin Gladstone documented on video the activities of QuAIA and the placards they carried not only stigmatizing Israel but displaying distinct neo-Nazi overtones. Little did I know that day what a journey Martin, his partner Frank Caruso, Denise, and I would take in endeavouring to stand up for Israel, and what a bond would be created between the four of us.

It was a few months after the 2009 Pride Parade that I was introduced to Martin through Carol Pasternak, whom I'd first met while attending her support group shortly after I'd come out in 2006. Carol found out about QuAIA when her cousin sent her a newspaper clipping and she offered to investigate. She met Martin through another gay woman, and before she knew it, she was "totally immersed in the battle" and even appeared in his movie. Carol knew very little about Israel's history or the conflict, but started reading and talking and watching. She says she picked up the ball to pay a debt to her Jewish ancestors who had suffered so much and fought so hard against anti-Semitism. Martin and Frank first noticed – to their horror – the presence of the QuAIA group in the 2008 Dyke March, in which Carol and her partner, Audrey Kouyoumdjian, always marched. While watching from the sidelines, they spotted two lesbians carrying a homemade sign that read "End Israeli Aparthied," followed by a ragtag assortment of dykes behind them sporting signs with similar messages. At the time, Martin was so incredulous about what he saw he thought it was a joke – they couldn't even spell the word *apartheid*, never mind understand what it meant. But the next day, at the Pride Parade, the couple saw a larger group of anti-Israel activists – which included skinheads proudly marching with T-shirts emblazoned with crossed-out swastikas. The crossed-out swastikas suggested to Martin that these white supremacists were implying that Israel was akin to Nazi Germany for what it was allegedly doing to the Palestinians and should be banned. But most importantly, here was a group using the venue of a publicly funded march and parade to spread a noxious message that had absolutely nothing to do with the celebration of gay rights. Martin thought at the time that the parade had been hijacked by a hate group whose singular demonization of Israel felt anti-Semitic. Their anti-apartheid message made absolutely no sense to him whatsoever. In 1977, he had studied the politics of South Africa at York University and knew about the hundreds of laws that segregated blacks and whites – on beaches, in hospitals, on buses – and the laws that did not allow inter-marriage between the two races. He also knew there was no apartheid system in Israel. Arabs and Jews share hospitals and every other public venue. Arabs vote for members of the Israeli parliament. No one is denied access to services based on race. Martin could not believe that Israel was being singled out when there are seventy-two countries where gays and lesbians can be thrown in jail, tortured, or executed simply for being homosexual.

A year later, on June 25, 2009, Martin bought a video camera and got a few quick lessons on how to use it so he could film the QuAIA contingent in the parade a few days later. On that Sunday, he stood in the rain and filmed everything himself. His lack of experience in filmmaking was moot. He was determined to create a film to show councillors and funders what was happening to the city's gay pride celebration. He wanted to educate and sensitize them to the hate that had infiltrated the parade. Martin hoped if they could see the QuAIA contingent for themselves – spreading their lies in a public forum subsidized with public money – the politicians would push for more accountability from Pride's organizers. He was to learn, as we all did, that he was giving city councillors, provincial funders, and the large corporate donors far too much credit. Since I was occupied with running for the Tories in August and Denise and I went on our real honeymoon to France in October, it wasn't really until Martin hosted a screening of his film at Christmas time that we all jumped into the fray – Denise and I, Carol, a woman by the name of Andrea Spindel, who was not gay but was a strong advocate for Israel, and of course, Martin's partner, Frank. Denise and I could not believe what a professional job Martin had done, even writing and performing the theme music himself. After the screening, we all decided that we had to get involved in our advocacy work as early as possible, and needed to target, in particular, all of the candidates running for mayor that next year. And so our grassroots campaign began with a vengeance. I was determined to help in any way I could, by building awareness of

QuAIA in my column and by directing Martin and others to any councillors and mayoralty candidates who could advocate for better accountability in the parade.

I still remember the first time Martin showed his video at City Hall, to Jewish councillor Mike Feldman and his executive assistant. The video was long because it was detailed, containing footage from the 2009 parade – the two hundred QuAIA marchers carrying signs condemning Israel, wearing shirts displaying swastikas, and chanting, "Fist by fist, blow by blow, apartheid state has got to go." Mr. Feldman, even though he planned not to run again in 2010, became a tremendous help in promoting the film and our efforts to other councillors. The momentum started to build. In February 2010, then PC MPP Peter Shurman brought a private member's motion before the Ontario legislature, condemning the use of the term *Israeli apartheid*. As he said that day, the term is as close to hate speech as anyone can get, and the "inflammatory and racist" term has no place in our hate-free political environment in Ontario and in Canada. In March, I wrote what would be the first of many columns fighting what I came to regard as a rising anti-Israel, anti-Semitic cancer.

As we suspected, with a feisty mayoralty campaign underway in 2010, our crusade, and particularly Martin's film, hit a responsive chord. Councillor Kyle Rae, to his credit, wrote then Pride executive director Tracey Sandilands a strongly worded letter noting he'd seen Martin's film and found the "intervention" of QuAIA in the 2009 parade completely not in keeping with the "spirit and values" of Pride Toronto. "If political dialogue and criticism is to be welcomed at Pride, surely we should be supporting our brothers and sisters who find themselves victims of institutionalized homophobia and transphobia," he wrote. "Free speech is to be encouraged but free speech of this nature is not in keeping with the expression of Pride." Amen. That would prove to be one of the few times I would agree with Mr. Rae. It wasn't long before the media pressure began to mount. All four newspapers agreed – for once – that QuAIA should be kicked out of the parade. My columnist colleagues and radio talk hosts like John Tory weighed in repeatedly on the subject, all contending that QuAIA had absolutely nothing to do with gay rights – that its sole purpose was to stigmatize Israel by portraying it as an apartheid state. There was general agreement in the mainstream media that this was not a freedom of speech issue, as QuAIA supporters and the radical leftists tried to make it. QuAIA only found support in the fringe left-wing media, particularly radical leftist *Xtra* magazine and its resident reporter at the time, a woman named Andrea Houston, who, without the slightest bit of shame, would soon come to be the mouthpiece of and advocate for QuAIA. But the cowardly bureaucrats at City Hall continued to pander to QuAIA, issuing a milquetoast briefing note at the end of April indicating that while Pride likely violated the city's anti-discrimination policies by allowing QuAIA to participate in the 2009 parade, they were "satisfied" and convinced that Pride had put a plan in place to monitor the (hate) messaging of all participants for 2010. We were not informed what that plan was, but as we were to quickly discover, the briefing note was just a stalling tactic. We soon realized that, in addition to the almost incestuous relationship between the city's culture bureaucrats and the Pride organizers, city bureaucrats were far more concerned with being branded what they thought was politically incorrect than with doing what was right. The officials who ran Pride, particularly Ms. Sandilands, played games with the media, saying one thing until their funding was in the bank, and then, unable to stand up to the bullying from the QuAIA contingent, doing the exact opposite.

In May, Councillor Giorgio Mammoliti, who was still in the race for mayor at that point, led the charge at council to force Pride's organizers to prove by mid-June that they had received, and rejected, an application from QuAIA to march in that year's parade. By May 30, the board of Pride, conceding they'd experienced an "operational crisis" as a result of the negative media attention over the QuAIA issue – a loss of funding, lower participation rates, and lower staff morale – agreed to ban the group from the July 4 parade. But this was just a clever ruse. On June 22, one week after the city's weak-kneed culture officials handed them their grant cheque (instead of waiting until after the parade as they should have), Pride's organizers flip-flopped, saying QuAIA could march, provided they signed a document committing to respect the city's anti-discrimination policies. Once again, the city's cowardly bureaucrats were complicit in enabling this hate group to march.

It was no surprise that QuAIA doubled down on their hate messaging in the July 4 Pride Parade, with support from the Canadian Auto Workers union and the city's outside workers, CUPE 416, who not only marched with the group but prepared signs of support with their union logos on them. *Xtra* magazine made it pretty clear where it stood by handing out signs that read "My Pride Includes Free Speech" – as if this was nothing more than a free speech issue. Denise and I marched with Kulanu that day, braving searing heat as we danced and sang Israeli songs along the Yonge Street parade route. Some five hundred members of

Toronto's Jewish community and a few community leaders joined us that year, along with mayoralty candidate Rocco Rossi. It was an excellent turnout – but securing support from Jewish community leaders would be an uphill battle, and their participation would be hit and miss, with key (and well-funded) Jewish groups like the Canadian Jewish Congress (and its successor the Centre for Israel and Jewish Affairs) and the Canadian Jewish Political Action Committee (CJPAC) more often than not MIA at crucial points in our fight. A strong and sustained showing of support from these groups would have given us a far better chance of getting QuAIA out of the parade much, much sooner.

The most frustrating missed opportunity was the race for councillor in Ward 27 in the fall of 2010. It was a very close fight between gay centrist Ken Chan (who was anti-QuAIA) and NDPer Kristyn Wong-Tam, a radical leftist lesbian art gallery owner and real estate agent with ties to QuAIA. Ms. Wong-Tam had strong support from CUPE 416, whose members were spotted working in her campaign office. In late September 2010, I revealed that Ms. Wong-Tam wasn't just linked to QuAIA but appeared to be one of its founding members, having been the registered owner of the group's website for fourteen months until that was suddenly changed in late August 2010, just before the municipal election. When I finally tracked her down after days of unreturned phone calls and e-mails, she claimed she'd only lent QuAIA her credit card – for fourteen long months, it seems. At that point, CJPAC and Bernie Farber, the former CEO of the Canadian Jewish Congress (a good talker, but not a doer) should have jumped into action to ensure Ms. Wong-Tam and her dangerous views didn't get into office. Mr. Chan lost by a mere 462 votes. It was so disheartening. Had a few Jewish groups taken the race seriously and advocated (even quietly behind the scenes) for Mr. Chan, as CUPE did for Ms. Wong-Tam, the result likely would have been different. As the representative of the ward in which Toronto's Gay Village is located, and as a lesbian, she was council's go-to person to set the tone for the gay agenda and the parade. Ms. Wong-Tam is too much of a politician to ever admit any disdain toward Israel or the Jews. Nevertheless, it was always darn clear through her actions that her sentiments were with QuAIA.

I will always have to give credit to Giorgio Mammoliti, who was so incensed that councillors had been duped and that QuAIA had marched in the July 4, 2010, parade that he called for Pride's organizers to pay back their $123,800 cultural grant. But knowing full well that this demand would never be supported by a leftist, pro-union (and likely anti-Israel) council, the organizers crafted a compromise stipulating that Pride wouldn't get any money until after the parade in 2011 – and would only receive it if all registered participants complied with the city's anti-discrimination policy. Still, when Ms. Wong-Tam got elected in October 2010, I suspected we were in for another circus in 2011.

Little did I know that the fight would get even dirtier and more personal. After the fiasco of 2010, Pride's organizers had named so-called gay community leaders to a community advisory panel (CAP) – headed by Reverend Brent Hawkes of the Metropolitan Community Church – to determine what to do about the parade's crisis of conscience. Rev. Hawkes was only too eager to have exposure for his church, given that his days as an activist for same-sex rights and marriage were long behind him. But in February 2011 – after nine months and hundreds of consultations – Rev. Hawkes's CAP delivered a 232-page report that deliberately skirted around the key issue of whether QuAIA should be marching in the Pride Parade. It was absolutely ludicrous. The whole reason for the panel was that the media attention and political pressure around QuAIA's involvement had created a crisis at Pride and had deeply divided the community. The panel was supposed to resolve that issue. But they couldn't, and wouldn't, do so – proposing instead to put in place some bogus dispute resolution process to air complaints about QuAIA's participation. I knew then and there that the process proposed by Rev. Hawkes would be an exercise in futility – and I was later proven right. It was on the night the CAP report was presented that I lost all respect for Rev. Hawkes. I saw him as nothing more than a shameless opportunist and I feel that way to this day. Instead of doing the right thing as the supposed moral leader of the gay community, he chose to play the part of politician and do what was right for him and his church. But whether he realized it at the time or not, choosing not to make a decision was in fact making decision. He was opting to sanction QuAIA's involvement in the parade. With the help of QuAIA's founder, Ms. Wong-Tam, Rev. Hawkes set about doing the rounds to try to intimidate councillors and bureaucrats into believing that any withdrawal of city funding for the Pride Parade would be an attack on the gay community and a "direct attack " on one of the LGBT community's beloved institutions. They knew that new mayor Rob Ford was prepared to stand up to Pride and not give the organizers their funding unless QuAIA and its hate speech agreed not to march in the 2011 parade. Knowing Ms. Wong-Tam, I have no doubt she was trying to leave the impression that Mr. Ford was homophobic for not wanting to fund Pride.

(Sadly, that whole issue did not end well for Mr. Ford. In 2011, he started the ball rolling by refusing to attend one single event during Pride Week, including the Pride Parade.)

As I saw Ms. Wong-Tam and Rev. Hawkes's reprehensible efforts ramping up with little pushback from the well-funded Jewish advocacy organizations, I grew more and more incensed and frustrated with them. Having chatted with the mayor's then director of stakeholder relations and now executive director of the Ontario Liberal Party, Earl Provost, I realized the so-called leaders of Toronto's Jewish organizations had to step up to the plate and express in no uncertain terms that QuAIA had no place in Toronto's Gay Pride Parade. In the heat of the moment, I wrote an e-mail to Avi Benlolo of the Simon Wiesenthal Center and to both Bernie Farber and Len Rudner of the then Canadian Jewish Congress. In it, I expressed concern that while Toronto's Jewish community had been absolutely silent on QuAIA, *Xtra* and Rev. Hawkes were working feverishly behind the scenes to ensure there were enough councillors prepared to vote to give Pride its funding that year. I also said it the way I saw it about Rev. Hawkes: that while he had promoted himself as the self-appointed leader of the gay community, he did not speak for Jewish gays and that his main concern was with saving face and keeping bums in the seats of his church. I urged them to get on board and start encouraging members of the Jewish community to send e-mails en masse to their councillors. My message was outspoken but heartfelt.

I meant well, and there was no question I was passionate about fighting QuAIA. My only mistake was writing that e-mail to Messrs. Farber, Rudner, and Benlolo on my *Toronto Sun* account. I should have done it from my personal e-mail address. I never did find out who leaked the e-mail, but I have my suspicions. Former *Xtra* reporter, Ms. Houston (she was let go in early 2014), who ironically still didn't see herself as an advocate for QuAIA, wrote a story full of hyperbole about the e-mail and how I'd been "censured" from reporting on Pride because of it. She never did ask me to comment – not that I was surprised. The president of the City Hall press gallery, David Nickle, who became part of the unrelenting and vicious mob obsessed with Rob Ford, preached about my ethics (or lack thereof) in the *Xtra* story. Poor Rev. Hawkes said he was "reeling" from the e-mail and resented the "impression" I painted of him. "This damages my reputation, the church and the entire community," he was quoted as saying. I wanted to tell him at the time that he'd already done that with his phony community advisory panel and his inability to do what was morally right about QuAIA. But knowing I'd said enough, I kept my mouth shut. Nevertheless, the hypocrisy abounded. It showed the double standard with which media are treated – those on the left handled with kid gloves while those on the right are subject to a virtual lynching, even by their own colleagues, for the slightest of transgressions.

I was not amused by Mr. Rudner's response. In the *Xtra* article, he claimed that my e-mail represented one approach and that they preferred to take a "different" one. To this day, I am not sure what he meant by "different," but their approach certainly was not to take a strong stand against QuAIA or to galvanize Toronto's Jewish community. The greatest support came from my editor-in-chief at the time, James Wallace, who said the contents of the e-mail contained nothing over and above what I'd said in my columns – and that I'd never hidden the fact that I wanted funding to Pride cut.

Nevertheless, to avoid an appearance of conflict of interest, I was asked not to report on the issue until after the funding decision was made, which I agreed to. Still, the whole episode was predictably over-the-top and done deliberately to try to change the channel from the real issue of QuAIA not belonging in the Pride parade. Even if I had written from my personal e-mail address, people would have known that I was a columnist for the *Toronto Sun* who was passionate about keeping QuAIA out of the parade, and I bet the e-mail would have still been an issue.

Meanwhile, Martin was celebrated with a well-deserved honour for his work at Simon Wiesenthal's Spirit of Hope gala at the end of May 2011. Denise and I were so proud as we watched him share the stage with Salman Rushdie and Elie Wiesel that night. A small group of us also formed a kitchen cabinet with a small but dogged group of activists who included David Nitkin and the very colourful Vivienne Ziner. We decided we'd also target some of the big funders of the parade – particularly TD Bank. Denise arranged to have signs made with catchy slogans like "Morally Bankrupt," "Investing in Hate Speech," and "Pa$$ing the Buck," and on a rainy Sunday a small group of us protested in front of the TD Bank in Lawrence Plaza. It was a tremendous grassroots effort, but as we were soon to discover, the man behind the funding of QuAIA, TD's vice-president of community relations, Scott Mullin, appeared not to care whether QuAIA was in the parade or not. Our pleas fell on deaf ears. I stayed out of the fray, not writing another column on the issue until mid-June of that year, happily missing a May executive committee meeting at which the pro-Israel contingent, the QuAIA supporters, and the supposed free speech advocates took each other on. The mayor and Mr. Mammoliti held firm on their plan to withhold Pride's $123,807 cultural grant until after the July 3 parade. At that same council meeting, Councillor James Pasternak, who represents a sizable Jewish community, got approval on a motion directing city manager Joe Pennachetti to craft an updated city anti-discrimination policy. Mr. Pasternak meant well, but we soon wished he'd left it alone. The new policy ended up being far worse. The July 3 parade was a win on one front: QuAIA did not participate. But neither did Mr. Ford – proof not that he was homophobic but that he failed to understand nuance and was his own worst enemy. His snub of Pride proved to be the tipping point that started what would become an extremely acrimonious relationship between the radical left in the gay community and the mayor's office. From that point on, Pride insiders felt justified calling him a homophobe and our fight started to lose steam. QuAIA, Ms. Wong-Tam, and the free speech advocates were able to successfully divert attention away from the real issue – anti-Israel hate in the parade – by pinning Pride's funding problems on a supposedly homophobic mayor. It was simplistic and ridiculous but it worked.

There was no doubt in my mind coming into 2012 that Ms. Wong-Tam was not prepared to allow the ban on QuAIA from participating in the parade to become a permanent ruling. She had too much invested in the group, and using Mr. Ford's snub of Pride as a basis, she wanted to be seen as the "progressive" (progressively Machiavellian, that is) voice on council. To this day, we are not sure where Ms. Wong-Tam's apparent antipathy toward Israel comes from. Born in Hong Kong, she was raised as a Buddhist and moved to Canada with her family at the age of three, settling in Regent Park. It became increasingly clear that she perceived those of us trying to fight QuAIA as the enemy. In early June 2012, Denise, attempting to do Martin a favour, arranged to drop off his second film – this one called *Why Is It Hate?* – to all city councillors. This film tried to illustrate the clear arguments made at City Hall by credible human rights groups and individuals showing why the messages and slogans of QuAIA were hateful and contrary to the city's own policies of tolerance and inclusion. Denise had become friends with Councillor Mike Del Grande through me, and with his kind permission, one of his assistants took her around to each councillor's office, including Ms. Wong-Tam's, where she was met with icy hostility. Ms. Wong-Tam must have let her pal at *Xtra*, Andrea Houston, know what was happening. Around 11:45 p.m. the night before we were due to catch an early flight to Vancouver, Ms. Houston called Denise for comment on whether she'd done the drop-off for me, claiming she was on deadline. Denise practically hung up on her, refusing to comment, and Ms. Houston's attempts to embarrass me by alleging that I was trying to lobby councillors through Denise (not true) never really got off the ground.

To add insult to injury, a woman by the name of Uzma Shakir, Toronto's new director of equity, diversity and human rights, was assigned by the city manager to revamp the city's anti-discrimination policy. After checking into her background, I discovered that Ms. Shakir had written several articles for rabble.ca, a virulently anti-Israel website that strongly supports Israeli Apartheid Week and the BDS movement. It was no surprise, given her apparent bias, that her report claimed the phrase *Israeli apartheid* did not violate the city's anti-discrimination policy. What happened next was entirely predictable. Once her secret was out, the city bureaucrats circled the wagons. Joe Pennachetti, the city manager, contended that Ms. Shakir was "very highly regarded" in the equity and human rights community. Then the cat-and-mouse game began. Martin said her report on the messages carried by QuAIA – he was far kinder than me in that I called it eight pages of drivel – had no human rights case law or authority behind it. He said by the standards of procedural fairness – which clearly don't exist at City Hall – the report should have been discredited and tossed out for its apparent bias. Believing she used her position to espouse her personal views, Martin and several others in the Jewish community filed detailed formal complaints about Ms. Shakir's apparent bias. The complaints were handed to her boss and the person who hired her, the very ambitious left-leaning (now retired) deputy city manager Brenda Patterson. I was never a fan of Ms. Patterson because I thought her one of those typical bureaucrats who was far more adept at doing what it took to survive and saying what was necessary to move up the ladder, than at actually doing her job competently. She had all the warmth of a block of ice. I remember practically chasing her into a washroom demanding to know whether Ms. Shakir had a conflict of interest. Ms. Patterson actually had the unmitigated gall to send Martin an e-mail in September 2012 indicating that Ms. Shakir did not pen the section of the city report that commented on whether the term *Israeli apartheid* is a violation of the city's anti-discrimination policy (even though Ms. Shakir's name is on the report). Then Ms. Patterson provided her ruling – that she found "no basis" for Martin's complaint against Ms. Shakir. Of course she didn't.

What this response told Martin was that City Hall was seriously broken and that personal agendas drove public policy, with few checks and balances. Ms. Shakir's report fit perfectly with the ideology of the left on council, their union supporters, and of course QuAIA, and so it suited them to embrace it. Other councillors simply did not have the depth to understand what QuAIA and their hate messenging meant for Pride and for gay Jews. And of course it came as absolutely no surprise that QuAIA was approved to march in the July 1 parade of 2012. Now councillors could hide behind Ms. Shakir's report and the sham of a dispute resolution panel set up by Rev. Hawkes to mediate any complaints.

The theme of the parade that year was "Celebrate and Demonstrate," which was why QuAIA was approved to march. No one saw it as ironic that their "demonstration" had absolutely nothing to do with gay rights, or that Israel is the only democracy in the Middle East that accepts homosexuality, has two gay pride parades (in Tel Aviv and Jerusalem), and grants asylum to many Arabs who can't be openly gay in their own countries. No one saw it as ludicrous that Israel was being singled out while no one "demonstrated" against the seventy-two countries in the world – including Egypt, where Mr. Greyson was held hostage for fifty days – where one can be imprisoned, tortured, or killed for being deemed homosexual. The farce continued when the so-called dispute resolution process cooked up by Rev. Hawkes and gay lawyer Doug Elliott, his partner in crime on the CAP, heard its first complaints just prior to the July 1 parade. B'nai Brith filed a complaint about QuAIA in good faith and found out pretty quickly they were wasting their time. To the surprise of Anita Bromberg, former national director of legal affairs

with the well-respected organization, one of the dispute resolution panel's allegedly unbiased arbitrators actually inter-
ceded during her testimony to present evidence as to why the
term *apartheid* could apply to Israel. Given our knowledge
of Ms. Bromberg's experience and those of others involved,
Mr. Elliott and Mr. Hawkes must have been delusional to
think Martin and I would be fooled by their kangaroo court.

By the spring of 2013, we were all growing weary of the
never-ending saga of QuAIA – even some councillors, like
James Pasternak, who'd been bravely behind efforts to get
the group out of the parade. Martin and I felt bruised and battered. Both of us had been repeatedly attacked personally in
Xtra, and labelled as members of the "Jewish lobby" and supporters of Rob Ford. Martin believes the intent was to make
what he was doing sound "nefarious and evil," even though
he was not associated with any organized community group.
Martin was speaking in his personal capacity as a gay man
worried about the anti-Semitism and hate that was infiltrat-
ing the parade. Even though he's gay, a devoted vegetarian,
an environmentalist, and a former Green Party member, he
was branded right-wing. The left-wing media and QuAIA
supporters attempted to denigrate my passion for Israel and
for doing what's right by labelling me a puppet of Rob Ford.
It didn't matter that I'd repeatedly criticized him for not supporting Pride events. Facts didn't matter, and that's what we
found so depressing.

Throughout this whole sad saga, I realized that those of us
fighting for the underdog – Israel – were also underdogs, even
though it should not have been that way. That didn't bother me,
and I know Martin felt the same way. What did incense me was
the tremendous hypocrisy of everyone who was either closely

allied with the QuAIA movement or had turned a blind eye to its hateful message. That hypocrisy came out loud and clear in early May 2014, when a cast of QuAIA enablers – Ms. Wong-Tam, Rev. Hawkes, Kevin Beaulieu (CEO of Pride), and TD Bank's Scott Mullin – spoke to the Empire Club about the impending WorldPride event in late June. I nearly choked as Mr. Beaulieu told the mostly gay and lesbian crowd and the requisite Pride supporters that the 2014 WorldPride event in Toronto would be the fourth that has occurred around the world as "part of a global movement" of LGBT folks seeking a strong identity. And where have the other three been held? Rome, London, and Jerusalem, Israel. Yes, WorldPride was held in Jerusalem in 2006. Beaulieu, forced to mention Jerusalem, tried to whisper it. But I heard him. I also heard him say the key aspect of WorldPride is "the struggle for human rights." Ms. Wong-Tam, without even considering the irony of her words, piped up that there are a lot of "countries where gays are persecuted and prosecuted" for what we are freely permitted to do in Toronto. I'm guessing she'd never admit that one of those areas is the Occupied Territories (Palestine), which QuAIA is so concerned to defend. Rev. Hawkes, promoting the human rights conference that would occur at WorldPride, told the Empire Club luncheon crowd that day that there are sixty-eight countries around the world where someone would be executed for being gay (the number is actually seventy-two) and that he hoped to use WorldPride to build a movement. He said they need to determine what is the "right way" to help countries like Uganda and Russia.

Then, after patting themselves on the back for all the wonderful human rights they would recognize at the fourth WorldPride event, following in the footsteps of Rome,

London, and Jerusalem, Mr. Beaulieu, Rev. Hawkes, and Ms. Wong-Tam very decisively deviated from what is normal practice at the Empire Club and refused to open up the floor to questions. I repeat, those very same people who advocated for QuAIA because of the group's supposed right to "free speech" chose not to take questions from the crowd because they knew they'd have to deal with questions about the presence of QuAIA at WorldPride. As for helping countries like Uganda and Russia, Rev. Hawkes might want to make a fresh start (now that QuAIA has disbanded) by speaking out against such countries for their lack of gay rights – after spending six long years pandering to a group that singled out Israel. That's what moral leaders are supposed to do.

CHAPTER TWELVE

Calling It as I See It

It began quite innocently on the night of October 22, 2012, when Denise and I decided to attend the last U.S. presidential debate being broadcast at an open-air theatre in Boca Raton, Florida.

The theatre at Mizner Park was just a few miles away from the security zone around Lynn University, where President Barack Obama and his opponent, Mitt Romney, were exchanging sharp words on foreign policy. I was particularly interested in hearing what Mr. Obama had to say about Israel, considering that during his first term he'd wasted no time visiting Turkey, Iraq, Saudi Arabia, and Egypt – all within six months of being sworn in. But not once during that term had he set foot in Israel. At the Summit of the Americas in Trinidad and Tobago, he warmly greeted Hugo Chavez – a notorious dictator and anti-Semite with strong ties to former Iranian president and despot Mahmoud Ahmadinejad. I'd hate to suggest that Mr. Obama gave a whole new meaning to that well-known expression adapted from the Book of Proverbs: "You are judged by the company you keep." But he certainly did.

I could not understand how the leader of the world's greatest superpower could pander to despots while treating the only real friend to America and the only democracy in the Middle East – Israel – like a reviled third cousin. Indeed, Obama showed his true colours in March 2010, when he endeavoured to publicly humiliate Israeli prime minister Benjamin "Bibi" Netanyahu during a White House visit. Leaving him to sit and stew with his aides, Mr. Obama told Mr. Netanyahu he was heading off to have dinner with his wife, Michelle, and his daughters. It was in this context that I wanted to see what Mr. Obama would have to say in the debate to convince America's liberal – and in my view, wilfully blind – Jewish community to return him to office.

I did not consider Mr. Obama a friend of Israel then, and he has done everything to convince me since that time that he's made a point of singling out Israel for alleged slights against its Arab neighbours. Still, I should not have taken my BlackBerry with me to the debate in Florida that night. What was I thinking? True to form, with the BlackBerry there and Twitter readily available, I couldn't sit silently without commenting as I listened to Mr. Obama, disingenuously, declare his devotion to the Jewish state. He wasn't just lying; he was insulting my, and the rest of the audience's, intelligence, even though he was just behaving like a typical politician, saying whatever needed to be said at the time to maintain Jewish support. "Obama says he will stand with Israel if attacked and they are a true friend. His nose is growing again. #MuslimBS," I tweeted. The tweet would have been absolutely fine if I had not added that hashtag. I don't know what possessed me to do so.

All I can say is that I should have anticipated it would be all the impetus my detractors on Twitter – and there are many – needed to attack me. And they certainly did, claiming I was suggesting Mr. Obama is a Muslim and calling me a "birther." At the time, I had no clue what the word *birther* meant. But I quickly learned that I was being likened to right-wing Tea Party wackos who believe Mr. Obama is not entitled to be president because he was not born in the United States. I didn't mean that at all. What I did mean by the hashtag was that I felt Obama, by his deeds and actions during his first term, had a soft spot for and an affiliation with Muslims. I also thought him narcissistic enough to believe that he, and he alone, without a shred of foreign policy experience before coming to the presidency, could actually sweet talk the dictators of the Arab world into making peace in the Middle East – ignoring, by design, the very fact that most of those countries will not rest until Israel is annihilated entirely. What was particularly disturbing to me was his speech in Cairo in 2009, in which he talked of a new beginning between the United States and Muslims around the world. It's not difficult to read between the lines.

Of course, none of these beliefs could be explained in a two-word hashtag or in a 140-word tweet. I opted not to delete the tweet that night, figuring I was damned if I did and damned if I didn't. Instead of endeavouring to explain my sentiments on Twitter, I angrily attacked my detractors. Twitter admittedly sometimes brings out the fighter in me. Things quickly escalated. The attacks on me continued throughout that night and for days. Unknown to me because

I was still in Florida and no one endeavoured to reach me for my side of the story, radio talk show hosts in Toronto, the *Huffington Post*, and other leftist online fringe news services and bloggers took turns taking shots at me. I made the wire services and CNN. My editor-in-chief at the time, James Wallace, was very understanding, notifying me in Florida that they intended to run a Twitter comment distancing themselves, understandably, from my inflammatory, politically incorrect tweet. When I returned to Toronto a few days later, I took the opportunity to explain what I meant on the radio during my stint with Talk 640's John Oakley. I said then, and I still believe more than ever, that Mr. Obama, while born in America, has very strong allegiances to Muslim culture and has deluded himself into thinking he can counteract Muslim extremism. I continue to believe he has no love for Israel and probably not for the Jews, especially given his attempts to interfere in the 2015 Israeli elections with the sole purpose of unseating Mr. Netanyahu. Thankfully, his efforts did not work. I'm sure he has never been above accepting campaign donations from anyone in the Jewish community who will cough them up, however. There are indeed still many liberal Jews in the United States who align themselves with the Obama camp.

To see evidence of Mr. Obama's stance, one has only to look at the influences on him and what he has done, or not done, since being re-elected to office in 2012. Barack Obama actually believes that the terrorist government in Iran will respect his calls to cut back on their nuclear program. They've done quite the opposite and I believe they will continue to do so, leaving Israel vulnerable to nuclear threats. The Iran nuclear deal has truly left Israel to defend itself. Photos of Mr. Obama on the phone trying to tell Vladimir Putin to get out of Crimea, or else he'll adopt some ridiculous weak-kneed sanctions, were laughable. Americans should be horrified at what a foreign relations joke their president has been. Yet while the world imploded around him in the spring of 2014, with the escalation of the civil war in Syria, Obama stepped up his rhetoric against Prime Minister Netanyahu and Israel. It was as if he alone had insights into how to craft a two-state solution when the only solution for the Palestinian terrorists and the Muslim Brotherhood was the absolute destruction of the Jewish state. To this day, I believe that while Twitter was not the right forum for expressing my opinion, I mouthed what so many others feel about Mr. Obama's ties to the Muslim world. What I became a victim of that October 2012 night was the absolute political correctness that comes into play when anyone dares question Muslims and the insidious ways the religious fanaticism of the extremists is being allowed to creep into and define our culture here in North America and in Western Europe.

But so what if Mr. Obama has Muslim sympathies or has had Muslim influences in his life? The question we should be asking is why he has gone out of his way to hide it so much. The reaction to my tweet showed me just how ready we Canadians are to bend over backwards at the mere mention of the "M" word and to attack anyone who dares question their politically correct view of Islamic extremism. The fact is, all of Mr. Obama's ties have shaped his view of foreign policy and the Jews, whether the liberal Jews or the so-called progressive media in the United States choose to turn a blind eye to it or not. It is my feeling that we are not doing ourselves a favour, here in Canada or in the United States, by simply accepting in the name of political correctness what the

Muslim community foists on us as our new Prime Minister Justin Trudeau seems bent on doing. We cannot ignore that what is happening in England and the terrible tragedy of November 2015 in France, along with the death and destruction in Belgium in early 2016, are warning signs, along with the parallel rise in anti-Semitism around the world, but particularly in Europe. Once the door is opened a crack, it is just a matter of time before Islamists start to impose their beliefs on our everyday lives in ways that are highly inappropriate. I'm afraid, in fact, that they already are. In the spring of 2014, a sign was posted in an east London park informing dog owners not to walk their dogs there anymore because it was an Islamic park and Muslims don't like dogs. I experienced something similar a few months before the Obama tweet incident. It could perhaps be considered a minor event in the grand scheme of things, but it is nevertheless very indicative of the hold Muslims have on us in Canada.

In the wee hours of the morning in July 2012, I arrived home from Florida with my dachshund, Kishka, in tow. Kishka, a cream-coloured dachsie with real attitude and, at eleven years old, more comfortable chasing squirrels than spending time with people, has several nicknames. The most politically incorrect one is "The Terrorist." He earned that name because when Denise and I met, Kishka decided he wasn't too happy to share me and proceeded to mark all of the Persian carpets in Denise's home and scratch up her leather couch. He also likes to tell everyone off who dares come to our home for having the nerve to invade his turf. A few years ago, I bought him a soft kennel on wheels that not only fits under the seat in front of me on the plane but makes it easier for me to transport him through customs and to the gate – given that he's a robust boy, earning him another three nicknames: "Kishka Craig" (à la Jenny Craig), "Shelley Winters," and "Boomba Butt." I came out of Pearson airport at 1:30 a.m. with Kishka in what we now jokingly call his "burka bag," looking for a limo to take us home. The bag is black, Kishka is totally covered, and only his eyes show through the black mesh. The limo driver started to load my luggage, the burka bag included, with Kishka fast asleep inside. The sudden movement made a startled Kishka pop his blond head out of his bag. Without missing a beat, the driver practically threw my luggage and Kishka back on my cart and waved me away with a decided, "No!" A second limo driver turned me down the moment I approached him, leaving me standing on the platform alone.

It didn't take me long, after I posted my plight on Facebook (I couldn't help myself), to realize I'd opened a real can of worms. My Facebook friends were not only upset that I was refused a ride at 1:30 a.m. but angry that drivers who were licensed to deal with the public were being permitted to pick and choose who they'd take (for reasons unbeknownst to me at that point). I was urged to do a column exposing what had happened and why. I soon discovered this wasn't an experience unique to me, and it was done for religious reasons. Muslims consider dogs unclean and believe that if they carry one in their cars, they must go home and shower afterward (before they pray). But the story got even better – or worse, depending on how one wants to look at it. The limo company that employed the drivers who turned me down passed the buck to the Greater Toronto Airports Authority (GTAA), saying they have to abide by that body's rules. I learned that the GTAA, which licenses the limos, has pandered to the drivers' religious demands, even though there is a limited pool of limos licensed to pick up passengers at the airport, and notwithstanding the fact that they are in a service job in Canada. Let's not forget either that dogs can't travel on an airplane without being housed in a soft kennel. So it's not as if Kishka himself would be sitting right on their seats or that he was some vicious breed that has a history of attacking cab drivers. He's Kishka, for heaven's sake: a little chubby, at that time of the morning very sleepy, and more often than not, afraid of his own shadow. But the GTAA told me the Muslim drivers – who, let's remember, are licensed to serve the public in the country of Canada, not in the Middle East – are "not required" to take passengers with animals, and if they do, they must give their vehicles a "full interior cleaning" after a ride to protect other passengers against dander and allergies. This was absolute hogwash. It sure sounded to me like a case of the tail wagging the dog, so to speak. These rules have been driven entirely by the religious demands of the Muslim drivers, proven all the more by the concerns addressed by the GTAA's Consultative Committee (*consultative* being the operative word) on Taxicabs and Limousines.

In recent years, that committee – stacked with drivers who are of Muslim and Hindu descent, which gives them strength in numbers – has focused on such issues as where to locate the Muslim prayer room in Pearson's Terminal 3 and whether special trailers should be set up in the winter months in the driver holding area for those who have to pray five times a day.

Many of the 750 limo drivers who are not licensed by the GTAA told me that the licensed drivers, the majority of them Muslims, get kid-glove treatment from the Airports Authority. Their compound has a full-service cafeteria, their own shower stall, a variety of washrooms, and special signage advising which flights have arrived. When I was taken by their compound, I noticed several GTAA drivers gathered under a shady overhang, some saying their prayers on mats while others played cards at bridge tables. By contrast, the unlicensed drivers – who must charge their fares an extra fifteen dollars simply for the privilege of picking them up – are expected to wait in a compound with no shade, two pop machines, and just two washroom stalls.

But here's the irony. The unlicensed drivers told me that despite the lack of a level playing field and the fact that they must charge fifteen dollars extra to pick up passengers at the airport, their business keeps increasing because passengers are not interested in feeding into the religious demands of the Muslim drivers and the nonsense I went through. After the stories of my experience appeared in the *Toronto Sun*, I discovered that passengers with dogs and alcohol are being turned away by Muslim drivers in Melbourne, Australia; in various parts of England; in select U.S. cities; and in Vancouver, Edmonton, and Calgary. In the spring of 2014, about two dozen Muslim cabbies in Cleveland, Ohio, refused to drive cars with advertising for the Gay Games atop them. I would have fired them all.

It is happening in the Toronto taxi industry too. Gail Beck-Souter, president of Beck Taxi, was forthright enough to tell me that a certain number of the drivers who operate the company's nine-hundred-car fleet refuse to take dogs in them. She told me that some drivers use allergies to dogs as an excuse, when she knows their concerns are really religious. While the company's owners don't like it, Ms. Beck-Souter says they do give drivers the option of not carrying a dog. I can understand Ms. Beck-Souter not wanting to stir up trouble with the drivers when every other company is pandering to their demands. Still, no one is asking these drivers to take Kishka or any other dog home and live with them (although that might change their minds about man's best friend).

Look, I realize that whether or not Muslim cab drivers refuse fares who have dogs with them is not on the same level of importance as world poverty (and I haven't been refused since I broke the story), but the very theme of it is right up my alley: weak-kneed officials and the politicians who oversee them (in this case those affiliated with the GTAA or the bureaucrats with municipal licensing who oversee Toronto cabbies) pandering to special interest groups in an attempt not to offend anyone, rather than protecting our rights and freedoms. It's a slippery bloody slope. Another example of this was the leftist councillors' strong showing of support for Toronto District School Board trustee Ausma Malik, a Muslim woman who wears a hijab and who was elected in the fall of 2014 to represent a very left-wing downtown Toronto ward. I couldn't care less whether Ms. Malik wears a head scarf. That is her right. What I did care about, and what I exposed in the fall of 2014, were her nefarious ties to Hezbollah. During the heat of the fighting between Israel and Hezbollah forces in Lebanon in July 2006, Ms. Malik was a keynote speaker at a peace rally denouncing both the conflict and Prime Minister Stephen Harper's support of Israel's right to defend itself against Hezbollah's missile fire. Standing outside the U.S. consulate beside Ali Mallah – a well-known pro-Palestinian, pro-Hamas activist – Ms. Malik characterized Israel's actions as "state-sanctioned murder." She also rebuked Mr. Harper, calling on him to "get a backbone" while those around her – sporting Lebanese flags and the yellow flag of the Hezbollah terrorist movement – chanted "shame" and jeered jubilantly when word came down that Hezbollah had killed another twenty-two Israeli Defense Forces soldiers. When I contacted her for comment, she did not deny her involvement in the 2006 rally or what she'd said, claiming at the same time that she does not "support anti-Semitism in any form." While participating in a report on the needs of Muslim students – one sponsored by the left-wing Canadian Federation of Students – Ms. Malik suggested she'd be much happier if Sharia law was brought into Ontario classrooms. What was concerning to me about her candidacy – besides the long list of leftist councillors who endorsed her, including QuAIA's founder Kristyn Wong-Tam, Mike Layton, and Joe Cressy – was the potential for her radical political views to make it into the school curriculum or into school policy. But the more I and one of her opponents, who happened to be Jewish, pointed out her questionable ties, the more her politically correct supporters circled the wagons, characterizing her as a victim of racism and Islamophobia. Literature was circulated in the ward highlighting her questionable background at around the same time, unfortunately, that reservist Nathan Cirillo was tragically shot and killed on Parliament Hill by a radicalized thirty-two-year-old Muslim man. The shooting occurred just five days before the municipal election and that's all Ms. Malik and her leftist supporters needed. While emotions were running high about an extremist killing a soldier in broad daylight, Ms. Malik and her leftist supporters were successfully able to plant the seeds of racism in voters' minds by claiming she was only being targeted for being Muslim as well. I've got to hand it to the leftist contingent. They played the situation with skill. Mr. Cressy even went on TV to ensure that everyone knew how terribly Ms. Malik was being treated by alleged Islamophobes. She won the election handily and I was accused of being an Islamophobe for weeks afterward. So this is what happens in Toronto when one merely tries to suggest that a Muslim with a highly questionable past might not be a suitable choice to determine policy or to set an example for schoolkids at Canada's largest school board.

In 2010, Denise and I travelled to Morocco as part of her fiftieth birthday trip that started in Spain. It was a feast for our senses but also clearly a country where all manner of dress was accepted for women. We met ladies dressed in Western garb, others wearing the hijab, and still others outfitted in the full burka or niqab. I'll never forget the day we sat in a taxi in Marrakech and, when I looked behind us, seeing a woman driving a car dressed in a full brown burka with glasses perched atop the only part of her showing – her eyes. I wondered, laughing, how that garb would affect her peripheral vision. But the point was, we fully expected to see women dressed like that in Morocco. But imagine my surprise when, upon returning to Canada, I saw a woman dressed in a full brown burka walking near the Eaton Centre, a couple of paces behind her husband. I have seen this all too many times since, more recently while jogging up Yonge Street and while conducting an interview with a female resident of Toronto Community Housing Corporation. When the woman took me up to her laundry room to show me some desperately needed repairs, there was another woman in there in full burka doing her laundry. I have to concede I found it creepy for more than one reason. For one thing, this woman is availing herself of the largesse of the Canadian taxpayer if she is living in social housing. But clearly she has no intention of assimilating to our culture. There is something dreadfully wrong with that picture.

I am certainly not talking about women wearing the hijab. To me that is no different than Orthodox Jewish women wearing shaytels (wigs) or Jewish men wearing black hats out of respect for the Lord. I'm talking about women wearing a full burka and walking a safe distance behind their men, or hiding everything but their eyes in a black tent. It makes a mockery of democracy in this country and of presumably the reason they came to Canada in the first place – for a better life. As women, we have fought for equality in the workplace and at home. It wasn't too long ago – less than twenty years ago – that I experienced sexism in my own place of employment. As a lesbian who wrestled with her own identity and lived in a closeted relationship for twenty years, I am incensed that we are so willing to accept a religious custom that harkens back to the Dark Ages and condones the near-abusive practices of patriarchal and oppressive fundamentalism. Dress it up any way you want, but that's what it is.

The ultimate in pandering to these archaic Muslim laws occurs at Canada Customs, where Muslim women in full burkas are allowed to breeze through customs clearance and security checks without once showing their faces. It is beyond ludicrous, but few will speak up about it, particularly our politicians. Yet it is perfectly acceptable in our crazy, upside down, politically correct country to treat the average non-Muslim traveller with absolute disdain while he or she is crossing the border. I have lost count how many times, en route to my second home in Florida, I've been subjected to aggressive questioning, bordering on bullying, from U.S. Customs officers who have accused me of everything from working in the States (even when I've shown them my latest *Toronto Sun* column) to having dog biscuits and carrots – allegedly a no-no – to feed Kishka on the plane. And that's after going through three months of screening to acquire a Trusted Traveller Nexus card. At security, we are asked to remove our shoes, belts, and jewellery, and each time I go through with Kishka in my arms, my palms are swabbed to ensure there is no harmful residue on them. While necessary, Denise and I find the whole customs/security exercise not just wearying but tremendously selective as to who is targeted.

Yet, I repeat, a woman in a full burka is often permitted to breeze through without question and without showing her face. If we are all to be treated equally, all of these women should be required to disrobe and show their faces in a special room staffed by a female customs or security agent, so we would actually know who was travelling with a corresponding passport. Or their irises could be scanned by the same machine that does ours when we go through customs with our Nexus cards. Yet by all accounts, it's hit and miss whether they are required to be checked. This has to be one of the worst cases of political correctness gone mad. I might add that it is also the custom in Ontario elections not to ask fully veiled women to show their faces before they vote. Yet I can't go into any poll and exercise my right to vote as a Canadian and Ontario citizen without first showing ID. Women in full burkas are also not required to show their faces when testifying in Ontario's courtrooms.

The best example of political correctness and pandering to extremist Muslims gone mad is the whole kerfuffle over Prime Minister Steven Harper's attempts to force an extremist Muslim woman to take off her niqab while swearing in as a Canadian citizen. Seems like a simple request, right? But in our topsy-turvy country – where pragmatism often gets thrown out the window whenever political correctness is involved – a three-judge appeal panel of the Federal Court declared in mid-September 2015 that the woman in question, Zunera Ishaq, had every right to stay hidden inside her mobile tent and not reveal her identity while engaged in a ceremony to become a citizen of a country that celebrates democratic rights and freedoms, not Third World archaic views. And many prominent feminists thought that was just fine. Clearly the desire to undermine a Conservative government and a stance that makes perfect sense trumped what should have been a strong voice against an oppressive practice. This is where the feminist movement loses me. It just makes absolutely no sense to support this archaic view of women, but Canada's bleeding hearts are adept at turning reason into ridiculousness. They repeatedly fail or choose not to see the long-term implications of allowing the door to open a little wider with each attempt of Muslim extremists to ram their religious views down our throats.

In the newly revitalized Regent Park in downtown Toronto, the publicly funded aquatic centre provides women-only swim times three times a week, which allow Muslim women to use the pool without being subject to men looking in or attending. I went one Saturday evening to see for myself what was provided and who attended. A drape was pulled across the whole glassed-in exterior of the building to guard the women from public view. As much as I went wanting to believe that this was yet another example of giving selective treatment to Muslims, I was shocked to see the pool completely full of women – some dressed in bathing gear, others in gym outfits covering their arms and legs. But they all looked happy and free – free of their mobile tents and free of the men and a culture that keeps them hidden. I saw the hour made available to them twice or three times a week as a welcome reprieve from what I consider an extremely oppressive and repressive life.

That is, of course, unless you believe a 2013 study by the Canadian Council of Muslim Women (CCMW) – funded to the tune of $191,000 by the Ontario Trillium Foundation – that suggests the women they surveyed enjoy being slaves to this archaic custom. In yet another example of political correctness, officials at the CCMW decided they needed to justify why some women have chosen to wear the niqab. This was prompted, they say, because they'd received many calls over the years from the public and the media asking why women living in Canada fully cover their faces (as if they were living in the Middle East), and they had no answer to give. Oh my. So they spent nearly $200,000 of taxpayer money speaking to and surveying eighty-one mostly Ontario women – or about $2,500 per member of their ridiculously small sample – who are "actively wearing" the niqab. Seeing as they chose not to speak to women who have actively forsaken the niqab, we can pretty well guess what their study would find.

And indeed it did. When they presented their report in February 2014 in front of a mosque in Guelph, the CCMW had six happy women there wearing their niqabs "by their own free will." The council acknowledges in the executive summary of their study findings that the practice of covering a women's body and hair and leaving only the eyes visible with a niqab has often been "problematized as symbol of

Islamic extremism, women's oppression and lastly the failure of Muslims to integrate." You think?

The findings were a mass of contradictions. While most of the eighty-one niqab-wearing women who responded to the study possessed a "high level of education" and worked in a range of fields, most did not believe in dating and found homosexuality an unacceptable practice. And get this: most of those who chose to continue wearing the niqab after arriving in Canada did not do so because their husbands said they had to. In fact, many of the women claimed they faced opposition from their spouses to the idea. According to the findings, most of the participants expressed a "strong affinity" to Canada, praising its multiculturalism and its "freedom and life changing opportunities." I repeat. They praised the freedom and life-changing opportunities they have in Canadian democracy, *but* they continue to hide their identities in a mobile tent, as if they should be ashamed of who they are. You've got to ask yourself what kind of pressure is felt by daughters born in Canada to mothers who still wear the niqab. Do they turn against their mothers' strong beliefs carried over from the old country or do they feel ostracized among their peer group, or at school? How many stories do we hear of girls who leave their homes in the morning dressed in a head scarf and, just before they arrive at school, change into typical Western dress just to fit in with this new world of freedom and democracy?

CCMW officials say they hope to expand the survey – with the help of public funding, of course – to include other niqab wearers who don't speak English, don't have access to the Internet, or live in rural communities. I can hardly wait. I only hope that the CCMW sees fit, considering they are using public money, to speak to those who have decided to assimilate into this country, come into the twenty-first century and have ditched the niqab. After all, if the eighty-one participants in this first study mean what they say about coming here for freedom and life-changing opportunities, then I would think the first act of freedom would be to cast aside the shackles that have kept them bound to eras gone by. That means facing the realities of their new chosen home. Now if we could just get our public policy-makers, our politicians, and the media not to be held ransom by this religious extremism in the name of political correctness. All it takes is a few people to speak up about the Muslim limo drivers trying to ban my little dachsie "terrorist" to expose the ridiculous demands of a group imposing their archaic religious customs on a country that is supposed be a democracy. No one forced them to come and live in a country with twenty-first century values. Our society should not be expected to change to accommodate their beliefs. If they don't like the way things are in Canada, they have an alternative.

CHAPTER THIRTEEN

Manufacturing Outrage

Nothing is cuter to Denise and me than our three dachshunds – Kishka, Flora, and our adoptee, a sweet rescue we've named Fritzy – running side by side on their short little legs, their furry little bodies pressed together on a walk in our midtown Toronto neighbourhood. They form their own little pack, although Flora, being female, dominant, tinier, and extremely athletic, usually takes the lead, and Kishka, being lazy and chubby, always struggles to keep up. Reminds me of how my fellow journalists at City Hall chased after Mayor Rob Ford, their bodies pressed up to each other moving in a synchronized pack, almost from the moment he came to office. They prowled the halls outside the mayor's office hoping to sniff out any councillor who was eager to disparage the mayor on camera or in print. They never had to look far. There were always the yappy, self-serving, attention-seeking councillors – Shelley Carroll, Joe Mihevc, Josh Matlow, and Adam Vaughan, to name just a few – positively panting at the idea of giving a nasty sound bite. In contrast to my gorgeous, sweet, and always loyal pack of long-haired dachsies, there was never anything cute about this media pack, who as time went on became increasingly dogged about one thing only: dishing the latest dirt on Rob Ford, even if it meant stalking his family at his home or the family cottage. The usual boundaries were maintained for most politicians, particularly those on the political left, but any and all sense of propriety was thrown out the window once Mr. Ford's troubles started coming to light.

To be honest, the pack journalism didn't begin with the most controversial and highly troubled mayor Toronto has ever seen. My media colleagues at City Hall made it quite clear by their actions long before Rob Ford came on the scene as mayor that many of them did not have an interest in sinking their teeth into any complex issue. They preferred to cover the sideshow, the day-to-day dose of political "he said, she said" and anything that would require only minimal effort to produce a story. The more stories and story material they could be spoon-fed, the better. Reading meeting agendas from beginning to end was far too taxing. Attending council and committee meetings proved far easier if they could find the requisite number of councillors and professional protesters to manufacture outrage. Outrage certainly played better on TV and to an audience that often suffers from attention deficit disorder. These colleagues were largely what I now call repeaters, not reporters. What I found particularly disconcerting during my fifteen years in the press gallery at City Hall was how their tongues would wag continuously – forever gossiping, checking out what each other was doing, and sharing information that would help each of them cobble together what they regularly and shamelessly decided by consensus would be the story or stories of the day. Many times at council, I wondered if they were as attention-challenged as the politicians they covered, seeing as they talked with each other and councillors so much they couldn't possibly be following the proceedings. Now, to be fair, often in council meetings councillors rarely added anything new to the discussion. They just enjoyed hearing the sound of their own voices. Still, I never got tired of hearing their political rhetoric because I felt it defined what they were all about.

The media pack mentality at City Hall bothered me so much that I made a conscious decision to keep to myself and do my own thing pretty much throughout my fifteen years there. As the unofficial opposition during the Miller years, I produced some of my best critical opinion pieces and repeatedly broke stories and scooped the competition. I really had to dig to get whatever I got, but there were stories galore if one just searched for them. I read city reports, pursued tips, answered e-mails, and talked to anyone and everyone at City Hall, including the security guards. I regularly had coffee with my trusted clerk friends to keep up on the latest scuttlebutt. I didn't mind the challenge. After all, when I got into the business – almost ten years later in life than most of my media colleagues – I was naive enough to think it was my job to compete with Toronto's other mainstream media for the best stories on any subject.

It *was* very much like that in my early days at the *Toronto Sun*. I still remember one of my first assignments, when I'd finally convinced editor-in-chief Les Pyette to hire me as a general assignment reporter in late 1989, after an eleven-year career in corporate communications. A couple of young people had been snowmobiling on thin ice on a lake north of Oshawa and had gone through, dying instantly. I was assigned to do the "pickup," as we called it then – to get words and, hopefully, pictures of the deceased from their shell-shocked families. It was the least favourite assignment, and since I was the newbie in the newsroom, it was handed to me.

It was made clear that I was in a race with the *Toronto Star*, whose editors had the flexibility to assign a couple of reporters to be the first on the scene to get the same pictures and words from the bereaved families. I had a heck of a time when I got to the first family's home. But I managed to talk my way into the house and get a good story, even though the family refused to provide a picture of their deceased loved one. At the second family's home, they practically shut the door on my foot. When I returned to the newsroom without any photos, my editors put one of my more seasoned colleagues on the story to "bat clean-up." It was reassuring to later find out he wasn't any more successful than me. But there was tremendous pressure back then to beat the *Toronto Star* and other media outlets on stories like these and to hopefully not end up reading a story we'd missed on the front page of the competition. The race to be first was very real in those days.

To be fair, the way we report has changed a tremendous amount in the twenty-six years I've been in the business. The Internet and social media have had the greatest impact on those of us who have made print journalism the mainstay of our careers. When I started at the *Toronto Sun* in 1989, there was no such thing as social media, and our deadlines were geared toward getting a morning print edition off the floor by midnight. We actually had three editions in those days and something called "re-plate," which allowed us to insert a late-breaking story at 2 a.m. Cost-cutting and the Internet have put an end to that. Although our Canoe.ca website has been up and running since 1996, I don't really remember having to adjust to online deadlines until about five years ago. Somewhere around 2006, we started doing videos with a vengeance. These videos were used to accompany our stories online. In fact, one of my first was of Denise, when I wrote a column about her troubles with City Hall in July 2006. When I ran for MPP in August 2009, I was introduced to Twitter and Facebook for the first time. Before I knew it, our jobs and deadlines had changed, re-plate was long gone, our newsroom had shrunk considerably due to a series of layoffs, and the demands on our time had increased exponentially. Researching and reporting a story or writing a column is not enough anymore. There is constant pressure throughout the day – more on reporters than on columnists – to do web hits for the *Sun* online site and to be the first to break a story on the web. Often when I conduct an interview with a photographer, I am required to do video hits. Attending a press scrum, conference, or meeting and simply taking notes is a thing of the past as well. We are encouraged to give a running commentary on Twitter – so much so that it is not uncommon to see the heads of journalists focused more on their smartphones than on the subject at hand. As much as I use social media, I believe the immediacy of the Internet has not been good for journalism. It's not just that there are countless bloggers and amateur news gatherers masquerading as journalists. It has also affected how we actually focus on the story. Instead of really working a story, many journalists – and I certainly can't completely exempt myself from this – due to the demands placed on them, are more intent on delivering a steady stream of online commentary, mostly on Twitter. Their attention in scrums and at press events is often divided. As good as one may be at multi-tasking, it is impossible to tweet regularly and really concentrate on what is unfolding at a meeting or ask follow-up questions in scrums. Too often, sloppy reporting shows the superficiality of the media focus. The ability to remain anonymous on Twitter has led to a certain aggressiveness online as well. As Rob Ford found out many times – the hard way – the advent of sophisticated cellphone cameras has created a "gotcha" kind of journalism in which no one is immune from scrutiny, even when individuals are out in public on their own time. Again, I confess I've caught more than one picture of city workers asleep in their trucks or four standing around and observing while one works, and then posted the pictures on Twitter. It's just too tempting. If he were still alive today, my journalism law and ethics professor from my Carleton days, Wilf Kesterton – an honourable and well-respected man – would be shaking his head in disgust (and at me as well) at how often the lines of professionalism and common courtesy are crossed in the name of getting a story.

Even e-mail has had both its negative and positive points. I welcomed it initially because it allowed readers or contacts to e-mail me with story ideas, instead of spending considerable time on the phone. I am able to easily weed out what is a potential story and set up interviews by e-mail, saving valuable time needed for research. But it has also been problematic, and more often than not frustrating, for an investigative reporter like me, who is seasoned at follow-up questions and digging out valuable information in a telephone or face-to-face interview. A telephone or in-person interview provides context and a window into a subject's tone and speech patterns, and allows me to better judge whether my interviewees are telling the truth or not. Kathleen Wynne's Liberals are absolutely adept at manipulating the message by choosing only to respond via e-mail – so they can contain and spin the information and address only the questions they select. I can count on the fingers of one hand the number of times during my six months at Queen's Park, and since then in my new investigative role, I've been given direct access to a cabinet minister or a senior official to grill by phone or in person. The Liberals know what they are doing. They didn't and don't want to lose control of the message by submitting to phone or face-to-face interviews. Not only that, but initially, at least, they would more often than not deliver the answers just before what they thought was my deadline, making it impossible time-wise for me to respond with follow-up questions. Soon, I started to try to trick them at their own game by telling them my deadline was much earlier than it was, even by a day, and I continue to do that.

My *Sun* editor and friend, Zen Ruryk, often jokes that in our business, reporters and editors have their own form of attention deficit disorder – namely that we are easily distracted by the latest "shiny penny" that is tossed our way. The Liberals are skilled at taking advantage of that disposition. The situation with the discovery of the gas plant e-mails is a perfect example. When in September 2012 the gas plant scandal was heating up, Neala Barton – then media relations director in Premier McGuinty's office – decided to try to change the channel (and distract journalists from the gas plant issue) by proposing that the premier have a press conference to voice sudden support for a private member's bill banning the use of tanning beds by Ontario youth under eighteen. Barton even mused, in an e-mail obtained as part of the gas plant document dump, that the tanning bed story is "really good" and would "make a fabulous headline in Saturday's papers." And so they trotted out cancer survivors and announced the legislation to grand applause at Sunnybrook's cancer centre. Then nothing happened with the bill, mostly because Mr. McGuinty prorogued the legislature the next month. The following March, after Kathleen Wynne became leader, health minister Deb Matthews held her own photo opportunity at Princess Margaret Hospital with more cancer survivors to resurrect the legislation. Again nothing happened, until my uncle, Jeff Lyons (who was involved with the Melanoma Network of Canada as a survivor himself), brought the issue to my attention and I did a column attempting to embarrass the Liberals about dragging out cancer patients for their "political gain." I was very pleased, as was Jeff, when the Skin Cancer Prevention Act passed less than two months later. This time, the Liberals got caught at their own game.

Sadly, however, the Liberal style of avoidance – or shall we say their ability to adeptly massage the message – has trickled down to many government departments and agencies now, including those at Toronto City Hall, where a phalanx of communications flacks control the information flow. The Pan Am people used it continuously. I was only granted one sit-down interview with former TO2015 CEO Saad Rafi – never to be invited again after I asked him hard questions. In the summer of 2015, when I attempted to approach Pamela Spencer, the former general counsel for Toronto Community Housing Corporation, to ask her a question directly, one of the housing authority's PR agents tried to push me away. I was at a press conference, I saw her there, and since I was writing about a consultant study she'd allowed to go over budget, it made perfect sense to try to catch her for comment when I saw her. But Ms. Spencer refused to answer any of my questions, tried to bully me for approaching her directly, and insisted I send her an e-mail with my questions (so she could spin the answers the way she saw fit).

Despite the many changes in my profession and the pressures on us to be multi-media journalists, I experienced a rude awakening when I first got to City Hall in 1998. The pack journalism was so pervasive that I quickly got labelled as the outsider because of my less than popular views on so many subjects. I often likened myself to a salmon endeavouring to swim upstream. On the flipside, these are the very aspects of my writing that my readers can't get enough of and that I've built my reputation on. Former *Globe and Mail* city columnist John Barber took an instant dislike to me, not just because of my politics but because I happened to be Jeff Lyons's niece. Jeff, a well-known lobbyist, was tight with the Mel Lastman regime – a connection of mine that I never hid. There were whispers of nepotism since Jeff's friend Paul Godfrey was our publisher at the time (and, with the Postmedia takeover of Sun Media in April of 2015, is once again in charge). I'm not sure whether that rumour was started by Mr. Barber or by former Sun Media journalist Don Wanagas, who thought he'd be a shoo-in for the *Sun*'s City Hall columnist job. This wouldn't be the first time in my career that an issue was created from nothing. In any event, Mr. Barber had a mad-on for Jeff, as he did for all those he perceived to be the "enemy," and particularly those he considered behind-the-scenes dealmakers. While an excellent writer, he was a bitter and often angry man, who would savagely attack politicians who didn't agree with his world view, without ever getting their side of the story. I never understood how he got away with it. He seemed to forever get a free ride either because politicians were afraid of him or because he worked for a left-of-centre newspaper where his then wife held a senior position. Just saying.

Everyone gave Mr. Barber the kid-glove treatment, the City Hall security and my press gallery colleagues included. I will never forget the day in 2002 when he urinated in a press gallery plant to a captive audience of cheering media colleagues. His intent was to mock Rob Ford, who mere hours before had begged his fellow councillors to get rid of plant-watering services to save seventy-eight thousand dollars in that year's budget – a plea to pinch pennies that was met with scorn and much derision by council and Mayor Lastman. The media in the press gallery stood howling over Mr. Barber's puerile stunt like the "cool kids" at high school, enjoying a good laugh at Mr. Ford's expense. Not one of them dared to suggest that Mr. Barber's behaviour was classless, unprofessional, and downright disgusting – or, heaven forbid, that Mr. Ford might have had a point. The culture of entitlement was so ingrained at City Hall that most of my media colleagues saw nothing wrong with the perks of office or with Mr. Barber's stunt. But Mr. Barber's most infamous moment came in 2004, when, in the heat of a scrum at council, he was, shall we say, pissed off with the answers councillors Case Ootes and Rob Ford gave him. In a fit of pique, Mr. Barber mouthed the slur "fat fuck" at then councillor Ford. It wasn't actually the first time he'd used the "f" word in front of the media and politicians. In November of 2002, after arbitrator Tim Armstrong delivered his ruling on the CUPE union contract, Mr. Barber got incensed when then deputy mayor Ootes and Mayor Lastman contended that the arbitrator had allowed the union to continue with their generous "jobs for life" clause. For some reason, he didn't like Mr. Lastman and Mr. Ootes using the term "jobs for life," even though that described the union clause perfectly, considering it referred to the fact that no CUPE jobs could be contracted out after ten years of service. That term had certainly resonated with the public. Mr. Barber's classless 2004 "fat fuck" lip-sync was captured in a YouTube video that made the rounds for years. Again, he got off easy – no doubt because he was a *Globe and Mail* columnist attacking two right-wing councillors. The security staff didn't even intervene in what was a very public scene. Yet a few years later, during the David Miller era, I was "written up" and a letter sent to my editor for having had the gall to get upset with a security guard who gave me a hard time for wanting to get into my office on Remembrance Day (a day off for City Hall staffers but not for us). I can only imagine how I would have been treated had I made the same very public remarks as Mr. Barber did to any of the more portly members of council. That double standard was always prevalent throughout my years as an outspoken right-wing columnist, and I forever felt I had to be doubly careful about what I did – even to the point of not eating or drinking anything when I attended public events – for fear it would be reported by a media or political detractor.

The CBC used to regularly ask me on air to fulfill their small right-wing quota – particularly during the Lastman, Miller, and Ford eras – and I rarely turned them down when asked, even though I knew full well I could count on getting more than a few angry e-mails afterward from the usual suspects. At least the CBC made an effort to appear balanced. Canada's National Newspaper Awards (NNA) and the Ontario Press Council have never even made a pretence of being inclusive. This is by no means sour grapes. It is merely a statement of reality. As a columnist and investigative journalist for the *Toronto Sun*, who has scooped the competition many times over the years, I always knew it was a waste of my time to even put in for an NNA. We would never be nominated by the media snobs/elitists who sit on the judging panels in any of the "serious" news categories, regardless of the impact or fallout of our stories. I was talked into entering my investigative stories on spending abuses by executives with Toronto's Pan Am Games in the fall of 2013 – a series that every media outlet followed for days, which caused Premier Kathleen Wynne to be put on the hot seat in the legislature more than once, led to policy changes, and caused the firing of three senior brass with TO2015, including CEO Ian Troop. I set the agenda on that story for months. Yet I didn't even get nominated in the investigative category. As for the Press Council, after several biased rulings against the *Toronto Sun* – including one ridiculous decision when the firefighters complained about a story I broke on their secret pay hike in 2007 – I was so glad when Sun Media later pulled out of the organization in protest.

I regularly attended press scrums during the Lastman, Miller, and Ford years, feeling it was my job – all the more as a columnist – to be scrappy, to ask tough questions, and to try to set the agenda. But as time went on, I found myself growing more and more exasperated at these press opportunities.

While the press were all perfectly adept at being aggressive, bordering on vicious, with Rob Ford (no doubt because there was safety in numbers), few of them had the balls to ask the really tough questions of any other politician, or to look at any issue beyond the very superficial. Little wonder the bureaucrats and politicians felt no pressure to clean up their act. It wasn't that I minded being in the lonely position of asking tough questions, but I truly felt the public was and still is being short-changed by this kind of selective journalism.

Still, the scrums were always an excellent insight into the characters of each of my media colleagues and how they approached their jobs. Long-time *Toronto Star* city columnist Royson James, a smug, self-righteous, and lazy man, would stand just outside the pack, smirking haughtily at the media gathered and leaning in only when he might want to hear an answer or two to a question someone else had asked. Having been a city columnist since the Stone Age, he was too taken with his own importance to ask his own questions and preferred to scribble a few notes instead of using a tape recorder – the odd time he actually showed up to meetings or scrums, that is. Getting down and dirty was not for Royson – nor was hard work, for that matter. There were also the various cameramen who would aggressively push the print reporters aside to get the same shot over and over and over again from the same angle. When Adam Vaughan was still trying to get the world to notice him as a journalist for CP24, he'd ask the most ridiculous questions in an effort to appear as if he had some sort of exclusive angle. He never did. He just wanted – no, demanded – attention like a spoiled child. Most times, he was nothing more than a mediocre reporter trying to throw his weight around or appear more intelligent than he really was. I shared an office with his late father, Colin, during my first year at City Hall and found that Adam had none of the charm or the news savvy of his dad. He actually had, and has, an extremely nasty and humourless side to him. In 1999, while at CBC, he was overheard in city council gossiping about Marilyn Lastman's depression and the fact that she'd shoplifted a pair of Jones New York pants from Eaton's at the Promenade Mall a few weeks before. Some even suggested he'd leaked the story to the now available only online – but in its heyday, extremely cheeky – *Frank* magazine, something that would not surprise me. Mr. Lastman was so incensed with Mr. Vaughan's behaviour, he threatened to kill him, and justifiably so.

There were and still are the Barbies/talking heads from the all-day news channels, both female and male, who'd ask the most vacuous or silly "soft ball" questions, having done no homework before turning up at City Hall. They'd regularly do their "segment" purring into the camera, a good number of their facts wrong. But they looked good or filled the station's diversity quota and that was all that mattered. It was not news, it was info-tainment, and unfortunately it's only getting worse. When the Rob Ford soap opera reached crisis proportions, one was forced to listen to the news channels repeat their vacuous musings over and over again. There was always the long-time general news reporter from the TV station who was so taken with his own importance, he'd launch into some long-winded question merely to hear the sound of his own voice. By the time he was done, none of us were really sure of the question, let alone the answer. There were the members of the fringe (leftist) media – the bloggers and the Twitter crowd – who hung around the scrums mostly for the gossip factor. They seemed to produce noth-ing more than predictable, often slanderous attacks on Ford, fawning comments about David Miller, and personal digs at journalists – me included – who dared call them out for their behaviour. As time went on during the Rob Ford years, Twitter and obscure blogs were such hacks' preferred mode of communication, where they knew they'd find themselves in like-minded company and could get away with very nasty comments that would never be published in the mainstream media. Now don't get me wrong. I loved being part of the action at City Hall, no matter how down and dirty and per-sonal my colleagues could get, but there's only so much of that you can take. Notwithstanding my political leanings, I always laboured to get both sides of the story, even when I was well aware that the subjects of my stories would likely not give me the privilege of a response. As the years went by, the list got longer and longer – a list I wore like a badge of hon-our – of councillors who refused to talk to me, blocked me on Twitter, and would brag about it: Kyle Rae, Howard Moscoe, Janet Davis, Paula Fletcher, Shelley Carroll, Maria Augimeri, Kristyn Wong-Tam, Pam McConnell etc. They called me "mean," as if we were all in high school and it was a popular-ity contest. Didn't I know the drill? No matter what, I'd phone and e-mail them two, three, and four times for comment. If they chose to ignore me, that was their decision. Their delib-erate silence regularly got mentioned in my column.

When I was asked to come back to the *Toronto Sun* head-quarters to take on the challenge of investigative reporting in early 2014 – after nearly sixteen years at City Hall and Queen's Park – I wasn't at all thrilled about having to give up the sometimes daily or at least four-times weekly connection

I had with my readers as a columnist, not to mention my ongoing efforts to poke politicians, especially those who refused to talk to me. I absolutely loved being controversial and, even more, I loved getting feedback, both positive and negative. However, as a columnist, with the daily demands on me to follow the news, I did not have much time to investigate issues that came to my attention, as much as I tried. The only times in my career that I'd truly been able to dig into a story were in 2002 and 2012, when I was given a few weeks off to take a look at the homelessness situation in Toronto and to investigate who had bought into the newly revitalized Regent Park. Both efforts earned me awards for investigative reporting from Sun Media. I soon realized this was a great opportunity and a luxury very few in any media have, particularly the print media – either due to the lack of editorial resources or lack of space. A job that involved creating news and stirring up the dirt, rather than following the news, after twenty-five years of covering the education and political beats and being privy to so much mismanagement wherever I turned, was made for me. If I truly wanted to champion the rights of the underdog, to change policy, to set the agenda, and to expose waste and corruption, I needed the time to follow leads and do intense research using the many contacts I'd built up over the years. I've realized in the two years I've been involved in the investigative beat – as the story tips and the requests for assistance from those who don't have a voice pour in every day – that this kind of journalism is needed now more than ever.

The Wynne government and the McGuinty government before it, sadly, have set the bar so low as far as transparency, accountability, and fair play are concerned that many in the public have lost hope that their politicians are in it for the right reasons and can be counted on to do the right thing. Never mind even listening to what their constituents want. That should be a given, but it happens less often than we care to imagine. What I'm talking about is the lowering of all standards when it comes to being ethical and trustworthy. Public trust in what were once sacred institutions is at an all-time low. No wonder. How the heck can the public trust a premier who managed to walk away with no apparent remorse from the Sudbury election scandal and who covered her tracks on the gas plant scandal and then pretends not to know anything about it? How can the public trust a mayor who vows to contract out garbage east of Toronto's Yonge Street and then backs down on his pledge for no other reason than that he wants to make nice-nice with council's petulant left-wing politicians? What are we to make of an association called the Ontario Association of Community Care Access Centres that issues a press release blaming the government for not putting in the proper legislation and patting themselves on the back for delivering good care following the release of a scathing Ontario auditor general's report that says the exact opposite – that community care is poorly managed and the people who run it are grossly overpaid? I'd laugh if such examples weren't so revealing of the cavalier attitude with which bureaucrats in helping professions treat their clients, and of the culture of entitlement that runs rampant throughout government bureaucracies at both the provincial and municipal levels. Sadly, it has gotten to the point where the public is surprised if politicians actually make good on their election promises and if bureaucrats actually care about the people they are supposed to help. If I can do my part to hold the feet of politicians and bureaucrats to the fire, so much the better. Let the media pack chase after whomever they wish for the spin of the day. There's a place for all of us in a profession that has been under siege financially for years. Who knows whether newspapers will even be around in ten years? But for the time being, I am thrilled to have this opportunity to dig up the dirt.

EPILOGUE

I've come to call her The Incredible Shrinking Woman.

In the late fall of 2015, I started to notice the subtle changes in Carla Jamadar every time I popped by the Toronto branch where I do my banking and she is assistant manager.

At first I didn't want to say anything. But when I saw her face had changed dramatically – so much so that she looks like she could be on a Roman coin – I asked her if she'd lost weight.

That's when she confided to me that she'd undergone gastric bypass surgery in August of 2014 and had already shed seventy pounds. It took me a few weeks to broach the subject, and with good reason. Though it may seem surprising in someone so unafraid of saying it the way she sees it and who has conquered so many demons and obstacles in her life, the issue of weight is and always will be a highly sensitive one for me.

It has probably been one of my toughest life battles. There's no getting around it. I love food and I'm addicted to sweets. I've been in a lifelong struggle to keep off the thirty pounds that keep creeping up on me like someone else's bad debt. I've been on Weight Watchers so many times I've lost count – always successful until a few years go by and I find myself becoming less vigilant about maintaining portion control or keeping my sweet tooth in check.

Because of my body type – my friend Moira MacDonald likes to tease me that I have Eastern European hips – I have to watch everything I eat. I joke sometimes that I only have to look at junk or snack food, cakes or candies, or breads, bagels, and pasta to gain weight. I consider myself the classic yo-yo dieter. I even took diet pills while I was in my teens.

As able as I am to laugh off the perpetual criticism I get for my controversial opinions and as unafraid as I am to hold politicians' feet to the fire, I still find myself almost reduced to tears whenever someone calls me fat or chubby. My metabolism is so slow, I can train endlessly for my half marathons and run thirty-five kilometres a week, but unless I'm also very careful about what I eat, I won't lose weight. It only gets worse as I grow older.

I assumed Carla had to be equally sensitive about her body image, especially surrounded by a culture that displays images of near-anorexic size 0 women on the front cover of every women's magazine, and that isn't adverse to fat shaming. Consider how Rob Ford, or the singer Adele were treated. I'm betting it certainly doesn't help that Carla works in an area of Toronto where spas and fitness facilities outnumber stores and restaurants, or that women in our neighbourhood are known to calorie count as sport, some of them, sadly, so anorexic they resemble Holocaust survivors.

But Carla wasn't shy about telling me that after years and years of battling obesity, trying every diet imaginable – Weight Watchers, Atkins, Jenny Craig, Dr. Bernstein,

L.A. Weight Loss – and not sticking to any of them, she had to do something for the sake of her health and for her two children. Although she was putting on about ten pounds a year, she really packed the weight on after she had her daughter, Grace, now ten, and her son, Dillon Jr., eight.

As her weight crept up to 365 pounds, Carla found that she held herself back socially – afraid to fly partly due to the embarrassment of having to ask for a seatbelt extender or going to a party for fear of sitting in a flimsy chair and breaking it. She knew that despite her kind, warm, and engaging personality, far too often people would judge her by what they saw. She felt she was constantly on display. She'd even have strangers come up to her in the bank and tell her she had such a pretty face – if only she'd lose weight. "When you're overweight, you feel like you're constantly wearing a bikini . . . it doesn't matter if you're a nice person," Carla says. "Society is so obsessed about what we look like without considering what's inside."

She insists that she didn't do the gastric surgery out of vanity – although she appreciates the compliments she's been getting since she's lost weight. She confesses that she held off doing it for a few years, terrified that she wouldn't make it through the surgery. But she finally grew tired of being tired and of not being able to enjoy the most basic of activities with her kids – whether it meant not joining them on amusement rides or even walking with them to the local park, or having to send off her understanding hubby, Dillon, to play soccer with them. She knew she couldn't continue to live like that.

Once she breezed through the surgery, the real battle began. She can no longer process sugar and can't eat any junk food. She has to eat slowly so her food digests properly.

Her portions are now limited to those the size of a small bowl or salad plate. Even though she's down 152 pounds en route to a goal of 190 pounds in total, she still has to get used to not thinking like she's still 365 pounds.

If losing 30 pounds is hard, I can only imagine what a tough uphill battle it is for her. But every week when I check in with her, she is exuberant and full of hope. In the fall of 2015, she went on her first family vacation to Florida and had no trouble putting on a bathing suit or going on rides at Disney World. She's gone down four sizes on top and four on the bottom. She recently celebrated her fortieth birthday feeling like she has endless energy, so much so that her daughter recently told her she was walking so fast, she could barely keep up. "By no means do I have the perfect body, but I feel better for my kids and that's what makes me happy," she says.

I know Carla will reach her goal. She's come this far. There's no turning back. Carla is not one to seek attention, but she was so proud to tell me her story, thinking if she could inspire just one person to do what she's done, she'd be even happier.

She has certainly inspired me. I so respected her resilience, her discipline, and her positive attitude that she convinced me to tackle the 30 pounds I've put on since marrying Denise. If she can lose 190 pounds, surely to goodness I can shed at least 20, if not 25, pounds.

Still, I have gravitated toward Carla not merely because I identify with her weight loss battles. Despite her struggles – and there's no doubt that like me, she's an underdog – I admire her so much for her kindness, her decency, and her strength. She gives to others less fortunate, even though she is of modest means. She is hard-working, has a wonderful sense of humour, and I can see she is much loved by her customers.

I've come to realize, through the many obstacles I've had to overcome, that one should feel blessed in life to know people like the Carlas of the world. Whenever I confront the greed, the lack of concern for the vulnerable, the self-righteousness of those who think they're always right, and the obsessive pandering to political correctness – all too common traits in the politicians, the poverty pimps, and the faux feminists I write about – and I find myself getting passionately annoyed by the wilful blindness of the electorate to how they are being treated, people like Carla give me hope that there are those who dearly want to do the right thing and who are not afraid to fight back.

If only more people and more politicians had that kind of gumption and that kind of generosity of spirit.

ACKNOWLEDGEMENTS

I t was during the summer of 2012 after I'd finished three months investigating the $1-billion Regent Park revitalization that the gentle man I have jokingly adopted as a second brother, gay lawyer Martin Gladstone, started trying to convince me to write a book. He could see that the political discourse had become so polarized and that the media focus had become so fixated on the late Rob Ford's terribly unsophisticated but heartfelt attempts to stop the Gravy Train, that he felt a broader insight into what happens behind the scenes at City Hall was sorely needed. He believed I could and should write the inside story of City Hall to try to shape the agenda in the 2014 election. That was long before Mr. Ford's troubles with crack-cocaine and with drinking came to light. At that point Mr. Ford was merely – and I use the word "merely" tongue in cheek – being harassed and stalked continuously by the media and being dragged through the courts on frivolous charges. My wife, Denise, who has always been tremendously supportive even when she is forced to listen to the same political story for the fifth or sixth time at a dinner out or at a cocktail party, picked up where Martin left off, repeatedly pushing me to pursue a book.

It just so happened that around the same time I'd connected with the outspoken and politically astute Patti Starr, who'd written her own book *Tempting Fate* after taking the fall for David Peterson and his inner circle in the 1989 Patti Starr inquiry. When Patti wrote me to congratulate me for stirring it up with my exposé into Regent Park, we met for lunch and I spoke of the book idea. I had absolutely no clue where to start. She kindly offered to put me in touch with Don Bastian, formerly with Stoddard Publishing who now runs his own publishing house called BPS Books. With Don's help and his tremendous knowledge of the publishing business, I sat down during the 2012 Christmas holidays in Florida and crafted a book proposal that would be based on a tell-all about City Hall. Don and I worked together to fine tune the proposal and he found me agent Robert Lecker. After four months talking to various publishers, Doug Pepper at Penguin Random House Canada took me under wing and with his kind coaching we expanded my scope to *Underdog* – a tell-all no-holds-barred book about my life, the hurdles I've had to overcome, and my very controversial, outspoken views about left-wing politics, politicians, and political correctness.

Then the real hard work started – a marathon that took nearly three years of weekends and nights from start to finish. Throughout, I could not have done it without the wonderful and loving support of my wife Denise. I will never forget how, about six weeks into my initial two month book leave in Florida, a treasured gift showed up on my desk, an old Remington typewriter from the 1930s she found on eBay, along with a note congratulating me on my first book. I can't begin to say how lucky I got when I stepped up her driveway in 2006. Besides being intelligent, a multi-talented artist, designer, and singer, who knew what a great editor she could be? Being a quintessential Virgo, she read through each and every chapter and offered up fresh ideas and a fresh way of saying things. She always says god is in the details and that was indeed true as I watched her pore through chapter after chapter. But in addition to her keen insights and intelligence, she has a wonderful sense of humour. She always made me laugh especially when I got stressed out about meeting deadlines or frustrated with the long hours it took to write and edit this. I fully expect that she will be selling this book as much, if not more than me. She is absolutely adept at winning people over, so much so that I'm often asked if Denise will be accompanying me to political gatherings.

A very special thanks to my parents, Judy and Lou Levy for instilling in me a zest for life, a tremendous work ethic, a drive to be the best I can be and a real sense of social justice. There is no doubt I've inherited my outspokenness from my mother Judy.

Thanks must also go to Barb and Bob Covell, our special Florida friends, who made sure I had breaks at the beach and our favourite movie theatre during my two-month book leave. They are the kind of people one is so blessed to meet, who like Martin Gladstone and his partner Frank Caruso, we formed a bond with initially out of adversity. Special tributes must be paid to Dr. Karen Abrams, my emotional tour guide, for steering me down the road to recovery and for sharing far too many painful and bittersweet moments to count with me – and to Ellie Levine for offering me a lifeline when I so desperately needed it after my 2005 assault. To the many wonderful people who took me under wing during the year I spent fighting the justice system, most especially former Toronto auditor-general Jeff Griffiths and my dear late uncle Jeff Lyons, and to the friends, political and otherwise, who were there for me when I came out.

Thanks to gay Conservative Jamie Ellerton for taking the time to meet with me and share his thoughts on the federal and provincial Conservatives. And a special shout-out must go to our wonderful and now defunct *Toronto Sun* library system – so adeptly managed by Julie Kirsh. Julie was always there to boost my spirits during the drafts and revisions until she and her library ladies became unfortunate victims of the merger between Sun Media and Post Media in late 2015.

I will always be grateful for the kind encouragement of my editors at the *Toronto Sun*: editor emeritus Lorrie Goldstein, my mentor and my friend; editor-in-chief Adrienne Batra, who supported my many crusades, along with my weight loss leading up to the launch of this book; city editor Jonathan Kingstone; deputy editor Kevin Hann; and to everyone I've worked with at the *Toronto Sun*, past and present – James Wallace, Lou Clancy, the late Peter O'Sullivan and of course, the indomitable Les Pyette – who have allowed me to tell it the way I see it and to constantly stir it up. Special thanks to my dear long-time colleague and friend Zen Ruryk who has always had my back.

There are so many politicians, activists, advocates, union honchos, radical gays, public teat-suckers, poverty pimps, and media sheep who have fuelled my creativity, and often nearly drove me to drink over the years, that I would need an entire book to recognize them. Let's just say that I hope I've adequately reflected the madness and the constant lunacy exhibited by the Lib-left and their media sycophants during my years as a political journalist and a champion for the underdog. To my dear friend, contact, and confidante, former councillor and city budget chief Mike Del Grande, who always called me with "juicy juicies," and to Doug Holyday, the first councillor I told I was gay. He, too, has been a wonderful friend and contact over the years. I would be remiss if I didn't recognize the many clerks who shared coffee dates with me at City Hall during which we'd laugh, swap stories and gossip. Dear clerk Patsy Morris and her infectious laugh will always be in my heart. Patsy passed away of colon cancer at age 59, far before her time, in 2011.

But most of all, I am grateful for the many experiences that life has thrown my way, good and bad. Although I probably wouldn't have said it at the time, the obstacles have certainly shaped who I am and why I tell it like it is. As I've said in the book, I am living proof that what doesn't beat you down, or worse kill you, definitely makes you stronger.